D0319596

FOES TO TYRANNY

A History of the Amalgamated Union of Building Trade Workers

by

W. S. HILTON

Published by
The Amalgamated Union of Building Trade Workers.
Printed by the Co-operative Printing Society Limited.
7-11 *Tudor Street, London, E.C.*4. 1963

FOES TO TYRANNY

A History of the A.U.B.T.W.

CONTENTS

Foreword

by

GEORGE H. LOWTHIAN, C.B.E.

(*General Secretary of the Amalgamated Union of Building Trade Workers*)

THIS book is the first history to be written about the Amalgamated Union of Building Trade Workers and the unions which fused together to give it birth in 1921. Numbered among them are some of the finest workers' organisations of the last century.

In particular the old Operative Stonemasons' Society was, at one time, the most powerful and respected within the entire country. The records left by the Masons' Union are probably the best that remain in existence anywhere in the world. It is because other material is relatively scarce in the years up to 1860 that the O.S.M. necessarily figures largely in the pages dealing with that time.

To all of the unions which formed the A.U.B.T.W. however, and which struggled to uplift building workers, we owe a great debt. They were not anonymous bodies but gatherings of human beings who could suffer hardships, become dejected in defeat and rejoice at victory.

It was the human story we wanted to read, the author was requested. And in these pages we can see the men struggle grimly towards their objectives and feel the privations they and their families often endured.

Histories of our movement are sometimes uninteresting chonological records of changes in rules, wage rates and officials. This we felt should be avoided though, of course, it was recognised that it was necessary to set down the important events that had happened over the last 150 years.

In my opinion our Research Officer, Mr. W. S. Hilton, has excellently met the need for factual information married to the human and industrial circumstances which produced it. Here I must pay him a sincere tribute for the tremendous effort he has put in to complete this history. For over three years, researching into hundreds of volumes, he has devoted his spare time to doing this job for the A.U.B.T.W. Our members certainly owe him a debt of gratitude.

It is also obvious that he has a very great affection for the men about whom he writes though he has not allowed this to conceal any deficiences which they may have had. Because of this they appear to us as human beings with whom we can sympathise and with whom we can identify ourselves.

Book reading, it has been said, is one of our lost arts. But I would appeal to our members to read this—their **own** history. Having done so I know they will feel pride in their comrades of long ago and the heritage which they have passed to us.

G.H.L.

FOES TO TYRANNY

A History of the A.U.B.T.W.

CHAPTER 1

AFTER THE CONQUEST

THE longest and most dramatic battle in British history is that between capital and labour. For centuries there has been a continuing—and very often violent—struggle in which the workers have gradually sought to match the wealth and power of their opponents by building strong trade union organisations.

In this battle leaders have been thrown up from their ranks who more than compare in stature with the 'notables' whose ephemeral struggles for power are so diligently chronicled in orthodox histories.

Building workers were among the first to feel the effect of the wages system, and the clear division between employed and employer, which led to the antagonism and deep bitterness of industrial warfare. At a time when nearly all other craftsmen were self-employed, or small masters, the men in the building trades were wage earners with no opportunity for employer status.

In particular, "The stone building industry had a capitalistic organisation practically from the outset."* Not only was a large amount of capital required for the stone buildings of those days, but also a high concentration of labour.

It was the coming of William the Conqueror which greatly stimulated the activity of the stone building

**The Mediaeval Mason*, page 159.

industry. For not only did he bring with him a large number of highly skilled French masons, but the aftermath of the Conquest was to intensify the concentration of land and wealth in the hands of the king, his nobles and the church.

These were precisely the preconditions necessary for an expansion in building work and a corresponding increase in the number of masons. For building of this kind was both a lengthy and a costly business for which clients required long purses and reasonable immunity from any sudden or violent change in personal circumstances.

The system under which they hired building workers was almost exclusively direct labour. The men themselves were employed and paid directly by the religious or royal patron financing the building. Even the ' master mason ' was a wage-earner, hired to superintend the general constructional work and paid a higher wage for his extra responsibilities.

The early building worker found that his wage rates, with food prices at a low level, gave him little anxiety in maintaining a reasonable standard of life. In fact, the early mediaeval masons and carpenters were the recognised aristocrats among building craftsmen. And it was this very quality which found them immediately ranged against authority when their standards and status were challenged shortly after the Black Death had devastated the population of England. Spreading from the sea-port towns of Dorsetshire, where the ' foul death ' was first seen in August 1348, it travelled slowly throughout the rest of the country until it had claimed victim a large part of the population.

Apart from the personal tragedy and suffering that came in the wake of the Black Death, one other immediate and acute consequence was the desperate shortage of labour. Crops ripened and then rotted in the field for want of hands, and cattle and sheep roamed unattended at large over the countryside. The building of church and castle ground almost to a halt because of the dearth of skilled craftsmen.

The law of supply and demand, as far as labour was concerned, was heavily tipped in favour of the worker. Unable to tolerate this ' free market ' when it was so decidedly against them, the landowners demanded, and obtained, the Statute of Labourers in 1349. Among its other provisions this Statute made the state the supreme arbiter on wages and declared that all artificers should not be paid a higher rate of wages than was customary in the year before the Black Death.

But the cost of living had increased in the meantime. Wages which would have provided a reasonable living standard for building workers in 1347 were inadequate two years later. It was almost inevitable that the masons and the carpenters, proud almost to the point of arrogance, should revolt against the humiliating and crushing clauses of the Statute.

And their unique industrial position—wage-earners often working together in large numbers—enabled them to frequently combine for the forcing of higher wages from their employers than those laid down in the Statute. In this dangerous fight against authority the masons played a leading part. They were able to force up their wages to a higher level than any other building craft. " It is very probable that the combination which these artisans were able to effect, the regulations by which they might govern their trade, and the manner in which they were certainly associated together under the title of free masons . . . would have enabled them to take full advantage of the situation."*

These activities did not go unnoticed. The Statute of Labourers was reinforced in 1351 and had a clause specially aimed at restraining building workers.

" Carpenters, masons and tilers shall not take by the day for their work, but in such manner as they were wont "

---

* *Work and Wages*, page 21.

it threatened. And the scale of wages per day was firmly laid down: " A mason carpenter 3d. . . . a master free-stone mason 4d. and other masons 3d."*

Resistance to official wage regulations hardened, however, rather than weakened. And evidence that some form of organisation gradually took the place of isolated or spontaneous protest is shown in 1360 when the Statute of Labourers was made more repressive by increasing its penalties.

" Carpenters and masons shall from henceforth take wages by the day and not by the week or in any other manner " it ruled, and " all alliances and covines of masons and carpenters, and congregations, chapters,† ordinances and oaths between them made or to be made shall be from henceforth void and wholly annulled. So that every mason and carpenter, of whatever condition, may be compelled by his master whom he serves to do every work that pertains him to do."‡

This threat of punishment seems to have had little effect, at least as far as the masons were concerned. For, as an attempt to kill their efforts towards combination, another Act was passed in 1425 specially directed against them. This Act was based on the complaint that " by the yearly congregations and confederacies made by the masons in their general chapters assembled " the purpose of the Statute of Labourers was being defeated. Wages were being forced above the lawful limits. This Act§ forbade them to continue their congregations and chapters. Any mason who took an active part in holding them was to be adjudged a felon. The mason who took a more

*Stat. 25 Edw. III C.2.

†The term ' chapters ' probably refers to the lodges of building workers engaged in church work who would have regulations made for them by the church chapter. The inclusion of other ' congregations and covines ' implies that the organisation was reasonably widespread and by men employed on differing types of work. A ' covin ' is a secret meeting for arriving at " deceitful agreement between two or more to the hurt of another."

‡Stat. 34 Edw. III C.IX.

§Stat. 3 Henry VI C.1.

passive role by merely putting in an attendance was liable to be fined and clapped in prison.

Any law however is only effective to the extent that it can be enforced. Parliament, representative of the nobles and the landowning class, might well rage against combinations of the masons but the machinery to police its laws was inadequate. Masons' wages in general continued to exceed the limits laid down in the regulations. And it was not only over wages that they gave offence to authority.

"They conspire together that no man of their craft shall take less for a day than they fix" complained J. Wycliffe in the 14th Century, "though he should by good conscience take much less; that none of them shall do good steady work which might interfere with the earnings of other men of the craft, and that none of them shall do anything but cut stone, though he might profit his master twenty pounds by one day's work by laying a wall, without harm to himself."*

Wycliffe's complaint rings strangely and irritatingly familiar on the ears of 20th Century trade unionists! Were these forbidden congregations and chapters of the mediaeval mason then the first development towards trade unionism? Oddly enough they have been frequently confused with the old craft guilds, and dismissed out of hand as the possible embryo of the unions which made a permanent mark towards the beginning of the 19th Century.†

Yet the masons established certain customs and practices in those days which were not only subsequently found in the masons' trade union of 1831, but were

---

**Building in England*, page 42.

†In his *Builders' History*, page 4, Raymond Postgate abruptly decides that "these are not the forerunners of our modern trade union." The Webbs, however, are more cautious in their observations. Speaking of the chapters and fraternities of masons they conclude: "Such an association may, if further researches throw light upon its constitution and working, not improbably be found to possess some points of resemblance to the Friendly Society of Operative Stonemasons." *History of Trade Unionism*, page 8.

assimilated by other unions not even remotely connected with the building industry.*

Certainly no continuous and written record exists to satisfy the curiosity of the historian and his desire for accuracy. This, however, is due to a number of causes.

The ability to read and write was not nearly so widespread as it is today. Even if it had been, the masons were not likely to supply written evidence for those wishing to prosecute them. There was also the fact that the migratory nature of their industry ensured a continuation of their laws and customs without the necessity for having them written down.

This is not an attempt, however, to claim that their organisations were akin to the modern trade unions which were fashioned in the particular circumstances present at the turn of the 19th Century. But the evidence at least indicates that the economic conditions of the building industry, and the organisations of masons and other building workers, had led to some form of trade combination not altogether divorced—at least in intention—from our present-day trade unions.

" It is not until the changing conditions of industry had reduced to an infinitesimal chance the journeyman's prospect of becoming himself a master, that we find the passage of ephemeral combinations into permanent trade societies," wrote the Webbs. Not until, in other words, industry had developed to the stage where there was a strict class division between wage earners and employers.

When the Webbs wrote that passage they had the mediaeval craft guild in mind and were discussing whether it qualified as the forerunner of trade unions. They decided that these guilds had more of a capitalist basis.

*The word 'lodge,' for example almost exclusively meant the workshop of the mason, and later his union branch room. The conduct of the lodge—the officers in masonry gloves and aprons, with the symbolic tools of the trade—together with lodge door guards called 'tylers,' have only any real relation to the mason's craft. Yet many early trade unions of the 19th Century adopted the terminology and customs as practised by the masons' lodges.

They were formed and controlled by small masters who had gradually accumulated enough capital to purchase raw materials and hire labour for the production of finished commodities. Their income was derived from the margin of profit on these products. Their guilds, which were essentially town-based organisations, regulated and protected their interests and controlled the journeymen and apprentices employed by them.

Proof that the economic position of the early mason was radically different from the general mediaeval artificer, is shown by the almost complete non-existence of masons' guilds.* The simple fact is that there was almost no possibility for masons to earn a living and establish themselves in the towns of those days. Houses were mainly constructed of wood, and often the only stone building was the church. Under these conditions the carpenter and other building craftsmen could put down roots which might lead to the establishment of guilds, but the mason had to face the frequent necessity of tramping from job to job.

He did not acquire the stability to set himself up in business as a small master. There was no possibility, due to the heavy costs of stone and other materials, of his earning a living by selling finished products. Like his modern counterpart he could only offer to sell his labour power. For him the unit of organisation was not a masters' guild, but the workmen's lodge.

This lodge was the shed or shelter in which the masons worked. Here they prepared the stone for buildings generally commissioned by the church or crown. On a big job the lodge was of substantial size. At buildings like Vale Royal Abbey, York Minster and Westminster Abbey, there was considerable expenditure on the erection of lodges for the masons.†

*Various researchers have remarked on the absence of such guilds. Knoop and Jones (*The Mediaeval Mason*) and Salzman (*Building in England*) have found that only in London was there evidence of a masons' guild organisation.

† *The Mediaeval Mason*, pages 56-58.

The size of some of the lodges and the number of men employed in them once again emphasises the difference between the status of the mason and the town-based artificer engaged in small operations. In fact, from the very first large-scale building of ancient civilisation it is obvious that in the building industry great numbers of workers would be required to place themselves under the authority of others and have no chance of ever achieving ‘independence’ as master contractors. The barracks at the Great Pyramid in Egypt, for instance, provided accommodation for around 4,000 masons who were employed on the facing of the stone blocks alone.*

Though thousands of years lay between the English mediaeval building industry and the vast structures and slave labour of ancient Egypt, there were jobs of such a size that they might employ anything up to a thousand masons who would be working together in their lodges for some considerable time.

The lodge, in fact, became the centre of the mason's working life. It was to its door he turned his weary footsteps when on the tramp for a job. It was here he practised the ‘mysteries of his craft’ and formulated whatever rules he thought necessary for governing his relations with other masons.

There were some lodges which had a much more permanent character than those erected merely for the construction period of a building. These were usually set up at royal palaces and religious buildings for maintenance or alteration of the fabric. With good fortune and conduct the men in them would be provided with many years of continuous employment.

Working regulations for these lodges were drawn up by the religious or royal employer. For the churches, supervision of the men and enforcement of the regulations were likely to be in the hands of the church Chapter. Directly responsible to the Chapter was the master mason—or “master of the fabric” as he was sometimes called.

---

* *A Short History of Building Crafts*, page 12.

The arrangements at York reveal an even more extended form of control exercised by the Chapter over the lodge. Perhaps because of the risk that the master mason might develop sympathies with the men placed under him, or be negligent in his duties, a clergyman called the supervisor was delegated to keep a close eye on the lodge and see the masons kept up to scratch. " We may fairly see in him a mediaeval anticipation of the modern ' speed boss ' and in the conditions which produced him a similarity, in all but scale of operations, to those of modern capitalistic factory industry."*

It is in these more permanent lodges that we can suppose the evolution of customs and practices associated with the craft itself and those aimed at regulating the organisation formed by the men. For, in addition to the working rules imposed by their employers, the men had to devise their own code governing relations between them.

A tramp mason, for instance, might present himself asking for a job. But before admitting him to the lodge and the fellowship of the craft, it was necessary to obtain reasonable proof that he was a craftsman. And in those days it could not be done simply by asking him to produce written indentures! It was therefore necessary to arrive at some form of initiation, perhaps including a special hand-grip and password, for those qualifying as masons which would serve as an introduction wherever they might travel.

In course of time the working regulations and the rules of the masons in the lodge began to fuse together to give a general code of guidance for the craft. The constant movement of the masons from job to job would automatically ensure that the code became nationally known and observed.

The Crown also inadvertently assisted this activity by using a system of impressment—similar to the naval press gangs of later years—by which masons were drawn from various areas and forced to work on palace or castle.

---

* *The Mediaeval Mason*, pages 61-62.

When the royal will was intent on some new project a shortage of building workers in the immediate neighbourhood was not allowed to thwart it. Nor did the idea of attracting men to the job by higher wages and better conditions remotely suggest itself to the king. Instead a peremptory instruction was sent out to certain authorities that they had to select a certain number of men and send them as speedily as possible to the building site where they were required, to work at the " King's wages for as long as they should be needed."

Edward III was particularly fond of the system. For work at ' Wyndesore (Windsor) Castle ' he sent out an order on the 6th January, 1359, to certain sheriffs, mayors, bailiffs and others: " Know that we, trusting in the discretion and loyalty of Master Robert of Gloucester, our mason, have assigned and deputed him to take and arrest as many masons as may be necessary for the erection of our works in our castle of Wyndesore, wherever he can find them, within liberties or without, and to place them in our work aforesaid at our wages, and to take and arrest all masons whom he shall find contrary or rebellious in this matter and bring them to the aforesaid castle there to be held in prison until they shall find security to remain at those works according to the instructions of the said Robert on our behalf."*

Two years later in 1361, he ordered 17 sheriffs to send a total of 1,360 masons for work at Windsor.

The system of impressment was itself an indication of the prolific building activity, mainly for royal or religious lords, in relation to the number of masons available. Beginning early in the 14th Century it was frequently resorted to until it gradually died out about 300 years later.

But, by that time, many of the other customs in the industry had also changed. One of the chief events responsible for the transition was Henry VIII's dissolution of the monasteries due to his quarrels with the Pope and his desire to plunder the wealth they had accumulated.

---

* *The Mediaeval Mason*, page 244.

CHAPTER 2

RISE OF THE EMPLOYER

DURING their centuries of existence the religious orders had amassed great wealth. At the time of their dissolution the annual value of monastic lands alone was estimated at over £160,000 which indicates their tremendous capital value. Then there was also property and other items of wealth which had been accumulated through the years. Now, by officially breaking with the Pope and assuming the mantle of supreme head of the Church, Henry had conveniently made himself master of all its property, and he wasted no time in getting it into his own hands.

But he was by no means the sole recipient of the plunder. Others had to help, or acquiesce, in the deed. They also had to be paid for their services both in wealth and, ironically, 'honours.' It is said in fact that Henry founded a new nobility on the spoils of the mediaeval church. What is certain is that "the dissolution of the monasteries must have been, even from the effect of so vast an amount of property being suddenly transferred from one set of owners to a new and needy aristocracy, the cause of large disturbances in the economic condition of England."*

One immediate consequence was that the 'needy aristocracy' now had the wealth with which to fulfil their building desires. And as the industry began to respond to this redistribution of wealth the previous concentration of building workers on a relatively few

---

* *Six Centuries of Work and Wages*, page 323.

religious, royal or other constructions gave way to a more diverse labour force occupied on a much wider variety of work. In some cases the monasteries, out of which the occupants had been thrown, were used as easily accessible 'quarries' from which ready prepared stone was taken for new buildings.

There were, of course, other influences at work in the industry. Brickwork was coming increasingly into fashion. And Henry himself might well have qualified as the patron saint of building (presuming he was fit to be a saint of any description) for " he had twenty or thirty palaces on all of which pulling down and building was going on, in which an army of workmen, often by night and day, on Sundays and on the highest festivals of his Church, were incessantly employed."*

The total effect of these changes was to provide building craftsmen with a wider and more varied demand for their services. Not only did this enable some masons and bricklayers to put down roots in the towns and establish themselves as capitalist artisans, it also began to erode the traditional system of the client hiring his labour direct. In the competition for labour that was taking place, new practices were also creeping into the industry. Some clients were now making agreements for operatives to do work by the piece, and a number of small gangs of men were carrying out contracts on a labour-only basis—the client supplying the materials as was traditional. On some of the repair and maintenance work the tradesman was often supplying both labour and materials and sending in his account for the complete job.

These changes in industrial conditions were followed by a gradual transformation of the lodge organisation of the men. The dissolution had, for a start, meant the breaking up of some lodges which had been controlled by church chapters for maintenance of the fabric. In any case a single lodge, situated on one job, could no longer serve the interests of all operatives when they were dispersed

---

* *The Economic Interpretation of History*, page 35.

over a larger number of sites in the locality. The need now was for some central meeting point, and it was during this transitional period that the word ' lodge ' was gradually transferred from site usage and became applied to an appointed meeting-room within a town.

But though the building craftsman found himself affected by changes within the industry, and saw some of his own fellows assuming the role of employers, there was still not such a wide gap between them as to form complete class delineation. The erstwhile employer might frequently find himself one of the employed again, and many craftsmen were probably aiming at achieving the status of employer. There was, therefore, a general fluidity in the position which maintained an affinity of interests between the men. In the main, lodge members would still regard themselves as basically wage earners whose working rules must now cover the position of those who became employers for a time.

These new central lodges were not generally secret in their operations nor did they run much risk of suppression so long as they confined themselves to formulating working rules governing their craft. Highly skilled artisans like the masons were only liable to suffer punishment if they attempted to thwart legislation on the wages and hours that were laid down for them. Revolt on these matters was not likely because the mason, with his services and skill in great demand, had wages well above that of any other craftsmen. For example the magistrates at Warwick, meeting in April 1684, assessed a scale of wages for that year and fixed the general artisans' wages at 1s. a day except for the freemason. He was to be paid 1s. 4d. per day. This compared very favourably with the plasterer who was to have only 8d. per day.

The legislation under which the magistrates were empowered to fix rates of wages was a Statute which had been brought in under Elizabeth in 1563. Although it was partly welcomed by craftsmen, because it laid down regulations forbidding anyone to practise a craft without first serving a seven years' apprenticeship, the clauses dealing with assessment of wages simply committed working people to the mercy of their masters. Quite apart from the punitive discipline to which they were now subject, their wages were decided upon by the local magistrates. These magistrates might be employers themselves, or were, at least, from the same class or in sympathy with it.

The Elizabethan Act, in fact, consolidated all the early statutes which had followed the Black Death and made them much more rigid in application. The penalties which could be inflicted for any " conspiracy of workmen to raise wages " were severe. On the first conviction the fine was £10, or 20 days in prison on bread and water. If the offence was committed again the fine was £20 or the pillory. Any luckless wretch found guilty for the third time was fined £40, the pillory, the loss of one of his ears, and judicial infamy.

As this was at a time when even the smallest of the fines —the first of £10—might represent a year's earnings for some men, it was obvious that in most cases they would have to pay the alternative penalty.

Throughout the 17th and into the 18th Century the economy of Britain was developing towards its climax in the Industrial Revolution. The system of directly employed craftsmen in the building industry was now becoming almost obsolete and a much more clearly identifiable employer class emerging. Under these conditions the old basis of lodge life was gradually being destroyed. No longer were working regulations commonly agreed rules between craftsmen and those of them who might frequently employ others. Instead they were now being framed by operatives almost as defensive measures aimed at making their employers observe trade traditions and privileges. The character of the lodge was, in fact, becoming much more clearly a trade union one. And, as the fixing of wages by magistrates fell into disuse, a strong lodge of operatives would also use pressure—even if still adjudged illegal—to seek improvements in their wages and hours of work.

It was precisely because the masons and bricklayers were comparatively well paid tradesmen, with craft prestige behind them, that they—and other artisans like them—formed the first trade unions. For " though it is often assumed that trade unionism arose as a protest against intolerable industrial oppression this was not so. The first half of the 18th Century was certainly not a period of exceptional distress . . . The formation of independent associations to resist the will of employers required the possession of a certain degree of personal independence and strength of character. Thus we find the earliest trade unions arising among journeymen whose skill and standard of life had been for centuries encouraged and protected by legal or customary regulations as to apprenticeship, and by the limitation of their members which the high premiums and other conditions must have involved."*

New and profound problems faced the mason and bricklayer as an employer class rose from among their own ranks. In the old days of direct labour they were paid by an employer—the person commissioning the building—who did not interfere with their actual trade regulations. The new class of craft employers not only controlled hours and wages but also tried, because of their own experience in the industry, to direct men in their detailed working operations. This the operatives deeply resented.

For though they had been denied the right to determine their wages in the past, at least they had always been accorded self-responsibility in carrying out the processes in which they had been trained. It was this which was the source of their pride and dignity, and set them apart from the unskilled labourer. Not for the building craftsman a subservient role to some rudimentary machine with an overseer constantly directing his every movement. Instead the mason took the raw stone, worked on it with tools sharpened and maintained by himself, and applied his years of training and experience to fashioning the

* *History of Trade Unionism*, page 44.

finished surface. After this he would put it into place in the building of which it was a part.

Guiding their tools by a combination of hand and brain, they were in almost complete control over their own work and had only required slight supervision. The end-product was a completely unique construction in which the craftsmanship of the men was an integral part, and would perhaps remain to speak of their art long after they were gone.

The fight by those early lodges of building workers to enforce the regulations under which they were prepared to work, therefore, was an attempt to prevent the employers robbing them of their dignity as craftsmen. And this fight was being waged in face of a powerful economic climate which sought to destroy all these human values and replace them with a yardstick based on purely commercial considerations.

Nor was this fight confined to building craftsmen. It was also echoed in other traditional trades. To underline their refusal to submit to the degradation meted out to workers in the new factories, and to emphasise their craft status the millwrights for instance " had for their everyday garb a long frock-coat and tall hat."*

From the beginning of the 18th Century the local trades clubs and primitive trade union organisations began to make themselves much more effective. Employers were constantly complaining about combinations of workmen enforcing trade regulations and rules which, they claimed, were 'in restraint of trade.' From these people there were continual demands that more oppressive legislation be introduced to curb this new 'threat' from the workers. Towards the end of the 18th Century the prevailing economic and political conditions gave the Government the opportunity to take severe measures against the new unions. At home the capitalists complained the workers' organisations were a barrier to their desires to be able to exploit the opportunities of the

---

* *History of Trade Unionism*, page 45.

Industrial Revolution without restraint. Abroad, the French Revolution had led to a fear in the rulers of a great many European states—including Britain—that the same sequence of events might be repeated nearer home. Any gathering or combination of workmen was suspiciously regarded as a possible conspiracy which might breed revolution.

It was therefore the desires of the capitalists on the one hand, and the fears of the state on the other, which brought the passing of the Anti-Combination Act in 1799.

Under this Act all combinations of workmen were now prohibited—whether to purely discuss working regulations or not—and severe penalties were laid down for transgressors. The Act was, in fact, the extreme end-point of all the statutes levelled against the workers since the 14th Century.

But, like them, it was by no means successful in killing their organisations. The judicial machine was still not developed enough to rigidly enforce the Act throughout the country. There were also employers who did not wish to make use of the new legislation and, in areas where there had been no great turmoil, a form of union organisation was carried on and negotiations and strikes still took place. It was the employers in the factory districts of the Midlands and the North who eagerly seized the opportunities given them by the Anti-Combination Act and applied it with great severity. The major effect of the new legislation, however, was not that it destroyed trade unionism but that it probably delayed the growth of more widespread organisation.

For, though the spirit of the workers was such that they were prepared to take risks to retain their independence and their local unions and trade clubs, they knew it would be like committing immediate organisational suicide if they drew official notice to themselves by linking together to form more extensive societies.

The Anti-Combination Act remained in existence for 25 years. During those years the economic and political condition of the country had undergone great change. But by the end of that time there was a more settled atmosphere in which it was possible for the employers, and the ruling class, to look more objectively at the organisations of the workers.

There were still those who would take any steps, however ruthless, to keep the organisations of the workers under suppression, but the almost hysterical fear in which the Anti-Combination Act had been passed was now largely gone. This encouraged Francis Place and other political radicals to sponsor legislation aimed at repealing the measure and, assisted by the constant pressure of the workers themselves, their efforts were eventually rewarded in 1824 when Parliament repealed the Anti-Combination Act and the trade union movement was no longer adjudged illegal.

CHAPTER 3

THE FIGHT BACK

THE repeal of the Anti-Combination Acts removed restrictions which, from the Statute of Labourers in the 14th Century, had been aimed at suppressing combinations of workers. For the first time in nearly 500 years they had the right to co-operate with one another in fighting for better wages and working conditions.

Those local unions which had maintained their existence for some time in defiance of the penalties which might have been inflicted upon them, now gradually began to strengthen and widen their organisations. And a great part of the new-found strength of the trade union movement came from the reaction of the workers against their personal degradation and misery. The original drive towards union as a means of protecting craft status and working traditions was now given added impetus by the terrible conditions which accompanied the rapid expansion of the capitalist system.

The coal mines and stark factory chimneys which gradually scarred and blackened the green countryside of the Midlands were symbolic of a system which just as callously despoiled and degraded human beings; a system which crushed the spirit of the people and also claimed their children.

" I am convinced," said the eminent economic historian, Professor Thorold Rogers, " that at no period of English history for which authentic records exist, was the condition of manual labour worse than it was in the 40 years from

1782 to 1821, the period in which manufacturers and merchants accumulated fortune rapidly."*

It is to this period we trace back the origins of the A.U.B.T.W. For it heralded the birth of the unions of bricklayers and masons; two groups that were often to meet in head-on clashes in later years before they finally combined to form a far more powerful and influential organisation than either of them had dreamed of achieving in their separate years of existence.

The Friendly Society of Operative Bricklayers (F.S.O.B.) was founded in 1829, probably in Manchester. Unfortunately no direct record remains to speak to us of the Union's first 30 years of existence, apart from the two annual reports covering the years 1844 to '46. But from them, and newspaper comments of the time, it was obviously a society of national character with its main centres of strength in London and Manchester. The Union's general organisational structure would probably be similar to that of the Operative Stonemasons' Society (O.S.M.).

It was in the Autumn of 1831 that the O.S.M. was created to rapidly become the strongest and most powerful union in the country.† Within two years it had reached the then exceptional total of nearly 4,000 members—enrolled in 100 branches that stretched from Carlisle in the North, right down through the country to Plymouth. This was an indication of the extent to which masons—like the bricklayers—were able to capitalise from their long years of experience as wage earners banded together in their lodges and from their nomadic tramping the country in search of work.

It is the masons who have left us the finest and most continuous union records in existence.‡ They remain

---

* *Six Centuries of Work and Wages*, page 63.

† This date is different from the one given by R. Postgate—23rd March, 1833—in his *Builders' History*. Proofs for the 1831 date are contained in Appendix " A."

‡ In their *History of Trade Unionism*, page 233, the Webbs say: " The Stonemasons' Fortnightly Circular, which, regularly appearing as it has done since 1834, constitutes perhaps the most valuable single record of the Trade Union Movement."

the only accurate guide to much of the building union history of the early nineteenth Century.

The foundations of the O.S.M. were laid in the local organisation of masons which had a few years of pre-existence at Huddersfield, at that time a storm centre of the early Labour Movement.

One of the men who had resolved to do all he could to change the degrading nature of society was Thomas Fothergill of the Huddersfield Masons. Strong trade union organisations, he claimed, were needed to secure reasonable conditions and a softening of the grimness of life. Fired by these convictions he persuaded the other members of his local lodge to back him in trying to build a general union of masons throughout the country.

With a small group of willing helpers he travelled to "Manchester to open a lodge there, when they had the good luck of initiating close upon three hundred members into a bond of the union, during the three days they kept open lodge there. They next went to Bradford, Brighouse, Halifax, Dewsbury, and Leeds and thus commenced our invaluable Society."*

In 1831 these new lodges met and agreed the principle of general union between them. Rules for the society were laid down and the O.S.M. was launched with "Lodge No. 1 in the No. 1 District, under the title of Grand Lodge, now held at the house of Joseph Higgenbottom, Sign of the White Bear, Westgate, Huddersfield."

The pioneering work of Thomas Fothergill was not forgotten and, for the rest of his life, he was fondly regarded throughout the O.S.M. as the 'Grand Old Number One of our Society.'

No lodge could be opened under the title of O.S.M without the consent of Grand Lodge. And when members were made it was through the ritual laid down in the 'Making Parts Book'.

Much of the ritual and terms used were not unlike that of the old lodge regulations and customs of the mediaeval

---

* O.S.M. Fortnightly Returns, 2nd July, 1863.

masons. The earlier secrecy oaths, however, had been given a more dramatic and grotesque form due to the years of illegality under the Combination Acts. Then the oath had been necessary not merely to protect the 'mystery of the craft' but the personal liberty of those taking part in the union. Although the Combination Acts had been repealed, the swearing of the oath was carried on for some years by the force of tradition.

The initiation ceremony of the masons was something that new members were not likely to forget in a hurry.* And if it now seems more humorous than horrific it should be remembered that it was administered in a different age, and by men who generally viewed the proceedings with a grim respect.

The aspiring member was warned to wait attendance at the lodge room on the appointed meeting night. On his arrival his first challenge was from the outside tyler (doorkeeper) who was dressed in decorative apron, gloves and a tall peaked hat with a broad ribbon round it. Upon assuring the tyler of his honourable intentions, he was then taken to a small room just off the main lodge room where he met his sponsor who helped prepare him for the ordeal.

His jacket was unbuttoned so that his shirt could be arranged to " bare his naked breast on the heart side " and a blindfold was held ready. Then suddenly the communicating door to the lodge room was thrown open to reveal the even more awe-inspiring figure of the inside tyler, or conductor, wearing white gloves and apron. He had a brilliant sash across his chest, and in his hand was a lethal looking sword. If the candidate still had sufficient courage left at this stage he was blindfolded and led into the lodge. Standing before the president's table he was

* " It certainly terrified me," said Fred Jordan, one time Assistant General Secretary of the O.S.M. As described in this book it has been compiled from Fred Jordan's recollections when he was made a member, the *Making Parts Book* of 1831 and the various items of expenditure for swords, "guilding the axe" (these were used as part of the ceremony) which throw light on the subject.

then challenged about his craft status and whether, if worthy to be admitted as a member, he would " guard well the secrets of the lodge." Next he was asked to kneel down while the members sang a verse of their lodge hymn, " Praise God," and the president read the formal initiation address. After another verse of the hymn the president then commanded: " Give this stranger light! "

The blindfold was taken off and the bewildered candidate now had his first sight of the lodge room. Facing him were the president and other office bearers all dressed similarly to the tylers, except that their sashes and aprons were more resplendent in accordance with their rank. Before them was a low table on which were arranged the tools of the trade, a square and compass, and an open Bible.

To his left was a white shrouded figure and immediately in front of him was the inside tyler—who now held the sword point within an inch of his naked breast. In this position the candidate had to swear his oath of loyalty with one hand firmly on the Bible.

The sword was then lowered and the president leaned forward and whipped away the shroud on his left to reveal the gaunt figure of a skeleton. Pointing to the skeleton the president warned of the fate awaiting those who broke their oath:

" Stranger, mark well this shadow which now you see,
'Tis a faithful emblem of man's destiny.
Behold this head, once fill'd with pregnant wit;
These hollow holes once sparkling eyes did fit;
This empty mouth no tongue or lips contains;
Of a once well-furnished head see all that now remains;
Behold this breast where a generous heart once moved
Filled with affection loving, and behold—
Mark well these bones: the flesh hath left its place
These arms could once a tender wife embrace,
These legs in gay activity could roam.
But, alas, the spirit fled, and all is gone.
O Death, O Death, thy terror strikes us with dismay,

'Tis only the just spirit, that hath left its earthly clay,
Can set thee at defiance, and in triumph say:
O Death, where is thy sting, O grave where is thy victory?
The sting of death is sin, and we are sinners all:
The heavy stroke of death must one day on us fall."

After further warnings from other officials on the 'rewards' for disloyalty, the president completed the candidate's initiation. He was now a member of the Operative Stonemasons' Society, pledged to action on behalf of his brothers and to uphold the Union's rules.

These rules were divided into three sections. First were the Bye Laws. Here was laid down the duties of officials, the conduct expected of members in and out of the lodge room, and a rough set of standing orders for guidance of the chairman.

Some of the rules about members' conduct in the lodge now appear rather quaint but, in an age when the status of the old craftsman was rapidly declining and all sensitivity and human decency were being blunted, they were an attempt to establish relations between men on an honourable level. Fines were prescribed for the discourtesy of late or non-attendance. If the Warden was late he was forfeited sixpence. Failure to attend increased his fine to one shilling—at a time when masons' wages averaged only four shilling a day!

Swearing, drunkenness and lack of respect for officials or other members were frowned upon and carried fines. And "any Brother leaving the Lodge Room and not returning the same evening without addressing the Chair and wishing the officers and brothers good night in the room shall forfeit one penny."

After the bye-laws and list of fines were the "Government Rules" for the local lodge. Last of all were the "Grand Rules" which set down the pattern of national administration for the Society.

From these it was obvious that the Union's principal objective was to use the combined strength of the various lodges to support strike action. The main function of

Grand Lodge was to act simply as a collection and distribution centre for "Turn-out" funds.

The lodges collected members' subscriptions of 3d. per week, nearly an hour's wages at that time, and had the prior right of using the money to pay for local administration. These were secretarial and other expenses such as initiation regalia: Warrington branch paid the large sum of £4 12s. for "delegates expenses, regalia, etc." for its opening night on the 15th September, 1832.

There was also the expenditure on beer. Each week the lodge tylers were paid for their services in beer. Every time new members were admitted to the Union the lodge suitably celebrated its gathering strength with a drop of ale. When a large influx of members took place the expenditure on "Ale for new Members and Tylers" reached a respectable total. At a time when a few coppers were enough to provide a hangover, Warrington spent 13s. 1½d. on this item on what must have been a really Grand Opening Night.

Only after this expenditure had been met was there any likelihood of the remaining surplus being sent to Grand Lodge. The central fund was then used to channel assistance to any lodge which had members out on strike. If the fund was not sufficient to meet demand, and this was quite frequent because the lodges were reluctant to let any money out of their control, then an appeal was launched or a levy imposed on members.

The power and effectiveness of Grand Lodge was severely limited. In part this was due to the unwillingness of the local lodges to meet the expenses necessary for central administration. Basically it was because they were extremely hostile to any proposal which might tend to erode local autonomy. There was not even the opportunity for Grand Lodge to acquire stability or experience for, each year, it was moved so that it "be held at the principal Lodge in each District as they stand in Rotation." This rule both satisfied the demand that all the districts had a fair crack of the administrative whip and also the desire to avoid the expense of maintaining a fixed general office.

The structure of the Union was therefore fairly simple. Grouped in districts the lodges each sent a delegate to their district lodge meetings. From among themselves they elected a " Grand Master, a Deputy Grand Master and a Corresponding Secretary who shall retain office twelve months." This District committee met four times a year on the fourth Wednesday in March, June, September and December.

Each district was entitled to send one delegate to Grand Lodge meetings, which were held twice a year. Though it seems absurd to hold what was tantamount to two national delegate conferences every year, it should be understood that extensive policy making was not the purpose. Primarily it was a half-yearly audit in which the lodges satisfied themselves that the officials of Grand Lodge distributed the turnout income in the right way. The masons were similar to most other early trade unionists in one respect, they easily became suspicious about the character of anyone handling their precious funds.

The first Grand Lodge meeting in each year elected a " President, Vice, and Secretary . . . to retain their office 12 months." The fixed dates for meetings were the fourth Wednesday in September and March at 10 o'clock in the morning. If any delegate showed disrespect to the assembly by not being present before quarter past ten he was fined a shilling. " And for non-attendance 5s. The fines to go towards defraying Grand Lodge expenses."

One point of difference between the rules for district and Grand Lodge meetings shows the transitional nature of the Union. For district meetings the officers elected are given names reminiscent of the officials in the old operative masons' lodges: ' Grand Master and Deputy Grand Master.' The same two officers of Grand Lodge, however, are known in modern idiom as ' President and Vice.'

The Society's single-mindedness of purpose was revealed in the rule: " The object of this Society shall be to advance and equalise the price of labour in every Branch of the trade we admit into this Society." The only benefit payable was for strike action and a simple scale of payment, recognising family responsibilities, was laid down. " A turnout shall receive out of the funds of the Society if a single man 7s. per week. If a married man 8s. per week. If a wife and one child 9s. If a wife and two children 10s. per week but no more shall be allowed on any occasion whatever."

The skilled mason and bricklayer had gone through the same severe decline as other trades in living and working conditions. Hours of work lengthened rather than shortened. But the rise of the trade unions was a sign that the workers were beginning to fight back. The long decline was almost at its end. The organisations of the masons and the bricklayers met with early successes in obtaining increased wages. More important still, they quickly appreciated the benefits and power they had gained by combining within their separate trades. What greater objectives might they not achieve if they crossed the trade barrier or, at least, came to some sort of alliance with each other.

This new process of thought was to lead to a development within the building unions which immediately brought them to the forefront in the fight against capitalism and, for a few hopeful months, seemed to provide them with a solution to all of their problems. Their dream was of a powerful general union of all building trades.

CHAPTER 4

A GHOST ORGANISATION

AS far as official documents are concerned the Operative Builders Union of the years 1832-34 might well be a ghost organisation. Only one circular remains as a forlorn echo of one of the most exciting and moving periods in the history of building trades unionism.

Occasional and intriguing glimpses of the Union are caught from contemporary papers and periodicals. Even these, however, are often second-hand and unreliable reports in publications which were much more interested in the political ferment of the time. Nothing is certain about the organisation—its official name,* structure, membership, or the years of existence. It is around 1832 that reports of its activities are first seen in the press of the day. By 1834 it has reached a crisis and begins to disintegrate. After this there is silence.

Though other histories have generally agreed about the origins of the O.B.U. " being wrapped in mystery," what information we have seems to give us at least one clear, hard fact; that the masons and bricklayers were the men who took the first bold steps in the attempt to create a united union of all building workers. " It is supposed that the bricklayers and masons unions possess considerably the greatest number of members and their funds

*The "Operative Builders Union" is the title generally given to the organisation in press and periodical reports of the time, though sometimes it is referred to as the " General Union". Doubts about its official title are not resolved by the one remaining circular (printed as Appendix " B " to this book) for no title is given at all.

considerably more wealthy than other trades that have yet joined the union," commented the *Poor Man's Guardian.**

The Grand Rules of the masons adopted in 1831 also show that they possessed the vision to see that building workers would best be served by a united trade union organisation fighting for a common wage rate for all craftsmen. The first and second rules clearly express these principles. They ran:

> "(1st) That this Society be called the friendly Society of Operative Stone Masons and Builders in general.
>
> (2nd) That the object of this Society shall be to advance and equalise the price of Labour in every Branch of the trade we admit into this Society."

It is probable that the O.B.U. was based upon the organisations of the masons and bricklayers and that it soon attracted the adherence of other trades. It was still far from being a fully united single union, however. The remaining records of the masons and the sole surviving circular of the O.B.U., indicate that it probably had a loosely knit, federal basis with each separate trade union sending three delegates to the Grand Central Committee. At its strongest period there were seven of these trade union sections; masons, bricklayers, carpenters, plumbers, painters, plasterers and slaters.

The delegates from each of these seven sections made up a Grand Central Committee 21 strong, which elected a Grand Chairman and Grand Secretary. This Committee was responsible for federal decisions in between meetings of the 'Grand Parliament.' When the Parliament met it was attended by delegates from all districts of the unions affiliated to the O.B.U.

The power and influence of the Union was remarkable for its time, but has sometimes been over-rated by writers who wondered at the reason for its tragically early collapse. Only two of the affiliated organisations, the masons and the bricklayers, had established themselves on anything like a

*Page 379, November 1833.

national basis. The others were mainly confined to the areas of Lancashire and the Midlands generally. The majority of them were also so recent in origin that it is very doubtful if their internal organisation was anything but the most rudimentary.

The masons were indisputably the king-pins of the O.B.U. They took the lead in every major strike it conducted and had certainly the best developed administration of all the trades. To each of their own half-yearly Grand Lodge meetings, for instance, a printed financial statement was given to delegates showing the number of lodges in the O.S.M., their financial position and also the total finances of the Union together with membership. It is extremely unlikely that any of the other trades, perhaps with the exception of the bricklayers, could have presented such a detailed account of themselves.

And enthusiastic reports of "40 to 50 thousand members flooding in" to the O.B.U. must be tempered by the knowledge that, from the O.S.M.'s records, it seems as if its own membership was 5,000 at the peak of enthusiasm. Few of the other six trades, if any, would have reached this number and the total affiliation to the O.B.U. therefore is likely to have fallen short of the 40 to 50 thousand claimed for it.

Whatever its actual membership there is no doubt that the intense enthusiasm and loyalty it drew from building workers stimulated an equally intense fear among the master contractors. In the few years after the repeal of the Combination Acts, they had seen an upsurge of autonomous local unions followed by the gradual creation of organisations on a national scale. Now it seemed as if the new general union was to lead to a unification of all building workers which would possess an almost irresistible power and influence.

Little wonder that the smaller employers consulted anxiously between themselves and cast apprehensive eyes at the rapid development of the O.B.U. They were convinced—as were the jubilant and almost over-confident members affiliated to the general union—that once the organisation had soundly established itself there would be a challenge for supremacy.

Instead of a challenge they found themselves united, even if it were a somewhat surprised and uneasy unity, in an attempt to rid the industry of the rapidly developing general contracting system.

Both operatives and small craft masters knew their interests were threatened if the system extended widely. The master had his status and hard-earned capital to safeguard. The men knew with a grim certainty that under the general contractor they would have a greater struggle to maintain wages and conditions. For, while it was less onerous to have only one builder to deal with instead of making individual contracts with every craft master, the public or private client was not over willing to pay extra for the convenience. In practice this meant that the general contractor had to make his profit from a combination of better managerial efficiency plus holding down the wages and conditions of his workmen, or in trying to force a greater output from them. In addition to this the men knew that the more remote general contractor would not have the same trade relationship and understanding of the small craft masters.

Throughout the Midlands, therefore, the O.B.U. began to move against general contracting with a campaign to ensure " that no new building should be erected by contract with one person." When the men found the small masters almost completely united at their side they were cockahoop at the ' victory ' which they thought they had won.

But it was almost completely meaningless. They had not fought anyone: their campaign was basically an appeal to intending clients to preserve the old and cumbersome system of tendering by trades in preference to general contracting.

The masters were not so deceived by events. The more astute of them realised that, though the campaign had slightly retarded the spread of general contracting, business would be increasingly channelled to the general builder simply because it was far more convenient for the client.

If profit was to be made along this path then that was the way they would have to travel. Those who could began to accumulate extra capital and tendered for a wider range of work.

But the members of the unions within the O.B.U. still could not comprehend that the industry itself was changing, and the change was almost beyond them to control. They were not even conscious of the fact that their own formation of a federation was as much a sign of transition as the replacement of individual craft masters by the general contractor. To them the action of the masters who had gone over to general contracting was simply regarded as outright betrayal. Their indignation at this, allied to the general feeling of confidence and power they had acquired, now resulted in a vital and bitter challenge to the employers over conditions in the industry.

Liverpool saw the first of the conflict. Simultaneously each of the separate trades in the town sent a list of demands to their masters. A uniform wage was demanded for "each class of operatives, a limitation of apprentices, the prohibition of machinery and piecework, and other requirements special to each branch of the trade."

If these demands were hard for the employers to swallow, even more unpalatable was the aggressive and scornful manner in which the unions presented them. "We consider," they wrote, "that you have not treated our rules with that deference you ought to have done, we consider you highly culpable and deserving of being severely chastised."

Not content with admonishing the masters like an irate parent with a wayward child, the unions added further insult by the novel suggestion that they would make the employers responsible for any strike pay that might be incurred: "Further" they added, "each and every one in such strike shall be paid by you the sum of four shillings per day for every day you refuse to comply."* The employers were outraged by these demands. They

* *History of Trade Unionism*, page 129.

decided, perhaps not without justification, that they represented a declaration of war rather than a basis for negotiation. At a hastily summoned meeting in June 1833 they decided to take up the challenge flung at them by the O.B.U. There would be no discussion between them and the Union; their aim was its complete extinction. With this objective in view they publicly announced that employment would only be offered to those men who signed a formal declaration that they were not union members.

" We, the undersigned," it ran, " do hereby declare that we are not in any way connected with the General Union of the Building Trades and that we do not and will not contribute to the support of such members of the said union as are or may be out of work in consequence of belonging to such union."

The only way to work for the men lay through signing their names to the 'Document'—as it was soon to become notoriously known in the building industry. If the masters had felt that the initial demands of the Union made compromise impossible, their 'Document' was a retaliation in kind. The strike was immediate, and the two sides ranged antagonistically against each other across the silent yards and building sites of Liverpool.

Even at this stage the O.B.U. might have been able to force a compromise if the Grand Central Committee had been able to carry out its allotted function of collecting strike funds from the various affiliated unions and channelling them to the turnouts. But this presupposed a large number of members at work and able to pay the necessary levies. In Birmingham and Manchester, however, two of the main centres of strength for the O.B.U., events were rapidly echoing those in Liverpool.

The men made their demands and were given the same ultimatum; sign the 'Document' or else. . . . Soon the struggle had developed throughout the Midlands and the O.B.U. was faced with strike pay expenditure that it found impossible to meet from its own resources. Its member unions collected all they could from those not directly involved. Organisations outside the building industry, recognising the importance of the fight, also sent donations to the Grand Central Committee. The number of men on strike, however, was growing fast and funds were being quickly drained.

The situation now became extremely critical for the O.B.U. It had only been in existence a year or two and its federal structure was still far from perfected. Its member unions were not only financially involved in the Midlands struggle but in numerous other small strikes, triggered off by individual lodges which still possessed a great deal of autonomy. In London also a tense situation was developing between the employers and the men which might at any time lead to another major strike. For the various affiliated trades, vainly trying to keep the central turnout funds fully supported, it was like attempting to fill an outsize bath with a badly leaking bucket.

What had started as a bold challenge to the employers was fast becoming a battle for survival. It was a battle the unions might have won even with its heavy commitments at that stage. Though it would have meant a gradual disengagement from the struggle without securing any material gains, at least they would still have retained the valuable framework of the O.B.U. plus the hard-earned, if bitter, experience with which to improve its organisation and strength. It was just at this crucial moment, however, that the unions came under the influence of the famous Robert Owen and undertook further commitments which were to lead straight to the destruction of their federation.

CHAPTER 5

FAILURE OF AN IDEAL

FEW men have reached the authority and stature of Robert Owen at the time of his greatest influence on the trade union and co-operative movement. As a successful mill owner his first departure from the normal harshness and brutality of the day was to give comparatively civilised and humane conditions to the people he employed. Becoming increasingly involved in social problems he began to propound co-operative solutions to the terrible evils suffered by the mass of the people.

To many of them he appeared an almost heaven-sent saviour. Allied to their natural gratitude for his work was a sense of awe that someone of his wealth and position should condescend to become immediately concerned with their problems. Meetings were arranged for him throughout the country at which a triumphant Owen was acclaimed by his audience for showing them an apparently easy way of achieving a wonderful co-operative commonwealth in which their poverty and misery would be a thing of the past.

This was perhaps the greatest fault Owen had: simplifying the struggle and effort necessary for achieving his objectives to the extent that he encouraged people to take on tasks for which they were completely unprepared. It was this fault which assisted the destruction of the Builders Union.

Disillusioned by unsuccessful attempts he had made to build co-operative communities, Owen turned his attention to the trade unions as an alternative method of achieving his goal. There was no need, he urged, to engage in bitter warfare with the employers; the men could simply decide to join together in a co-operative productive society which they would themselves control. The employers, continued his theme which anticipated a similar one by some years, would just wither away. The general union of building workers excited his interest because he felt its federal structure provided the basis for a simple transformation into a co-operative unit.

Once he had decided the direction of his activities, one or two of Owen's disciples organised invitations for him to meet some of the more important district lodges of the unions affiliated to the O.B.U. At these meetings he had apparently little difficulty in converting the delegates to an enthusiastic acceptance of his proposals for a 'National Building Guild.'

To them Owen's scheme was most attractive. For a start the masters—both the small craft employer and the general contractor—would be swept out of existence by the simple expedient of the Guild offering the services of its members direct to the public. Unemployment, one of the greatest fears they had, would also be a thing of the past. "None of the Brethren will be unemployed when they desire to work," they confidently declared, "for when the public do not require their services they will be employed by the Guild to erect superior dwellings and other buildings for themselves."* *The Pioneer*, at that time semi-official journal of the O.B.U., exultantly reported Owen's meetings with the district lodges. "A grand secret has been unfolded to the world," its readers were told, "that Labour is the source of all wealth."†

Few of Owen's listeners seriously questioned his scheme or the validity of his proposals for avoiding unemployment—though it was almost like suggesting they could live by taking in each other's washing when there was no other work in hand. Instead they agreed with him that it was necessary to have the entire Builders Union behind the Guild before it could become a practicable proposition.

---

* *Builders' History*, page 464.

† *The Pioneer*, 21st September, 1833.

For this purpose it was arranged that Owen attend the next meeting of the Grand Parliament, which was to take place at Manchester in September 1833.

Two hundred and seventy-five delegates arrived for the Parliament and paraded the streets arm in arm before proceeding towards the meeting place at which Owen's proposals were extensively debated.* At this larger meeting Owen was not without his critics but, in the end, his supreme self-confidence and the authority with which he forced home his views rewarded him with a majority for the Guild. If Owen had been regarded merely as a wild visionary with impracticable ideals the delegates to the Grand Parliament might have exercised more caution. They gave great weight to his opinions, however, because they were well aware that he had an outstanding record of business success as a mill owner. It was not likely, they reasoned, that a man of his experience would propose a financially impracticable scheme.

Now that he had persuaded them to accept the principle of the Guild, Owen's final task was to induce the unions affiliated to the O.B.U. to relinquish their separate autonomy and transform themselves into a single organisation which would provide the basis for all his plans. After some debate the delegates reluctantly accepted the need for 'universal' as against 'exclusive' government and the Grand Central Committee was instructed to formulate plans for the change-over.

Owen's triumph seemed absolute but, in view of the rapidly deteriorating position of the O.B.U., it was almost worthless. The continuing strike throughout the Midlands had devastated its funds and was exposing the weakness of its shaky federal organisation. Yet here were its leaders and the union delegates seemingly prepared to accept that, in one simple stroke, they could move beyond federation into a united guild able to undertake heavy financial building commitments. Their decision seems even more incomprehensible in view of the acute awareness by most

* *Character, Objects and Effects of Trade Unions*, page 43.

of them that local lodges were so jealous of their independence they were even reluctant to give any real power to their own executive bodies. How then were they to be converted into surrendering their autonomy to an even more remote central control.

Possibly the very grimness of their circumstances drove them to accepting what seemed an easy way out. They had been so confident about the power of their new found unity in the O.B.U. to force better conditions from their employers. A loyal and enthusiastic membership had been ready to make a proud challenge under the banner of general union. Now weeks of sacrifice and suffering for the men and their families lay behind them and still the strike continued. Their high hopes of the O.B.U. were gradually being replaced with a desperate awareness of its obvious limitations. In the future they could only see a continuation of the same bitter struggle to win the meagre necessities of life.

To these men the National Building Guild must have seemed a miraculous way of avoiding almost certain defeat and the path along which they could completely emancipate themselves. They refused to face up to the great difficulties involved, or even the possibility of failure, because they fervently wanted the scheme to be as simple and certain of success as they had been assured by Owen.

Plans were therefore rushed through for headquarters worthy of the new National Building Guild, which was to be situated in Birmingham. On the 28th November, 1833, a brave procession, in which all the trades marched with colourful banners, proudly wound its way through the town to where the foundation stone of the new Grand Hall was to be laid at a site in Broad Street. The most pathetic comment on the situation is that the very same day, Thursday, 28th November, the Grand Central Committee met at Manchester and decided to send out an urgent circular warning the district lodges that they were finding it almost impossible to carry out " the Rules agreed upon at the last Delegate Meeting."* The laying

* This circular is printed as Appendix " B."

of the foundation stone was to signal the end, not the beginning, of an era.

The Society "is nearly eradicated for want of zealous co-operation" complained the Committee. Some lodges were neither sending true returns of membership nor the full financial levy agreed upon "at the last Delegate Meeting." This in turn was causing deep bitterness among those who were struggling to honour the decisions made at the September Parliament.

As the Builders Union became more and more paralysed in thought and action so the suffering of the strikers increased. Men who had already been existing for months on the pitifully inadequate turnout pay were now sometimes receiving as little as 4s. per week from the Union. "Families would not have suffered the privations they have from such miserable pittance received," bitterly complained the Central Committee members, "if other towns had paid as well as the bodies we represent."

This last complaint was perhaps the most significant indication of the weakening position of the O.B.U., for only four of the affiliated unions were signatories to the circular, the masons, plasterers, slaters and painters, who were each represented by three delegates. Just two months after the most important parliament they had ever held, and at a time when the Union was struggling to fight its way out of serious difficulties, the carpenters, plumbers and bricklayers had not sent a single delegate to what was an extremely vital meeting. Already, in spirit, there was a growing rejection of the 'Universal Government' principle that had been so enthusiastically acclaimed a short time ago.

The fight with the masters was now being complicated by an increasingly vicious struggle between those who supported the retention of 'exclusive' government and those who wanted to lay the necessary basis for the National Building Guild. Not only were the unions warring against each other; deep divisions were also appearing in the internal structure of those where there was a split on the issue. Apparently incensed at the leading part being played by some carpenters' lodges in the drive to retain exclusive government, the Birmingham carpenters responded by announcing that " we the Friendly Operative Carpenters and Joiners of Birmingham (in open lodge assembled) in co-operation with all the other building trades in union in this town, feel ourselves duty bound to abide by the degree (for universal government) of the delegates' meeting held in Manchester in September last."*

The affairs of the O.B.U., however, were gradually reaching such a state of confusion and near anarchy that some of the leading officials of the various unions must have tacitly accepted its death. Their immediate and growing concern was to ensure that their own trade organisations were not buried with it. And they soon found this fight for survival further complicated by Owen's sponsorship of another venture.

His success with the delegates of the Builders Union had fired him to even wider visions; why not a great all embracing union in which the various trades could produce their goods and exchange them among themselves. In time this union would become the real power in the land. With hardly a backward glance to see how the plans of the O.B.U. were working out in practice, he hurried to London and used the immense prestige he now had to persuade a number of unions to convene a conference to discuss his new proposals. At the beginning of 1834 the meeting was held and it was agreed to launch a new union which was given an impressive title symbolising Owen's desires—The Grand National Consolidated Trades Union.

Again there were enthusiastic reports of members pouring in to the new union. 500,000 was the figure claimed for it within a few months. But, in fact, the Grand National had not performed any recruiting miracle among the unorganised. Its membership was achieved, in the main, by the simple amalgamation of the already existing trade unions which gave it their allegiance. And

---

* *The Pioneer*, 7th December, 1833.

even then, knowing the relatively small membership of some of the strongest unions within the country, it is very doubtful if the figure of half a million was anywhere near the truth.

Where the unions taken over by the new organisation were entirely confined to the South no problem arose. For the national unions of the masons and bricklayers, however, now emeshed in the failing fortunes of the O.B.U., it was a severe blow when they found their London districts seceding to the Grand National.

The position was particularly serious for the Operative Stonemasons' Society. Not only had their London district gone, the Grand National had attracted other of their lodges to its banner. Even Worcester, only a few miles from the masons' stronghold of Birmingham, had gone over and one of its members had been elected to the new union's ' cabinet '.*

The masons had been the driving force behind the O.B.U. and their soundly based organisation had given the Builders Union the stability to carry on under increasing difficulties. Now the main prop itself was almost broken in two and the end was in sight. Already the men involved in the Midlands' strike were drifting back to work. Not because they lacked courage—they had already shown plenty of that—but because it was the only alternative to complete starvation. To get their families a piece of bread they now had to make possibly their greatest sacrifice: to sign the hated 'Document' in front of their victorious masters who, only a few short months ago, they had so confidently challenged for control of the industry.

Nor did they gain any consolation from progress made by the Grand National Consolidated Trades Union. Almost immediately it was involved in disputes over which it had almost no control. The weaknesses and inefficiencies of the separate unions could not be cured simply by fusing them all together. If the more compact builders federation had not the strength to achieve Owen's

---

* See O.S.M. Accounts for April/October 1834 and *The Crisis*, 12th July, 1834.

objectives, what chance had the larger and almost disorganised Grand National. Within a few months its fate was settled, and helped by a strike among the very builders' lodges it had attracted from the O.B.U.

The strike took place in London, where the brewery firm of Combe, Delafield & Co. had taken a strong stand against trade unionism. It would employ no man belonging to one it declared. This had a peculiar significance for building workers because it was a well established custom for beer to be brought in and drunk on the job. As just retaliation the men employed by the building firm of Messrs. Cubitt decided that they would not drink any beer which had been brewed by Combe, Delafield.

Cubitt's immediately reacted by saying that only Combe, Delafield's beer would be allowed on their jobs, and promptly locked out their workmen. Such a harsh decision can only be explained by the fact that the London employers were looking for any excuse to administer the lesson of the 'Document' they had learned from their Midlands' colleagues. All of the London masters now swung into line in an attempt to break the trade unions and the resistance of their members to sub-contracting and piecework. To regain employment the men were told they would have to come to terms on these matters and also sign the 'Document'. By July 1834, the dispute had spread throughout London and work was at a standstill.

The Grand National was completely powerless to assist. In fact it was so drained of strength by numerous other disputes that the London lock-out merely hastened its end. "One fatal blow succeeds another to accomplish the dissolution of the Grand Consolidated" mournfully reported *The Crisis* in July. "We have a melancholy tale to tell of the honesty of one at least of the Union cabinet. The Worcester delegate, Mr. Hall, a stonemason, and one of the four Executives, has already embarked for Sydney, New South Wales, and God knows how much of the money of the poor operatives he has taken along with him."*

* *The Crisis*, 12th July, 1834.

By the end of the summer of 1834 both the Builders Union and the Grand National were spent forces and Owen had begun to look in other directions for the building of his ' New Society '. His brief connection with the trade union movement was nearly ended.

In London the collapse of the Grand National left the building workers struggling alone, but still determined that they would not sign the ' Document ' or compromise on any of the other demands made by the employers.

At Birmingham the Stonemasons were being forced to face the fact that the Builders Union was already of historical rather than practical value. The wonderful Guild Hall, which was to have been the power house for the creation of a better society, remained a half-finished shell—a mocking reminder of the great ambitions of the O.B.U. Other sections of the Union had already begun to break up. They now knew there was no short cut to an efficient all-embracing organisation able to win and maintain a reasonable standard of life for building workers. Enthusiasm and courage alone could not make up for lack of experience and deficiencies in administration.

With the final defeat in the Midlands' strike, and the breakaway of part of the Union to the Grand National, the O.S.M. had almost reached a stage of inertia. Now it received a further blow. George Bevan who had been full-time Grand Correspondence Secretary for the past 18 months, had apparently become increasingly convinced that the O.S.M. would itself fall in the wreckage of the Builders Union; the remaining funds might just as well be his. He disappeared with a total haul of £35 3s. 9½d.

There was only a handful of delegates, nine plus the Grand Master and Grand Tyler, at the September 1834 Grand Delegate meeting of the O.S.M. and they heard with dismay of Bevan's treachery. From the records he had been preparing, and even these proved optimistic, they saw that membership had fallen to 1,941. The total amount of money possessed by the entire Union, Grand Lodge funds plus the balances in every lodge, came to only £54 15s. 4½d.* But this disaster, which might well have shattered the Union, at last stimulated the delegates to take the necessary steps to save it.

It forced them to accept officially what they had known in their hearts for some time; that the Builders Union was dead and their own fight for recovery would have to be under exclusive government. To lead them in that fight they managed to persuade one of the delegates to the meeting, Angus McGregor, to take over the vital position of full-time Grand Correspondence Secretary. It was an extremely wise decision for, in the few short years he was to hold the job, Angus proved himself one of the finest men who ever served his fellow trade unionists in the Stonemasons' Society.

---

* O.S.M. Reports, March/September 1834.

CHAPTER 6

ANGUS THE BUILDER

"BRADFORD District was in a state of confusion and almost ruin, partly between the strike and law suit. Newcastle was in the very heat of a strike, which has since cost them upwards of £40. Leeds had nothing in the funds and had since some difficulty in supporting their proportionate share of expenses. Plymouth was then in debt and has since had a strike, from which they are left to extricate themselves. York was in debt, Huddersfield, Chester and Carlisle Districts were extinct . . . such was the state of the Union at the Grand Delegate Meeting."

When Angus McGregor completed this gloomy survey of the shattered state of the O.S.M. he had no illusions left about the difficulty of his task in trying to rebuild the Union.* What gave him even greater concern than the poor physical state of the organisation was his realisation that the faith of the members in unionism as an ideal had been almost destroyed. Coupled with this was a heightened distrust of giving any power or money to the Central Committee; it would be some time before the lodges forgot George Bevan's plundering of the central funds.

McGregor's primary objective was the regeneration of confidence among the members; only when this had been accomplished could there be any revival of physical strength. As a first step he put every lodge fully in the picture on finances and general activity by sending each

* O.S.M. Returns, 11th December, 1834.

district lodge, every fortnight, a return of all income, expenditure and news about the strikes which were taking place. Beginning in September 1834, these Fortnightly Returns were issued without a break for 87 years until the O.S.M. merged with the unions of bricklayers in 1921. In the vital few years after the break up of the O.B.U. they were to give badly needed stability to the masons.

But the most valuable asset the Union had in its struggle for survival was Angus McGregor. It was his complete honesty and simplicity of character, allied to a canny shrewdness, which the other delegates realised were absolutely necessary qualities in a man holding the key position in the Union at that time. Perhaps it gave them even greater confidence to know that he was not particularly keen to take over the job. Angus had a quiet but deep pride in his craft and almost no desire for personal prominence or importance in any other sphere.

Now the hands that would much rather have been patiently carving stone were occupied, often far into the night, in painstakingly writing out the Returns to every district lodge. Apart from the financial statement with which he started each one, the rest of the Return would be a personal message suited to the needs of the particular district to which he was writing.

Even though the London District had seceded from the O.S.M. to join the Grand National, McGregor kept in touch with its officials in the hope that this once strong section of the Union would return to the fold. Now he received an appeal for help from them. Two hundred of their members were involved in the 'Beer strike' which had been dragging on for nearly four months and, though they had an income of £50 per week, expenses were twice that amount. Pleading for financial assistance they gave optimistic news of the strike. "Three masters gave in last week and we expect to conquer if we can keep our payments good for another fortnight."*

The Grand Committee of the O.S.M. was powerless to help: all it possessed were the debts it had inherited

* O.S.M. Returns, 16th September, 1834.

and constant pleas were being made to the districts for money to meet them. McGregor nevertheless wrote to the lodges and asked them to send any money they could possibly spare to London. But, by that time, the slight financial assistance from this source had little influence on the almost inevitable outcome. Having held out during the summer months the employers were not likely to capitulate when they knew the approach of winter would immeasurably weaken the position of the men. By November the dispute had fizzled out in a compromise more favourable to the employers than the unions; the men would not be forced to sign the Document but they had to give way on most of the other conditions demanded by the employers. With the Grand National now dead, the remnants of the masons' organisation in London made arrangements to rejoin the O.S.M.

The Friendly Society of Bricklayers was in a much worse position. Their central administration had fallen apart when the London area had gone over to the Grand National and the organisation in the Midlands seems to have collapsed completely with the break-up of the O.B.U. The end of the Beer dispute found the remaining lodges weak and dispirited. Not for some time were they strong enough to rebuild their organisation on anything like a national pattern.

By contrast the O.S.M. began to show amazing signs of revival. Several small strikes on wages were fought successfully and these victories were recorded in the Returns to give new heart to all of the lodges.

The strike at Blackburn was perhaps the most significant sign of the resurgence of the Union. For centuries it had been the custom that building workers' wages should be reduced in the winter months, generally from November to March. Recent years had seen a growing resentment against the practice and this was reflected in the outbreak of strikes which regularly took place toward the end of each year as the men resisted attempts to lower their wages.

Four shillings a day was the mason's rate in Blackburn, and this was normally cut to 3s. 6d. in November. The members of the O.S.M. met and agreed to strike if the masters refused to make it 3s. 9d. Ten of them turned out in support of their claim at the beginning of November and the rest prepared to join them. " But, to their surprise," reported McGregor, " all the Masters met and agreed to give them 4s." A document was drawn up and signed by all the employers agreeing to retain one rate throughout the year. To the jubilant Blackburn masons it was a totally unexpected victory.

When the employers had time to think about their promise to give more than had been demanded, however, they began to kick themselves for being fools. At the end of the first week's work they broke the agreement and told their men they could have the 3s. 9d. but no more. Forty masons immediately walked out of the yards on strike.

McGregor was far from happy about a strike taking place at that time of year, but he told the lodges that the Blackburn members must be supported in their resistance against ' an act of oppression.' £20 per week was needed in strike pay and he urged the districts to " do your utmost to raise the first week's support for them among your lodges. I am confident the Masters will give in." His optimism was justified for the fight was all over in three weeks and a jubilant McGregor reported that he had been able " to pay the turnouts up to the last farthing so that it is the first strike by which there has been no debt contracted."*

The ready response to McGregor's call for money to help Blackburn was a sign of the rapidly increasing confidence the districts had in him. They knew if he asked others to sacrifice he was more than prepared to do so himself. To drag the O.S.M. out of its morass of debt he both tried to husband its resources and bring in money from every possible source. In December 1834 he humbly informed the districts that: " I have commenced work when I have time, it is a saving to the Society and great

* O.S.M. Returns, 12th December, 1834.

satisfaction to me so I hope as long as you find the business done you will make no objection."

At that time his wage as Grand Correspondence Secretary was 27s. per week or roughly the mason's rate of wages in the better areas. After rushing through his Union work as quickly as possible McGregor would scour the Birmingham yards looking for a job. Regularly he was putting an average of 14s. per week back into the Central funds as payment for "Work by Secretary". In effect he was drawing less than half pay from the O.S.M.

By the middle of 1835 the old debts had been cleared off and membership had risen to 2,138.* Every one of the districts had been revived and the Union had re-established its connection with Ireland through the lodge at Armagh. And though there was no hard and fast agreement between them, extremely good relations had been established between the O.S.M. and the Scottish Masons Society.

A new spirit of militancy swept through the lodges. They began to look beyond the rate of wages as the only issue worth fighting about. Piecework, sub-contracting and working by candle-light became legitimate grounds for strike action. In particular the practice of working the dark winter hours by the light of candles aroused deep resentment. Apart from the affect on their eyesight the men looked upon it as an insult to their dignity and their craft.

In their growing confidence the masons began to re-establish their uncompromising attitude to blacklegs and non-unionists. In any town where they had reasonably strong organisation they would either drive a man into the Union or out of the locality. When a large job started at Northwich, for instance, the masons decided to make it a closed shop. Five men were brought into the works from outside the town and they refused to take out union cards. It cost the local masons a month's strike but they finally forced them to join; one of the blacks "being so

* O.S.M. Accounts, March/June 1835.

poorly was obliged to come to the lodge on horseback to enter as they would not have his money in his absence."*

As the Union developed McGregor realised that the old method of writing returns to each individual district was almost beyond his capacity and, in any case, did not provide a sufficiently strong enough link between all of the lodges and Grand Lodge. He campaigned for the returns to be printed so that a much more complete and extensive picture could be given to every lodge and the members generally. His main opposition came from the few districts who thought that their business might be betrayed by the printer to whom it was entrusted, though Manchester Lodge also objected " that a printed letter has not one-quarter the effect of the original one."

Angus retorted dryly that " as they are likely to be alone in their opinion we can accommodate them with the manuscript should they prefer it to the printed copy."

When the first printed Return was sent out on the 11th June, 1836, it ended with a paragraph typical of McGregor. In it he asked " whether you consider the Grand Secretary's wages ought to be reduced as it reduces his labours." It shows the regard in which he was held that not one of the lodges took up his offer.

The task Angus had set himself was now almost complete. Certainly there was still great room for expansion, but there was no longer any doubt about the survival of the O.S.M. " The prosperity of our society has been rapid in its progress," he wrote, " but still there are tracts of the country where the Union is comparatively unknown, and there are lodges which with difficulty maintain an existence. Surely there can be no greater proof of the utility and paramount necessity of the Union, than the marked contrast between such desolate deserts and those Districts in which Union presides! In the one we see the Masons working for low wages, slaves that seem to hug their chains, and cringing cowards at the nod of a tyrant, on the other hand let us refer you to the record of

---

* O.S.M. Returns, 6th August, 1835.

our struggles and victories, our successful resistance to oppression, the liberty we have wrested from the tyrants' grasp, and the high wages we have received as a proof that 'Union is Strength.'"*

In September 1836 he resigned as Corresponding Secretary and the grateful members of the Union voluntarily subscribed to a testimonial fund which raised enough to provide a farewell dinner at which Angus was presented with an engraved silver snuffbox. And of all the early secretaries he was the only one who left office in an atmosphere of goodwill and widespread regret at his departure.

No other secretary of the masons was to establish such a personal standing in only two years, or record such progress for the Union. From the crippling debts of 1834 the funds had climbed to a surplus in the lodges and Grand Lodge of over £1,108 in September 1836.†

In addition to reviving all the old district lodges new ones had been opened and there were now 20 of these in England with 84 local lodges attached to them. The organisation had also extended its activities in Ireland and there were three districts there, Belfast, Kingston and Armagh, encompassing 16 local lodges. Total membership of the Union had nearly doubled in the two years; from a questionable 1,941 at the time of Bevan's default to 3,570.

Progress was not only limited to a growth in numerical strength. The O.S.M.'s whole system of government had been placed on a much sounder basis and its activities extended so that members were offered a wider range of benefits.

One of the contributory factors to the Union's advance was the retention of Grand Lodge at Birmingham (though it could be removed annually if so decided by a majority vote) since the break-up of the O.B.U. This gave Grand Lodge members time to acquire executive experience.

---

* O.S.M. Returns, 7th July, 1836.

† O.S.M. Accounts, March/September 1836.

Due to lack of money they were not, as with modern executive councils, sent as representatives of the various districts. Instead they were chosen from the members of Grand Lodge wherever that happened to be. The removal of Grand Lodge from one district to another, therefore, would have meant an entirely new executive formed by members who had normally no previous experience in national responsibility. If such a move had been decided upon during the masons' struggle for recovery it might have had serious consequences.

Control over strikes had also been tightened and, except for resistance to wage cuts and attempts by employers to abolish established practices, any lodge wishing to strike had to state its case in the Returns and await the verdict of a national ballot. Once this sanction had been given the turnouts would receive strike pay from central funds. Generally the results of these ballots were announced within four weeks and the lodge concerned told whether or not it could proceed.

Not only was there quite often a list of proposed strikes on which the members had to ballot—occasionally a lodge would even request permission to strike some time in advance! " We have a particularly vicious employer we want to teach a lesson " they would say in effect. " However the winter is approaching and it would be suicidal to strike now, but next spring the employer takes over a big contract and we would like permission to strike then when it will embarrass him most." To these appeals, and nearly every other claim for official strike sanction, the worthy brothers usually responded with a handsome majority in favour.

A significant indication of the masons' still undaunted desire for general unionism was the fact that they were prepared to extend this strike coverage to other unions within the building industry. The first and most important Government Rule stated—and remained the same for many years—" That we, the members of the Friendly Society of Operative Masons, cordially agree to render support to all Building Trades in Union on legal strike making application for our support."*

This rule was used, on a number of occasions, to help plasterers, carpenters, plumbers and others. The original appeal would be made to the local lodge of the masons wherever the union concerned was on strike. This lodge then had the right to put the case in the Returns and appeal for a majority vote in favour on the same basis as if its own members had been involved in the dispute.

In addition to strike pay, McGregor's two years saw the creation of a sick scheme on a voluntary basis and the sounder establishment of tramp benefit. Unemployed members tramping around the country looking for work were entitled to draw a special relief card from their home lodge which was valid for three months. Union lodges situated about a convenient day's journey from one another were appointed relieving stations. On arrival in the town the tramp member would present his card to the lodge secretary who would initial it and then provide him with sixpence and a bed for the night.

This was increased to " one shilling and a bed for those members leaving town on strike." When the Union found itself involved in a long and costly dispute it would try to reduce the labour supply and the expense of strike pay by persuading some of the turnouts to go on the tramp looking for work elsewhere. The increase of sixpence in the relief allowance was intended as some small compensation for the voluntary sacrifice of home life and job they made to help the cause.

Appointed to take over this much smoother running organisation at the 1836 September Annual Delegate Meeting was James Rennie, the Manchester district representative. And if the delegates had actually been striving for contrast they could not have been more successful, for Rennie's character was almost the complete opposite of the man he succeeded.

* O.S.M. Rules, 1836 and onwards.

CHAPTER 7

ENTER THE 'BLACK PRINCE'

THERE was no doubt that James Rennie was a fair scribe and administrator, and no one more appreciated these qualities than himself. For a start he had his wages increased to thirty shillings per week on taking over the job and soon showed signs of being discontented with this. He also set the pattern for Grand Correspondence Secretaries abusing the Returns by airing their personal support or antagonism to any proposals put forward by the lodges. He further angered the members by preaching moderation to them at a time when the struggle to maintain wages was becoming increasingly bitter.

In particular the masons found that the big contractors constructing the new railways were proving hard task-masters. In 1830 George Stephenson had placed his famous steam engine, the "Rocket", on the Liverpool/Manchester line and its performance had sparked off a big railway boom. The men who rushed to invest their money in this new industrial development demanded both speed and low cost of construction from the contractors they employed. By 1836 a large number of masons were engaged in building bridges, tunnels and stations, and disputes connected with railway work were increasing as the men resisted attempts to introduce piecework and other practices to force up the pace of production while reducing costs.

Grissell & Peto, the big London firm, had secured a large slice of the construction work on the London and Birmingham railway. Opening up operations at the Birmingham end they put a notorious 'trouble-shooting' foreman in charge of the work, George Allen, 'a vindictive tyrant' who was such a sadistic bully that he was " known in London by the cognomen of the Black Prince."

Allen made a characteristic first attempt to drive down the rate of wages customary among the other contractors on the railway. He offered 4s. 6d. per day which was 6d. less than usual. Failing to get men at this rate he had to capitulate and agree to give 5s. But he decided to cheapen the job by other methods.

His men had to work " three hours per week more than any other brothers employed on the railway." Next Allen tried to force them to accept piecework and began to " treat them in the most degrading and insulting manner. Although there are good sheds erected, he would not allow them to work in them while it rained, and he compelled them to turn out of the sheds while it rained in torrents, or otherwise lose their time."*

The men finally revolted and came out on a two-week strike which succeeded in gaining them a personal interview with Peto, at which he agreed they should have the same conditions as the men employed by other railway contractors. " The strictest injunctions " he added, " had been given to the foreman to treat the men with every respect."

Not only was the Black Prince apparently to be restrained, there was even a hint that he might be dismissed if Peto thought he continued to be harsh. On this promise Peto certainly had his tongue well planted in his cheek for, a few years later, Allen was to serve the same employers in precipitating the most dramatic struggle in the history of the Masons' Union.

Rennie wrote glowingly about this victory over Peto which, he said, had compelled the firm " and their minion of tyranny to concede the rights of those they have not the power to enslave." But when the Coventry Lodge, only four months later, told him that its members working on the railway were thinking of striking for 5s. 6d. per day

* O.S.M. Returns, 12th May, 1837.

he sent them an angry admonition asking them to have more consideration for their employers! "In Mr. Peto's employment at Birmingham" an apparently short-memoried Rennie told the Coventry members, "were the men so inconsistent as to strike for 5s. 6d. per day, I have no doubt but he would soon be compelled to give it, being pushed with his work; still they are aware it would be taking advantage of him, and only cause him and all other employers to take every advantage of us in their power."*

The members of Coventry and the nearby lodges of Weeden and Rhode were enraged at Rennie's attitude. They had not asked for official strike assistance from the Union but had merely told Rennie of their plans and, in fact, had won their 5s. 6d. without much trouble. They certainly were not prepared to tolerate his supercilious preaching of consideration for employers who, they were fully aware, would not hesitate to take advantage if the boot was on the other foot. Their anger was intensified by the fact that Rennie had just demanded and obtained a rise in his wages to 33s. per week and was almost immediately pressing for another 3s.

"This secretary of ours, who wishes to have 6s. a day, had the audacity to write to Coventry, deprecating the brothers for what he calls inconsistency in taking an advantage of our employer in our unreasonable demand," they wrote in a letter which scorched the pages of the Returns. "Good God, is it inconsistent in working men to better their conditions? Men who are the real producers of wealth; men who, after toiling and bleeding to keep a set of lazy and indolent plunderers in luxury, are very frequently doomed to pass their declining years in some accursed bastille, or in obscurity, starvation and wretchedness! Ah! worthy brothers, we have hitherto been used worse than brutes, let us now strive to be men."

Within a few weeks nearly every lodge was embroiled in arguments about Rennie's attempt to increase his salary and the attitude he had taken on the Coventry strike.

---

* O.S.M. Returns, 29th September, 1837.

Some members pointed out that old McGregor had been quite well satisfied with 27s. per week and Rennie was certainly not a better man than McGregor. Others reminded Rennie that in Ireland, where conditions were always much worse than anywhere else, some skilled members had been cut to a wage of 18s. per week yet he wanted twice that amount.

The lodges of Preston, Liverpool, Weeden and Coventry took the lead in denouncing him. Even though powerful lodges rallied to his side, because they appreciated his qualities as an administrator, Rennie knew that he had lost the confidence of such a proportion of the membership that he could not possibly continue. "As I am not altogether dependent on the situation of secretary," he announced, "nor inclined to have my wages reduced for the gratification of the brothers of Preston, Liverpool, Weeden or Coventry, and as I should be exceedingly sorry were any ill-feeling or discord to be engendered in the society on my account I hereby give notice, that I shall resign the situation as soon as another can be elected, and I trust the society will elect one as soon as possible."*

Rennie's resignation had hardly been announced before an event took place which settled all the argument for and against moderation to the contractors, and also had the effect of cancelling Rennie's notice to quit. In Manchester the employers had been meeting secretly to discuss a united attack on the wages of the men. They decided that, with the approach of winter, the time was ripe to enforce a cut throughout every yard in the city. On the 18th November they gave their men notice that the new standard wage would be 25s. per week "thereby reducing them 2s. per week winter and summer."

There could only be one reply to this and, to a man, the Manchester members turned out with the complete approval of the entire membership of the O.S.M. It was the biggest strike since the famous Midlands and Lancashire dispute fought by the Builders Union. For

* O.S.M. Returns, 29th September, 1837.

four months an average of 200 to 300 men were out on strike and the Union had poured its entire central funds into Manchester. Its debts to the other trades and lodge house keepers—whom it had been unable to pay for tramp relief—came to a total of £634. By March of 1838 both sides in the dispute were completely exhausted and some employers had even gone bankrupt because the strikers had been so successful in preventing blacklegs doing work. A compromise on 4s. 6d. per day was agreed and the men went back.*

The dispute had seriously weakened the Union, while increasing the bitter debate about Rennie's attitude. A large number of the lodges thought the only way to recovery lay through radical changes in the Union's rules and constitution. Liverpool lodge was still leading a bitter attack on Rennie's demand for an increase in pay and this culminated in a proposal in the June Returns that "some method should be adopted to lessen the expense and the only method we can devise is to have no seat of government, then we would have no Grand Committee nor Grand Secretary, but carry on our business by the district lodges which would save us the sum of £200 or more."

There was little support for this proposal, which, in effect, was aimed at getting rid of the Grand Secretary by the simple but extreme process of almost destroying the Union itself. But Birkenhead lodge thought it might be done more subtly by the removal of Grand Lodge from Birmingham to Manchester and demanded a ballot on this proposal. This again was defeated by 834 to 247 votes.

If Rennie had merely been calling his attackers' bluff with the earlier announcement of his resignation, by now he was well aware that the only thing for him to do was to get out of office. At the September 1838 Grand Delegate Meeting Thomas Shortt from the Plymouth district was elected in his place, but his wages were cut to 30s. per

---

* O.S.M. Returns, 16th March, 1838.

week which indicated that the majority of delegates were in sympathy with the general attack on Rennie's previous demands.

A cut in salary was of small concern to Shortt. A man of medium build and fiery temper, which he tried hard to restrain, Shortt had spent most of his life in the active service of the O.S.M. Whatever the wages offered him he looked upon his new position as a great opportunity to advance the Union.

Shortt was held in uncertain regard by some of his comrades. They knew he was a much better than average writer and fond of inserting poetry in the Fortnightly Returns until he got his knuckles rapped by some of the more sober lodges who thought that "everything should be kept out of the Returns unless it pertained to the Union." Yet for a man who could turn a poetic phrase he was extremely handy with his fists.

In Plymouth he had been so well known for his aggressive leadership of the men that he had been blacklisted in every yard and had been unable to get a job in the town. He was also unique in that, a few years before, he was the first man to have his legal expenses paid by the Union when he was involved in a fight with a blackleg. There had been a strike at Johnson's job in Plymouth and a number of blacklegs had been brought in. One of them, Henry Versus, had been a member of the Union at one time, but was so often seen working on struck jobs that he was nicknamed the 'Black Reptile.'

He ran up against Thomas Shortt in the pub which also served as Union lodge house. Shortt was well aware of Versus's activities and expressed his contempt by refusing to drink in his company. Versus became so angry that he cursed and swore at him. Shortt's natural inclination was to retaliate, but he realised that, as secretary of the Plymouth lodge, he was a marked man as far as the employers and police were concerned. He therefore treated the insolence of Versus with disdain and left the pub.

Versus was apparently unaware of Shortt's reputation and hurried after him thinking he could have a bit of easy sport and act big in front of the rest of the company. However, Thomas Shortt had made his effort at dignity on behalf of the Union and now gave in to his natural temper. Versus received such a thrashing that Shortt was hauled before the local magistrates who were anxious to clap him in gaol on any pretext. Only after two hours evidence by witnesses in his favour was he released.

In the years that Shortt was secretary of the O.S.M. this tremendous drive and temperament was harnessed to fighting on behalf of the Union. He would not make the mistake that Rennie had of appealing for moderation to the employers.

Shortt, in fact, found the employers were using a new tactic against men on strike which was proving very effective. When men struck a job it had been a regular practice for the employers to advertise in various parts of the country—or send out agents—in an attempt to attract substitute labour to the job. Often these men came unaware that a dispute was taking place, but the pickets soon put them in the picture and attempted to turn them back.

The employers were now asking their agents to get these men to sign legal contracts for a three months period before they came to the job. When the men arrived they were then faced with the alternative of braving the wrath of the strike pickets or the consequences of breaking a legal contract.

When a strike took place at Bristol just after Shortt had taken office, the masters scoured Wales and Scotland looking for masons and managed to get a number to sign their three months agreement. Three Welsh masons only realised they were walking into a dispute when they arrived at the job in Bristol. When they found they were expected to act as blacklegs they immediately boarded a steam packet. Alerted by the employers the police took the men from the ship and they were tried and committed for one month each to the treadmill for breaking their agreement.

The alternative was to work out the three months for the employer. "Which latter they refused by informing the magistrates that they would rather stop the three months in prison than strike a blow for such deceitful masters" reported Shortt to the members in a successful appeal for their families to be allowed 18s. per week from the funds while the three masons served their sentence.*

Aware of the dangers of this new step by the employers Shortt took speedy counteraction by circularising the lodges with copies of the document and so publicised the case that few masons were left unaware of the dangers of putting their signature to such a contract.

Though Shortt tried to exercise restraint in his dealings with the various lodges he found the London district resentful of any 'interference'. In fact the few years since the re-affiliation of this district, after the fall of the Grand National, had still not served to heal completely the breach that had existed between it and the rest of the lodges. If he felt compelled to give advice to the London district at any time he only did so after considerably weighing up the circumstances involved. The fact that he was usually proved right did not help relations and a clash finally came over the question of hours.

The London district had already had a dispute with Messrs. Cubitts towards the winter of 1837 when the firm tried to reduce all the building workers working on Euston Station to a nine-hour day in the winter. While the shorter hours might have been welcome the consequent drop of 6d. per day in pay was certainly not. After a ten-day strike Cubitts had given in and promised they would not again attempt to reduce hours and pay in winter.

The next year again, however, the men were told they would be put on a nine-hour day and their wages cut. The masons came out on strike and succeeded in obtaining an interview with the firm. Cubitts said that while they had a great admiration for the masons on the job if they

* O.S.M. Returns, 11th April, 1839.

gave them the benefit of shorter hours at normal pay the other crafts would want it too, and they were not prepared to give such a privilege.

Faced with this answer the men continued their strike until Cubitts again agreed to stop the practice. But the London masons felt that a general district agreement should be obtained from the employers and put forward a resolution to the Committee of The Master Builders' Association " that 5s. per day be the wages in winter, for which we agree to work ten hours; our employers to make such arrangements as they deem necessary to carry the same into effect."*

This caused an immediate uproar in the O.S.M. and Shortt told the London district that it was lending itself to payment by the hour—a system which was fiercely resented by the members generally who believed that they ought to retain wages on a day basis. The other district lodges in fact were attempting to obtain a reduction in the winter to nine hours for a wage of 5s. per day.

Shortt dropped all restraint and jumped in with a blistering attack on the London members for the " imbecile and mean-spirited proceedings " which, he said, implied that they would work to 7 p.m. in the winter and it was almost an invitation to the employers to resume the detested practice of working by candlelight.

Did they not realise, he demanded, that such a resolution could be conveyed from master to master " with the velocity of a train of gunpowder, igniting every mason's yard as it passed." Grand Lodge and all the others in the Union " would rather see our funds exhausted . . . in endeavouring to lessen the hours of labour (which we feel convinced is the only source by which our society can be made permanent) than give countenance to such a resolution."

On this occasion Shortt was certainly speaking for the rest of the members for, when the matter was referred to a ballot vote, few favoured the London proposal. But

* O.S.M. Returns, 3rd January, 1839.

2,008 members took the trouble to vote against it and, in addition, there were 21 indignant protests sent to Grand Lodge from the other districts.* Over this particular case the London district felt that it was completely estranged from the Union generally and relations deteriorated sharply. While trying to smooth over this dispute Shortt suddenly found himself plunged into another with Ireland.

The other districts of the O.S.M. had been becoming increasingly hostile to the Irish lodges, which, they claimed, were acting as an open tap steadily draining away the funds of the society. The Irish members too, they accused, were almost completely resistant to any form of discipline in accordance with Union rules. Now there appeared cause for believing that there had been downright fraud in which not a few of the Irish lodge officials must have been implicated. Anger by the English and Welsh members was heightened because the fraud concerned the accident rule. This laid down:

"That should any member of this Society . . . get disabled by accident so as to incapacitate him from earning his living by his trade, all the members of this society shall contribute 6d. each to raise a sum of money, that he may turn himself to some business by which he may earn a livelihood, without depending on public charity or parish relief."†

Under this rule a member who had proved his case with the aid of witnesses and a medical certificate, and after a ballot vote of the whole membership, could usually count on receiving about £80—£100. Considering this might equal nearly 18 months' normal earnings it was certainly enough to set him up in a small business.

To investigate the charges of fraud and review general affairs in Ireland, Shortt went across for a few days in December of 1839. He was horrified at the casual

---

* O.S.M. Returns, 31st January, 1839.

† Rule XXXI in 1836 and which applied for some years afterwards without being modified.

irresponsibility of the lodge officers. Not one of the lodges appeared to have reasonably clear accounting books. Dublin especially could not give a satisfactory explanation about the disposal of their income and two masons, Bellew and Nugent, who had recently benefited under the accident rule receiving £80 each, had only ever paid a few shillings into the society and were well in arrears at the time their lodge secretaries had forwarded the appeal for them. Nor had their 'accidents' been explained and witnessed according to rule.

When Shortt laid his report before the Union it strengthened the determination of certain lodges to get rid of the Irish section. Birmingham convened a special meeting from which was sent a very lengthy resolution asking that the Irish masons be completely cut off from the O.S.M. They emphasised that in the last financial year a total of only £47 10s. had been received from the Irish lodges " and that £535 had been sent them during the same period; of this £160 was for Bros. Bellew and Nugent, leaving for other purposes £375."*

Liverpool replied with a reasonable amendment asking that the question of a break with Ireland should be left to the next annual meeting. This was better, they said, than the " very rash, premature, and dishonourable proceedings to cut off part of our society at a month's notice through the misconduct of a few individuals."

At this Shortt and the Grand Committee exploded with anger; there were only a few individuals in Ireland they raged who were capable of trust. In general " such company, on the whole, is not much to our profit, or entitled to our confidence." They asked the members to vote for Birmingham's motion and in March the result was announced. 923 were in favour of Birmingham's proposal and 784 for the Liverpool amendment. By a majority of 139 the Irish lodges were to be expelled with the " hope that our brethren in Ireland will exert themselves in preparing for their own future government."

* O.S.M. Returns, 2nd June, 1840.

These events left a bitterness between the lodges and a suspicion that not only the Irish were capable of taking advantage of the accident rule. Aware that the members were now in a state of mind receptive for a complete change in the rules, the Grand Committee took advantage by putting forward a long argument for a " Union of the Trade and Sick Funds."

This, they claimed, would make the O.S.M. a more valuable institution to its members than ever before and provide it with a greater stability. Not only would they be able to help their sick and disabled members, but such a wide range of immediate benefits could be offered by the Union that new members would come pouring in.

Shortt claimed that this " acquisition of numbers from the enemy's ranks " would enable them to abolish overtime working, leading to a general reduction in the hours of labour. This, in turn, would provide work for the unemployed and ultimately would be the " forerunner to an improvement in our mental faculties."*

All opposition to the new proposal, especially on the grounds that it would mean increased weekly subscriptions, was met by impassioned argument from Shortt. In his enthusiasm, however, he overlooked the most important fact of all. The old voluntary sick section started by McGregor had never been a great success. Shortt must have seen from the Annual Returns for September 1839/40 that only 354 out of a total membership of 5,226 were paying into the section.

What should have been a more realistic indication to him of the real feelings of the members was ignored as he exhorted supporters to get a big majority for the proposal that the delegates to the annual meeting go ahead and alter the appropriate rules. From May to September the votes were being continually sent in to the Grand Committee and a triumphant Shortt finally announced the result as 2,182 in favour with 797 against. This majority was big enough to sway the delegates attending the September

* O.S.M. Returns, 21st May, 1840.

Annual Meeting, and they drew up an extensive code of rules for combined trade, sick and funeral benefits.

Also, in response to demands from a considerable number of lodges, the entrance fee to the Union was dropped from £1 to 10s. To pay for the amalgamated benefits, however, subscriptions were doubled from 3d. to 6d. per week. In quite a number of areas this was equal to 1½ hours wages—when a man could secure work.

Within 12 months Shortt and the Grand Committee were completely disillusioned about their great new scheme attracting large numbers from the "enemy's ranks". By September 1841, membership had slumped by 1,517 to a total of 3,709, and it was still ominously falling.

The new scheme also led to an intensification of the squabble with London. Protesting that they were generally being given a raw deal by the Grand Committee a number of the London masons broke away and formed an Anti-Society which threatened once more to lead to a severance of the entire district.

Just as Shortt began to think that things could not possibly get any worse, the Union found itself in a fresh uproar over an accusation of fraud against T. Reed, secretary of the Manchester district. When Shortt tried to have the books examined he was not only resisted by Reed, but other members of the Committee, and Manchester district filled pages of the Returns with long diatribes about the "inability" of Grand Lodge Committee members. Reed also decided that the best defence against attack by Shortt was to accuse him, in turn, of taking too much money from the Union for various delegations.

The complete bitterness which now immersed the O.S.M. led to Short becoming so exasperated that he announced his intention to resign as secretary at the next annual delegate meeting. The Birmingham Grand Lodge Committee members also said that they could no longer take the maliciousness of Manchester and other lodges and they would also be giving up their executive responsibilities.

To prepare for the transfer of power from Birmingham—which had been Grand Lodge ever since the end of the Operative Builders Union—a vote was held to decide whether Liverpool or London should be the next seat of government. In this ballot London won by 539 votes to 434 and was to take office in September 1841. This at least partially solved one of the problems in that it helped to stay the influence of the London Anti-Society members.

It was also opportune in that the most dramatic strike the masons ever faced was to take place in London during the same month that it was created Grand Lodge. It was a strike of such importance that it immediately demanded all of Shortt's particular abilities and put all thoughts of resignation out of his mind.

CHAPTER 8

FOES TO TYRANNY

IN an attempt to keep their Lordships warm during the chilly month of October 1834 two workmen at the Houses of Parliament had been burning cartloads of timber to heat a flue leading to the Peers' Chamber. Gradually the flue, which was made of wood, overheated and caught fire. The blaze quickly spread through the building and the House of Commons and the House of Lords were both destroyed.

When the plans had finally been completed for the rebuilding of Parliament, the contract for the job was given by the Lords Commissioners of Woods and Forests to Grissell and Peto, the large and nationally known contractors. Grissell, the dominant partner, was extremely proud of having secured a job which he thought reflected great honour on the firm. He decided that the rebuilding of this national edifice could not be treated as an ordinary contract. To maintain control over the large number of men who would be employed, and ensure efficient completion of every stage of the work, he asserted that there must be " the discipline of the quarter-deck."

And he knew just the man whose reputation fitted him perfectly for the role of Captain Bligh. The general foreman he appointed for the most important job ever handled by the firm was George Allen—the 'Black Prince.'

By the summer of 1841 the job had reached the stage where 230 masons were employed on the site dressing and fixing the stone. Although resentment had been developing between the men and Allen, Grissell and Peto were so anxious that nothing should hold up work they had exercised a restraining hand on him. But as the labour force began to build up to its peak Allen resorted increasingly to his old bullying attitude in trying to exercise strict control over the job.

As the months wore on relations on the site gradually deteriorated and finally reached explosive point over the treatment young Ambrose Prothero received when he asked Allen for leave of absence to travel to Manchester for his mother's funeral. Prothero had been his mother's sole support for some years and he asked Allen for " a week or a fortnight to go and see her interred and settle some other business connected with her death."

" I be damned," roared Allen in reply, " but one day to go to Manchester, one to bury her and another to come back is enough."

When the men on the site heard of this they indignantly called a protest meeting. At this they heard of another example of Allen's brutal inhumanity. One of the masons had a wife seriously ill, with no hope of recovery. An under-foreman had given him permission to remain at home " to close the eyes of his dying wife." When he returned to the job he was pounced upon by Allen who dismissed his explanation with an oath and the remark that he should " go home and die with her and be damned."

When the meeting decided to lodge a protest against Allen his reply was to sack the chairman and two or three others who had taken a prominent part. As a last resort the men now wrote direct to Grissell and Peto. Apart from the tyranny of Allen there was also his other actions which were calculated to browbeat and degrade them. For instance, only one firm was allowed to sell beer on the site and the men claimed that it was abusing its monopoly position by selling them a poor brew. Not only did the ' Black Prince ' threaten to sack men buying from any other brewery, he even went so far as to lock up the pump so that the masons could only ease their thirst at the expense of buying beer.

This time Grissell arranged to hear a deputation from the men. But he flatly refused to believe or consider their charges against Allen. He also revealed that the firm itself was conniving at the monopoly supply of beer. He could not allow them to purchase beer from anyone else, he said, " inasmuch as there exists an understanding between the firm and the brewers."

Treated with such inconsideration by the head of the firm the masons on the job decided to present an ultimatum. " If Allen is not removed from the job by Saturday, the 11th September," they wrote, " we will no longer work under him."

Grissell and Peto refused to take the threat seriously. They claimed the trouble was entirely the work of a few agitators who were members of the Union. But when they went to the Westminster site on Monday the 13th September they found it as quiet as a grave. Every one of the masons employed by them had quit the job as one man.

It was the beginning of a nine months' battle, and the most intensive and widespread strike ever waged by the O.S.M. Yet it was not an attempt to raise wages or reduce hours. Thomas Shortt, General Secretary of the Union, put the issue squarely when he said that the struggle was over a much more fundamental principle. Employers not only expected to purchase the labour of a man, but also his soul. In addition to grim working conditions, the men had also to suffer degradation as human beings.

The masons on the Houses of Parliament job, he said, were striving for the principle of human decency and dignity. They were fighting for a cause which would fire the whole of the working-class throughout Britain and he felt confident that the other unions " would respond by giving financial support to ensure that this fundamental principle was settled once and for all time."

In Shortt the masons had a general secretary who might have been created for just such a fight as this. His pugnacious character, his vitriolic pen and his flair for organisation were the very qualities needed for the battle in which they were now engaged.

From the very start of the conflict Shortt realised that its length would depend greatly on the attitude of the government, as expressed through the Lords Commissioners of Woods and Forests. He therefore wrote to the Earl of Lincoln, First Commissioner, explaining the reasons for withdrawing labour and expressed the hope " that your Lordships' minds may not be prejudiced against us."

It was a vain hope. The Earl of Lincoln and the aristocracy generally were firm believers that the duty of the ' lower orders ' was to accept unquestioningly the commands of their superiors. They might have given some consideration to the men over a dispute on hours or wages, but they were distinctly hostile to a strike which had as its objective the partial destruction of the social order in which they believed.

To them the brutality of Allen was quite irrelevant to their fundamental principle of obtaining obedience of workmen to masters. The masons, therefore, received a brusque reply from the Commissioners that the " Board declines to interfere between the complaintants and their immediate employers."

But this policy of non-intervention was completely one sided. To Grissell and Peto the Commissioners expressed a letter of sympathy and an assurance of " support in maintaining that authority and control over your workmen which is so essential in an undertaking of such importance and magnitude."

And to make it quite plain where the Commissioners stood the Earl of Lincoln declared that " employers must be protected from the union of workmen." In effect the government had decided to accept a standstill on the Westminster site rather than embarrass the firm's attempt to crush the strike.

Shortt now knew that the masons faced a long and costly battle. In fact he was too shrewd a man not to know that, with the government ranged against them, it would be difficult to succeed. Yet he recognised that the masons must continue this struggle simply because to give way in face of tyranny and brutality would only make their position worse. And the quick and warm response of the rest of the unions throughout the country showed that the masons carried the hopes and loyalty of every other worker in this fight.

To Shortt's appeal for help donations poured in from individuals and organisations, and famous Chartist speakers and Radical Members of Parliament appeared on the platforms of meetings organised by the O.S.M. and also helped to stimulate financial support from middle class sympathisers. The press, however, generally took an unsympathetic view of the claims of the men and Shortt by-passed their editorial columns by taking out advertisements in which he castigated the employers, specified the oaths and deeds of Allen, and thundered challenges to the government to hold a public inquiry into the dispute. When the papers refused to publish letters from the strike committee—as did *The Times* and others—Shortt had them printed as lurid posters and decorated the street corners of London with them.

In addition to his appeals for money to pay the strikers—then draining the Union's funds by over £120 a week—he held huge balls and benefit nights. The amount of work he managed to do at this time was incredible. Apart from the tremendous responsibility of the strike, he still carried the administrative burden of the Union. There were also half a dozen other strikes on wages and hours taking place in the provinces and the wrangling with the London Anti-Society was still continuing.

When Grissell and Peto realised that there would be no easy capitulation by the men they proceeded to widen the area of conflict. Encouraged by the financial and other assistance of the Lords Commissioners they sent agents all over Britain seeking masons to take the place of the strikers. Posters and newspaper advertisements in every town and village were used to attack the men, while offering financial inducements to black labour.

The masons retaliated by forming defence committees of sympathisers throughout the country which counter-attacked with the same weapons. When the firm's agents arrived in Newcastle on Tyne, for instance, they received a fierce reception from the local branch of the O.S.M. which also wrote a bitter letter of condemnation to Grissell and Peto warning the firm that it should " not again disgrace the walls of Newcastle with your delusive, transparent, paltry placards."

But with all this activity and support the Union could not prevent an increasing number of ' black ' masons making their way to London from as far afield as Scotland and Ireland. Times were bad and many of these men had been idle for a considerable period, and the attractive wages of 5s. per day being offered by Grissell and Peto were a great inducement.

Even though strike pickets in London managed to turn many of them away, at the cost of badly needed funds, a small labour force was gradually built up on the Westminster site. It was a bleak moment for Shortt and the strikers. They faced the enmity of Grissell and Peto with unlimited capital at their disposal and, ranged with them, a government determined to assist the employers as much as possible. An extensive police guard, for instance, had been provided to escort blacklegs as they went to and from the job. Grissell and Peto were now openly boasting that their troubles were over and the men would have to toe the line in the very near future.

They were a little premature in their optimism however. For some time the masons working on Nelson's Column and the Woolwich Dockyard, other government contracts held by the firm, had been closely watching the struggle and helping the strikers financially. Shortt had, in fact, asked them to stay at work so they could provide this monetary assistance. But the time had come for more direct action and at both jobs the masons downed tools and walked out in support of their comrades.

Now Grissell and Peto were worse off for labour than they had been previously. Frantic appeals were sent to their agents to recruit more men.

Shortt also entered the fight with renewed vigour, though he was well aware of the immense task now facing the Union. The demonstration of solidarity by the masons from the Column and the Dockyard had put new heart into the men—but it also increased the weekly strike pay requirements to over £200. In addition to this more money was needed for turning away intending blacklegs and for carrying on the general administrative work of the strike.

It was only a matter of a few weeks more in fact when the unequal balance of money between the two forces again began to tell and Grissell and Peto steadily built up a fresh supply of blacklegs. The end, in fact, might then have come very quickly for the masons. The months of fighting had sapped funds until almost nothing was left in the special strike account, or the coffers of the O.S.M. The men were almost prepared for defeat.

Then the Scottish Masons' Society stepped into the picture. In a wonderful gesture of unity and sacrifice, which finally resulted in its own bankruptcy and near extinction, the Union donated money totalling £500 to help its English comrades carry on the fight. At the same time it warned its members not to help defeat the strikers by accepting the financial blandishments of Grissell and Peto; " Shall it be said that one mason in Scotland heaped eternal disgrace on himself by acting as a tool to these tyrants? Let the universal answer be No! No!! No!!! "

Rallied by this selfless act of the Scottish masons the strikers heard further encouraging news. The men working at the Dartmoor quarries which supplied the stone for Nelson's Column and Woolwich Dockyard had come out on strike and declared to their employers that they would not supply materials for masters who were " determined to reduce the condition of their workmen to worse than that of the negro."

But what might have been a serious blow to Grissell and Peto resulted in the Admiralty coming to their aid. Stone of another quality would be perfectly acceptable for the work they were assured. The Admiralty even instructed its own engineers to help the firm obtain an alternative supply of material.

Knowing that they were likely to meet opposition from the men at each quarry where they tried to obtain stone, the Admiralty agents held a meeting with the granite merchants at Penryn in Cornwall and formed a plan for breaking down the resistance of the workers. Commencing at one of the biggest quarries they selected two of the oldest hands and ordered them to prepare specimens of granite for Grissell and Peto.

Without hesitation the men refused. They were immediately discharged and the next two hands in order of seniority were ordered to do the work. Finally all the men in the quarry had been put through the same process, but the answer was unanimous. They refused to supply granite for employers who were trying to crush their fellows in London. And at every other quarry in the area the same scene was enacted—with the same result.

Frustrated at Penryn, Grissell and Peto sent men all over the country to the stone quarries from Devon in the South to Aberdeen in the North. Shortt countered this step by getting Union delegates to follow the employer's agents and appeal to the quarrymen not to supply material for ' black ' work. " Collisions between the antagonistic parties " he reported dryly to his strike committee, " are quite frequent."

Both sides were, in fact, now locked in an all-out battle which had spread countrywide. Fresh reports of quarrymen refusing to help their masters supply stone to Grissell and Peto heartened the masons, but it also meant an increasing number of men out on strike and looking to the O.S.M. for turnout pay.

Shortt, who had collapsed with exhaustion and been confined to bed for a week, summoned what remaining strength he had and set about raising more funds to pay the men.

In addition to intensifying appeals to other unions he took the novel step of hiring the Victoria Theatre for a night and had the patrons paying to hear a dramatised version of the case for the men. One of the strikers stood on the stage declaiming a long poetic argument, which ended:

> " They would have made us slaves, nay worse; but then
> We struck to show them that we still were men.
> And all who value worth and manliness
> Have sympathised with us, except the Press—
> The Press! that engine to enlarge the slave,
> Can it refuse when truth and justice crave?
> Alas! Oppression sways the venal pen—
> Corruption backs the master—not the men!
> But time will come when these things will not be—
> When heaven will give success to honesty.
> And those who worked at Nelson's Monument,
> And Woolwich too—by slavery unbent,
> Shall with their brethren raise a noble name
> That tyranny shall daunt, and treachery shame.
> Oh, may the members of the Houses be,
> As were the builders, foes to tyranny."

From this benefit night over £50 was raised. But even more important the masons began to receive increasing support from the public for their stand against Grissell and Peto.

The firm was now reduced, with the limited supply of materials and labour available, to making a pathetic pretence of carrying on 'business as usual.' An apt comment was the satirical report in the weekly periodical *Charivari*. Under the heading " Nelson's Column " it informed its readers:

" This national testimony to our greatest naval hero is formed of a square enclosure, composed of deal planks, profusely emblazoned with posting bills. The interior contains a stone erection, nearly six feet high, and has been used for some time past as a promenade for two respectable journeyman stonemasons and their labourer. It is confidently expected that the next generation will be enabled to see it without looking over the palings by which it is surrounded."

But the end in fact was in sight. No matter the solidarity and loyalty of the men, and those supporting them, they could not hold out for ever. On the other hand the government seemed determined never to have another Houses of Parliament, or a column for Nelson, if it meant Grissell and Peto having to concede victory to the men.

By April the strikers were almost at the end of their resistance. From Dartmoor the lodge secretary wrote: " The privation these men and their families are enduring in defence of their fellows is, so far as my knowledge extends, without parallel in the history of strikes."

Lack of money was also crippling the ability of the Union delegates to bribe blacklegs to keep out of struck quarries. " I never had the ' hammer ' worse in my life than I have it now," the delegate reported from Penryn. " I have walked twenty miles this day to stop three blacks without any money in my pocket. Hoskins has added three blacks to his number, which if I had had a little money I could have prevented."

The struggle had dragged on through a long winter and the coming of spring found the men and the Masons' funds completely exhausted. The strikers themselves had shown great endurance and loyalty. Of the masons who had struck at the House of Commons only five had defected. Shortt's efforts had raised a total of nearly £5,000 for the men, but he knew they had now reached the end of the road. The O.S.M. was heavily in debt and other unions had given all they could spare.

Shortt's personal position was no less desperate. At the start of the fight he had levied himself 2s. 6d. per week but now he no longer had sufficient income to pay his own wages. Every penny the Union collected had been given to the strike fund.

Shortt was a fighter and he showed great courage in a battle. But it took even greater courage for him to face the fact that they would never force Grissell and Peto to concede to the men by dismissing Allen. He therefore began finding other employment for the strikers so that the drain on the funds would be lessened. Soon he had reduced their numbers to just under 80. Gradually the men who were left also realised that they had no hope of enforcing Allen's dismissal. The government was not only accepting inferior work and materials to accommodate the masters, but had also greatly extended the time originally agreed for completion of the contracts.

The remaining strikers held a meeting at which they came to a decision that, while they would never again work under Allen, they would relieve their comrades of the burden of supporting them. From this meeting Shortt sent out his last request to the unions and others who had given so generously throughout the struggle.

He asked for £150 to enable his 'ragged little army' to depart in search of other work. "Give us this money" he appealed, so that the masons "although exhibiting evidence from the crown to the toe, of bitter persecution, cruelty and privation, will be enabled to quit the battlefield after a struggle of eight months, without tarnishing the honour of trade societies, or sullying their own character as determined and decided men."

And on the 25th May the strike ended. The 'Black Prince' perhaps still remained general foreman at the Houses of Parliament, but his power had definitely been curbed. Grissell and Peto might show the appearance of victory but its substance lay largely with the men, for the firm was later to make important concessions without a fight—simply because they were afraid to precipitate another strike of the same magnitude.

And to "the Public and the Trades of Great Britain and Ireland" Thomas Shortt drove home the moral of the whole conflict between labour and capital, and pointed the way ahead for future generations, in his last strike bulletin.

"The subordinate and humiliating station in society we at present occupy can only be the effect of our own servility—a want of self respect—a lack of confidence in ourselves," he wrote. "We have long had the power if we had had the will to improve our condition to a much greater extent than we have experienced, but have been either too indolent or too careless fully to exercise it. This apathetic conduct must be abandoned. The mutual dependency of the trades, and the identity of their interests should stimulate them to gather up their energies and consolidate their strength, that an unbroken front may be presented to the common foe. It is by our own efforts only—by being true and faithful to each other—that our regeneration can be effected."

CHAPTER 9

3,600 MEN AGAINST THE 'DOCUMENT'

THE strike at the Houses of Parliament had drained the finances of every lodge in the Union. Not one of them had sufficient income to meet normal expenditure. The money being sent to the Grand Committee therefore dwindled until the final depth was plumbed when there was no longer enough to pay the benefits which had been promised under the new sick fund rules.

Shortt desperately attempted to draw money in from every possible source. He even wrote a history of the nine months' strike from which he hoped to raise £50 in profits for the Union. Now he made an urgent appeal to every lodge: " Let the boxes be emptied—turn out the last shot in the locker rather than hear of a shopmate's wants, or the widow or the orphan's cry."

Finally a proposal from the Central Committee urged that a 6d. levy be imposed on all members to clear off the crushing debts that the Union had incurred. But the amount raised by the levy was completely insufficient and throughout 1842 the Union went from one crisis to another until it reached a point where members began to withhold their contributions because they feared that the O.S.M. would soon be numbered among the ' things that were.'

Orlingbury lodge emphasised that it was not merely the after effects of a lengthy strike from which the Union was suffering. The real disaster had been the amalgamation of the trade and sick funds. The lodge suggested that at the Annual Delegate Meeting in June, delegates should consider changing the rules so that " it be left to the pleasure of those who may join our society to contribute to the trade and sick fund, or to the trade fund only."*

There was great support from the other lodges for this proposal and when the annual meeting was held in London—only seven delegates plus the chairman attending because of the impoverished state of the districts—it was agreed to implement Orlingbury's proposals.

Members could now choose between two classes of membership. For trade benefit only the entrance fee was cut to 5s. and the weekly contribution lowered to 3d. Those wishing joint trade and sick benefits had to pay 6d. per week and an entrance fee of 10s. if under 30 years of age. This was raised to a £1 for new members over 30. And among other changes that were made to make the sickness benefits more attractive to members was the adoption of a Liverpool proposal " that leeches be supplied to members requiring them."

At this annual meeting Shortt was given a significant reminder that Manchester had not forgotten its old grudge against him. The lodge proposed that his wages be reduced to 30s. and that for this sum of money he should also act as secretary of the London district in addition to being secretary of the Grand Committee.

Shortt angrily retaliated with an attack on the Manchester members and anyone else who thought that his wages should be reduced. He reminded them that not long ago he had completely exhausted himself fighting the greatest battle engaged in by the Union. £5,000 had been raised for the strikers in London and the struggle had only been carried on for so long due to his own personal efforts. To help the Union out of its burden of debt he had burned the midnight oil writing a book on the strike which had brought in a fair amount for the funds while he himself had not benefited by a penny. He claimed that his wages should be increased rather than cut.

* O.S.M. Returns, 20th April, 1843.

Though Shortt managed to beat off this attack his failing health, coupled with a deep and somewhat justified resentment against his persecutors, gradually made him bitter and cynical. His relations with his own committee became extremely difficult and he was inclined to carry on petty grudges against individual members. The end came with a terse statement in September 1843. "We have found it necessary to suspend Bro. Thomas Shortt from office," announced the Central Committee, "the particulars of which will appear in the next Returns."

Two weeks later the lodges were informed that Shortt had been accused of petty fraud over payments involving the printer and, although protesting his innocence, he had refused to hand over documents and receipts which were demanded as proof by the Central Committee. Shortt replied to this with a bitter circular to all the lodges in which he attacked individual members of the Committee and swore that he would not stand any kind of trial before them.

Finally the Central Committee had to take a step which they acknowledged to be the reverse of the normal process of justice. They had no other alternative, they announced, but to presume him guilty until he produced evidence to show his innocence. That they still were appreciative of his efforts, and acknowledged the great abilities that he possessed, was expressed in their desire that he should prove himself innocent "for his character, in this respect, is much dearer to us than all the others." In the meantime they appointed one of the members of the Committee, Thomas Carter, as the secretary pro tem.

As Shortt continued to hurl threats without taking advantage of any of the opportunities to clear himself the Central Committee had ultimately no alternative but to lay the matter before the members of the Union for their verdict. On a ballot vote there were 140 for "Guilty" and 46 "Not Guilty." It was a pathetic end to the career of a man who had given so much for the O.S.M. The total vote of 186 was also a pitiful indication of the Union's weakness and the apathy into which the members had sunk even over such a crucial issue.

The Central Committee now took steps to appoint a new secretary. The first national vote ever held for this position (previous secretaries being appointed by annual meeting delegates) took place with five candidates in the field. In the first ballot Thomas Carter was returned with a majority over the other four. It was also decided that the seat of government should be removed to Liverpool.

Thomas Carter soon made it clear to the lodges that, in his opinion, their only hope of survival was to remain quiescent. "We think our members must plainly see the necessity of giving up all thoughts of strikes, under existing circumstances," he wrote. "They must direct their attention to the best means of extending our organisation, and let us see whether more good can be done by our moral power than by those ulterior measures. Strikes in few instances have ever been attended with very beneficial results, but almost invariably have tended to create enemies to our cause."

When the head office was transferred to Liverpool in April 1844 membership had shrunk to a total of 1,765, but the separation of the sick and trade benefits began to have the beneficial effect prophesied by Orlingbury. A year later the numbers had risen to 3,525 and were continually increasing. The funds also were in a much healthier state and many of the old debts paid off.

It was due to this quick recovery that the masons were able to respond to an appeal for help from the Friendly Society of Bricklayers. The F.S.O.B. had been engaged in a number of disputes which had completely depleted their central funds and plunged the Society into debt. The masons still had only a small credit balance on hand but they loaned £30 of this to the bricklayers.

This was only a small amount when compared with the debts of the bricklayers but it reduced immediate pressure on them to such an extent that James Locket, their General Secretary, wrote an effusive (and prophetic) letter of thanks which concluded: "May that day come, and with it a unity of purpose, between the two societies, as shall present a phalanx worthy of the cause in which we are engaged."*

Though pressed for money the position of the bricklayers was by no means completely desperate. By 1845, in fact, they had recovered some semblance of their old national organisation with five divisions—London, Manchester, Sheffield, Nottingham and Derby—to which were attached a total of 23 lodges. They had also evolved a system of accounting which, though more complicated than the masons, was much more accurate in the financial demand it made on each member. At the end of every year the accounts were made up and total expenditure divided into the amounts spent on tramp relief, turnouts and administration and each member had to pay an equal proportion. The divisions were responsible for collecting this money according to the number of members attached to the lodges in their areas.

This method meant an assessment of the average number of members during the year on which the lodges should pay rather than the number in them at any one time. During the financial year, July 1844-45, the average number of members in the Union was 1,369, but the possibility of an upward trend was evident in the total of 2,050 members at August 1845.

The gradual recovery of strength by the O.S.M., and a lessening of the bitterness at their defeat in the Houses of Parliament strike, found the masons once more turning their attention to improving their working conditions. In January 1846, a meeting was held in the Concert Hall, Lord Nelson Street, Liverpool, with between 600 and 700 members attending to debate whether the Union should go for a rise in wages or a reduction in hours.

Carter thought that a claim for a shorter working day was preferable to a wage advance in that it would incite less opposition from the employers. At the meeting he appealed for support on the grounds that it would also give employment to more men.

---

* O.S.M. Returns, 22nd August, 1844.

There were 8,000 masons in England, he claimed*, but 2,000 of them were only partially employed. The other 6,000 by giving up one hour per day could provide regular employment for 600 of them. These sentiments were unanimously acclaimed by every mason present and Liverpool decided to take the lead in going for shorter hours. The lodge formally proposed in the Returns of January 1846 that it be given a grant to strike for nine hours " on or after the 9th March next." At the same time, however, the lodge took steps to try and avoid a possible conflict by sending a reasoned letter asking the employers to concede their claim for a nine hour day. It would provide more leisure for the working man and a chance for him to reach better cultural and educational attainment, they urged. From this surely both employers and men would benefit and, even if granted the nine hour day, it would still mean a week of 54 hours for the masons.

Even Liverpool lodge was staggered by the large majority it received in favour of striking, if necessary, for the nine hour day. The only proviso made was that Liverpool members should not begin their strike until the Birkenhead lodge had made its move for an advance in wages; a majority ballot vote having already sanctioned the members in Birkenhead attempting to increase their wages from 26s. to 28s. per week.

With this plan of campaign agreed, 585 masons came out at Birkenhead on Monday, 9th March, and told their masters they would not go back without the increase of 2s. The joiners were already on strike for an almost similar claim. When the bricklayers also decided to turn out at the same time as the masons it seemed that a solid front had been presented to the masters which would result in early victory for the men.

Three employers, in fact, had conceded the wage demand when events suddenly took an unexpected turn. The joiners decided to go back; " some of them getting an advance of 1s. per week, others only their former wages,

* This estimate of the number of masons in England was far from accurate.

and some even less than that " wrote an indignant Thomas Carter.

The masons immediately took steps to lighten the heavy expenditure on strike pay in what they now expected would become a protracted struggle. Between the employers who had conceded their demands, members who volunteered to go on the tramp and those who secured alternative employment, they finally got the number on strike funds down to 230. The bricklayers, much more financially insecure than the masons, also took the same action. And, even with the joiners unexpected return to work, the masons and bricklayers and other trades involved might have succeeded in winning the struggle within a reasonable time but for the intervention of the Liverpool employers.

Far from responding amicably to the appeal from the Liverpool masons to shorten the working day they were incensed at the proposal. They were also well aware of the plan agreed by the Birkenhead and Liverpool lodges and decided they were not going to wait to be picked off on an hour's dispute after the masons had beat the Birkenhead employers on wages. Conscious that the operatives had been confused and divided when the joiners went back, they thought the time was more than opportune for coming to an agreement with the Birkenhead employers to completely crush the unions.

The decision reached by the masters was that the 'Document' should be presented throughout the entire area. The masons, bricklayers and all the other trades now found themselves faced with a tremendous fight as their members refused to sign the document and were turned out on to the streets. But the apathetic spirit which had so recently reduced the lodges almost to impotence was now completely gone. From every part of the country declarations of allegiance came pouring in. The Scottish masons sent a donation to assist in the struggle and appealed to the Liverpool unions engaged in the 'Document' struggle to fight to the end rather than sign.

The determination within the O.S.M. was reflected in a national ballot which decided by 999 votes to 255 that a sixpence levy be taken from every member to supply the 'sinews of war.' Even in areas which had suffered drastically during the Houses of Parliament strike, and where wages were only 15s. or 16s. per week, there was no lesser determination to win the struggle.

From Penryn lodge the secretary wrote direct to Liverpool that a meeting attended by almost every member had found them willing to sacrifice to pay the levy so that their brothers at Liverpool might succeed. "Another said he would sacrifice his beer but he would pay his sixpence; and another would give up his tobacco but he would pay his," he wrote. "It was then put to the vote and there were 36 for paying the levy and 2 against. We then moved for a donation, and I am glad to tell you that we got in £1 18s. I know that the men here are poor, but if we allow this tyrannical system to prevail we shall soon be poorer."

At Liverpool the masters threw everything they could into the struggle to ensure that this time the operatives would be forced to renounce their unions. Their leading figures raked up all the old arguments of the great 1833 strike in an attempt to inflame themselves and their colleagues, and also the public, against the operatives. Having forced 3,600 men out against the 'Document' they made no secret that their ultimate aim was to crush every building trade union.

To spread the conflict, the Birmingham masters then presented the 'Document' at their yards on Monday, 4th May. The reaction of the men, however, was so swift and concerted that they had little heart to pursue the matter and the fight was all over within seven days, and the 'Document' in Birmingham unconditionally withdrawn. The bricklayers, no less opportunists than the masters, took advantage of their sudden victory to demand a wage increase before they went back and secured an extra 6d. per day!

Any sudden termination of the dispute in Liverpool, however, looked so far from possibility that the stipendiary magistrate, Mr. Rushton, finally took action to bring both sides together. On the 27th May he invited a deputation from the masters and the men to meet him at the Sessions House. Eight employers attended and eleven delegates represented the masons, joiners, bricklayers, plasterers, plumbers and labourers.

In a heated and acrimonious discussion the employers first of all tried to get the men to renounce national union organisations, and then attempted to alter the hours of labour to suit themselves. These moves were completely rejected by the men, but a compromise was finally reached. On the actual question of hours of labour it was decided that it should be a "matter for adjustment between the masters of the several trades and the men."*

And, upon agreement by the employers to withdraw the 'Document', the men promised to return to work and leave unmolested those who had signed it and acted as blacklegs during the dispute. The next day all the trades turned out for a resumption of work—with the exception of the masons. They had refused to accept the agreement come to at the Sessions House conference.

Carter and the two delegates who attended the conference had agreed to try and get them to resume work upon the withdrawal of the 'Document', but when they reported back to a mass meeting of masons this proposal met with a hostile reception.

At Birkenhead and Liverpool their comrades had been out for weeks, said their spokesman, and nearly £1,500 had been poured into these two areas to support the strikers. The presentation of the 'Document' by the masters had merely been a cunning trick to forestall their strike for shorter hours. The men declared they were adamant that they were not going to spend so much money, and extract such sacrifice from their members, merely to achieve a standstill on conditions. They were "entitled to something by way of remuneration for the losses they had sustained."

* O.S.M. Returns, 14th May, 1846.

For this apparent about-face the masons' conference representatives came under verbal fire from the masters and members of the public. They were accused of dishonesty in negotiations and discourtesy to the stipendiary magistrate who had tried to assist them. Even from the other building trades there was a measure of hostility because the masters were reluctant to let anyone start while the masons remained out.

A spokesman for the master masons expressed great indignation at a subsequent meeting with Carter and members of the Central Committee. The men had agreed to return upon withdrawal of the 'Document', he claimed. But Carter and his Committee pointed out that the question of hours had been left to the various trades—and the masons wanted a decision before they returned to work.

Rushton, the magistrate, made it clear that although he regretted the masons remaining on strike their representatives at the Sessions House conference had warned him that, while they would try to get the men back to work, they were bound by whatever the will of the majority might be.

And there was no doubt about the will of the masons in Liverpool, Birkenhead, or anywhere else throughout the country. The other trades might be in no fit state to continue the fight—even the masters might be weary of the conflict they had started—but almost the entire membership of the O.S.M. was behind the continuance of the dispute if necessary.

The employers blustered that they would not surrender to such a "contemptible trade union" but, faced with the obvious determination of the masons not to capitulate, they gave in after another three weeks. On the 17th June the Birkenhead men returned to work having secured their rise of 2s. per week and also the additional concession of 40 minutes for breakfast instead of 30.

At Liverpool however the men had to retreat from their demand for a nine-hour day though they won a considerable advance in conditions. The masters made it clear that on the hours issue they would have continued to resist because it meant conceding it not only to the masons but every trade, and this they just would not do. However, the Liverpool settlement on the 19th June gave the masons an increase of 1s. per week in wages and a meal break of half-an-hour at 4 o'clock.

Having demonstrated the power of the Union to achieve results, the masons found members pouring in. By the end of the year in which they won their victories at Birkenhead and Liverpool there were 1,120 members of the trade and sick fund section, and 6,036 in the trade only section—giving a total of 7,856 members in the O.S.M. And even more comforting to a Union which had been almost constantly scraping the barrel for money was the total balance of over £4,082 in the hands of the Central Committee and the various lodges.

The 'Document' strike however had a much more serious effect on the already strained resources of the Friendly Society of Operative Bricklayers. In that year the Union paid out almost £2,212 to turnouts compared with only £51 in the previous 12 months. Even so the bricklayers were not discontented for they had also reaped the benefits of the enthusiasm engendered by the successful outcome. The number of divisions in the Society had increased to nine, with forty lodges attached to them. The average membership was up to 2,362, and the annual report ended enthusiastically: " We have infinite gratification in directing your particular attention to the fact that the average number of members for the year ending 1846, exceed the average of 1845, by nearly One Thousand members, and a further increase is certain."*

It was not only the operatives, however, who were being taught the benefit of union. In face of the growing strength of the men the employers had been driven to a recognition of their own weakness organisationally. Apart from London, Manchester and a few other places, the masters generally had shown a reluctance to come to

* F.S.O.B. Financial Reports 1845/46.

formal associations between themselves. In the past they had, in fact, frequently acted in a disunited way in face of attack from the men.

Now their hopes of crushing the unions had completely disappeared with their defeat in the second big 'Document' dispute to take place since 1833. They had to accept that the unions had established themselves and they must also sink any individual differences or else be constantly in an inferior position to the men. During the Liverpool and Birkenhead strikes they had in fact held a big meeting at Newton at which they thrashed out their differences. Finally they issued a lengthy statement which began by acknowledging that the operatives had a legal right to combine to raise the price of labour. It continued:

"It is equally clear that it is also the right of those who have to purchase it to combine to prevent that price being unjust, or more than they can afford to pay. While the trades unions make no unreasonable demands, this association will remain quiescent, but united. When those unions are dissolved, this will also expire; but while individual employers are interfered with, or particular localities selected for a strike, this association will be ready to act with promptness, and to take such determined steps as will bring strikes to a speedy termination."*

* O.S.M. Returns, 30th April, 1846.

CHAPTER 10

THE PANIC OF '47

HAVING defeated the employers in a second major battle on the 'Document' the masons now confidently settled down to building the O.S.M. up to a peak of membership and financial strength it had never known before. And in Carter they had a secretary well suited to this purpose. An honest, if rather humourless, man he took an almost purely administrative attitude to his job. In his opinion the value of the Union lay mainly in the friendly benefits it provided. Unlike Shortt he did not view it as a weapon to be used against employers for social advance. In fact he was very hostile to the use of strike action and considered that wage increases should be obtained by taking discreet advantage of the labour supply and demand position.

Hardly a Return was issued during his period of office without a sharp sermon on the stupidity of strikes, or an attempt to prevent an aggressive lodge turning out against an employer. He constantly resorted to the rules to refuse strike benefit to men who had not followed the correct procedure in making application for it. When the members of Fishponds lodge came out on sudden strike because their employer attempted to reduce the regular price for coping from 1s. 6d. to 1s. per foot run, Carter said: "They are by no means entitled to the support of the Society, and not having received any information from them on the subject, they must be conscious of the fact."

By this time he even felt so assured of the general support for his attitude that he further admonished the men at

Fishponds with a scornful reference to the fate of the Houses of Parliament strikers. Carter reminded them that in a few days it would be the anniversary of the walk out at Westminster. " What a boasting of strength, what an evident intoxication of power prevailed amongst the indignant and determined turnouts " sneered Carter. " But mark what a change was wrought in the four succeeding months; all was disappointment. Shame might well be the portion " of those who had so idiotically taken the lead in the strike he added; finally urging all members to " labour on in peace and comfort doing justice to our employers and securing the same for ourselves."*

Yet only the members of Fishponds—who won their dispute after eight days on strike—protested at this attack by Carter on what had been a proud and dignified struggle by the London masons. The rest of the society apparently was prepared to acquiesce in anything he might do, and even provide a large vote in favour when it was proposed that his wages be increased to 35s. per week.

The masons, with an almost continuous record of fighting since the Union started in 1831, now seemed content to have proved themselves. Trade was reasonably good and the members were agreed with Carter and the Liverpool Central Committee on a policy of peaceful stabilisation. The effort of the O.S.M. was turned towards a great organising drive and paid delegates were sent touring the Midlands and the North, from Doncaster to Carlisle, to build up membership. The Union even took the step of publishing the rules in Welsh for, as Carter explained, " although there are considerable numbers entering weekly, those would be doubled if the natives could understand the laws."

In response to an urgent appeal from the National Committee of the Scottish Operative Masons Society, the English Union also gave them organising assistance. Although there was no formal link between the unions

* O.S.M. Returns, 20th August, 1846.

extremely cordial relations existed and, in the Houses of Parliament strike and the 1846 Lancashire document dispute, the Scottish masons had lent support and given money almost as if they had been fighting for their own existence.

Now their resources were gone and the organisation almost shattered. " For a number of years when the great mass of our members were in position of virtuous resolution, great improvements were affected " reported their secretary Donald McLeod. " But the decay of virtue, accumulation of surplus hands, and unfavourable conditions of trade, disorganised us; leaving us a prey in dull seasons to the greed of employers and the dishonesty of our fellow workers." The Union had hardly any members capable or willing to act as delegates to recruit new members.

But the English masons had not forgotten their debt of gratitude. By 1,036 to 107 votes it was agreed that they would pay all expenses for a delegate to travel from England and link up with McLeod and they would then go on an organising tour to rebuild the Society.

The delegate finally selected by the O.S.M. was a member of the Craven Head lodge in London called Robert MacDonald. " The English Brethren might have sent us as good a man to help us, but could not send a better," reported Donald McLeod to Carter. " The Scottish Brethren are under a deep debt of gratitude to you, not only for sending us a delegate, but for the choice you have made."

McLeod had travelled to Dumfries where he met MacDonald, and the two men had begun an amazing marathon of organising to put the Scottish Union back on its feet. From Dumfries they travelled through South Ayrshire, up to Kilmarnock, then across to Glasgow and back again to comb the lowlands area around Galashiels and Hawick. In just over a fortnight they had covered hundreds of miles and opened thirteen new lodges.

The pleasure of the English masons at the success of MacDonald was heightened because their own membership and finances were also increasing rapidly. To a great extent this was due to the tight discipline imposed by Carter and the members of the Central Committee. Carter's position had become almost impregnable. It seemed as if the secretaryship of the Union was his as long as he cared to hold it.

In the 1847 nominations for the job, in fact, he had received a very much larger number of nominations than any other contestant. Then suddenly the Manchester lodge created an uproar when they protested against his re-election due to their discovery that his wife had become the proprietor of a spirit vaults. They were adamant in their opinion that this business must also take up some of his time which should be exclusively devoted to the Union.

Carter was bitterly indignant at this criticism and declared that he had done a great amount of work to strengthen and stabilise the Union. He immediately tendered his resignation and protested that he had never allowed his wife's business to interfere with the duties of his office. The Central Committee and a large number of lodges tried to get him to change his mind and Manchester only received abuse for their alleged attempt to protect the interests of the O.S.M. If the matter had been taken to a ballot vote it was obvious that Carter would have defeated the lodge heavily.

Instead he refused to withdraw his resignation and stated that his "private arrangements are now such as will not admit of retraction." Now convinced that he would not change his mind the lodges reluctantly proceeded to the election of a new secretary. Seven candidates were nominated and, in the subsequent ballot, Richard Harnott of Liverpool was elected. Harnott was no newcomer to the national scene. In fact his election, in competition with outstanding men such as Robert MacDonald, was a sign that his work as chairman of the Central Committee was well recognised and appreciated.

Of stocky build and stern appearance, he had a blunt manner and directness of speech which would normally have indicated an inflexible, dogmatic attitude. Yet he was much more guided by expediency than Carter. If the O.S.M. was temporarily financially embarrassed and trade was bad, he could caution against striking just as fiercely. But when funds were good and trade improved Harnott had no hesitation in counselling direct action to better wages and working conditions.

His first objective was to draw the local lodges and the Central Committee even closer together and make the Union a more efficient and united force. From his election as secretary at the age of 40, till death removed him from the position 25 years later, his sole purpose was devoted to making the O.S.M. a model of trade unionism; a powerful organisation that would command loyalty from the men in the trade and respect from the masters.

He started out on this task in 1847 when the masons' membership had reached 9,070 and there was a balance of over £6,059 in the hands of the Central Committee and the various lodges. Harnott was, in fact, taking over the most powerful trade union in the country. And the power of the O.S.M. was not merely in its membership and finances. Trade was good and there was a demand for masons. This was reflected in the successful strikes that had been taking place over the past twelve months—many of them on local responsibility because Carter had successfully repudiated Central Committee responsibility for turn-out pay—which had resulted in wage increases ranging from sixpence to one shilling per day. The railways and various large public undertakings were less resistant to wage demands in order not to disturb the progress of work.

Taking advantage of these circumstances the London masons held a mass meeting in June 1847 from which they sent a memorandum to the employers stating their case for a reduction of hours. This to be achieved by finishing on Saturday at 4 o'clock, thereby reducing the working week to 58½ hours. The masons also asked that there should be no reduction in wages.

This demand for a 4 o'clock Saturday had, in fact, been a national target for some time and a "4 o'clock movement " held meetings throughout the country to put over the case to building workers. In some areas the demand had already been conceded and the Halifax lodge, shortly after the London masons presented their demand, reported that after some months agitation the employers had now come to " an amicable settlement for the men to leave off at 4 o'clock instead of five on Saturdays." And the London masons were surprised when they also found the principal builders peacefully acceding to their request. The only major contractor standing out against the men was the old and most bitter enemy, Grissell and Peto, still building the Houses of Parliament.

The men employed by them decided on a firm plan of action. In the week that all the operatives in the other yards finished at four o'clock on Saturday, the 360 masons on the Westminster site walked out at the same time. On the following Monday they reported back to work as if nothing had happened and then quietly waited to see what the firm would do. " If he stops the time they are determined to come out on strike until he gives the four o'clock Saturday," reported Harnott, and added a warning that a very serious position could develop with this large number of men out on strike.

But Grissell and Peto did not want another major disturbance at the Houses of Parliament. After trying to bluff their way up to the point of a strike they saw the men were adamant and conceded the shorter hours. " Now it has become general in London to leave off at four o'clock on Saturdays " Harnott told the lodges. His pleasure at this success was justified for the London members had achieved a remarkable advance without the necessity for even one turnout. And 150 of them, dressed in their best, attended a dinner at the White Conduit House Tavern, Pentonville, to celebrate the great event.

The general picture was less pleasing to the Central Committee however. During Carter's term of office a strict control had been kept over strikes but the lodges, sensing Harnott's greater sympathy with them, had become more militant. " In many cases the Central Committee is never consulted on the subject of any premeditated dispute," its members tartly complained. "They strike and then apply for a proportion of the Society's funds. If this is going to be the part that some of our members intend to act, our use here as the Executive is at an end."

Then, suddenly, what had been a note of caution became one of desperation as the 1847 financial crisis gripped the country. "There is such a panic in the monetary question that it is really frightful," Harnott warned the lodges, as he appealed to them to accept a slight reduction in wages where inevitable rather than plunge the society into further strike expenses. The Union was already paying out over £200 a fortnight for several strikes in progress, he added.

As the crisis developed, frightened investors led to a suspension of work on railways and other large constructions. Where jobs continued employers quickly took advantage of the severely weakened position of the men. Reports came in that reductions of 6d. per day had been accepted by the masons of Cardiff, Bristol, Berwick and other areas simply because the men recognised the futility of attempting to fight their employers in the midst of economic depression. The position of the Union as a serious fighting force became even more gravely weakened when the Liverpool Banking Company, in which the O.S.M. had over £2,000, suddenly announced a suspension of all payments.

Harnott now recognised that the only way to prevent a major catastrophe was to conserve the funds as much as possible and his energies were spent in frantically trying to bring the various strikes to an end as expenditure quickly began to outstrip income. Do not strike, he urged the lodges, "unless compelled to by oppression in its worst form."*

Then in the midst of this anxiety Harnott found himself faced with an even greater threat to the security of the remaining funds. The lodges of Carlisle and Manchester put forward proposals that substantial sums of money be

* O.S.M. Returns, 25th November, 1847.

invested in the National Land and Labour Bank—a brainchild of the famous Chartist, Feargus O'Connor. His idea was that land should be bought out of subscribed capital and worked by "settlers" who would each have his own small-holding. The rents charged from them would be fair and equitable but still allow for a reasonable dividend return to investors.

Carlisle lodge claimed that this bank would actually be more secure than others because it would be guaranteed by the property it owned. Manchester added that the labour absorbed by the settlements would tend to swing the demand in favour of the unions and wages everywhere would be forced up.

Carlisle proposed that £500 be invested. But Manchester lodge, whose inability to safeguard its own funds was shown by the succession of frauds and thefts perpetrated by its officials, wanted the remaining £2,000 in the Central Committee's funds to be plunged into O'Connor's scheme. Harnott, who was well aware of the sketchy and impracticable character of the Land Bank, found himself in a serious and completely unexpected dilemma when his Central Committee members voted five to three for recommending the proposal.

This made an outright attack on it by himself in the Returns extremely impolitic. Instead he pointed out that the majority of the trustees "are men of long standing in society—men of sterling worth, and they have every confidence in the present system of Banking our funds." With this Harnott could do no more than hope that the lodges would oppose the proposition. The subsequent furore more than fulfilled his hopes. The pages of the next Returns were full of protests from a large number of lodges attacking the Carlisle and Manchester lodges for suggesting such a dangerous step. In the subsequent ballot vote the proposals were defeated and the masons, at least, were not numbered among those who lost their investments when O'Connor's scheme finally crashed. Safely over this crisis Harnott concentrated on controlling the amount of money pouring out in strike pay, and gradually was successful in bringing it down nearer the income position of the society.

Other unions which were less powerful and influential than the masons had been seriously affected by the crisis, and they inevitably looked to the O.S.M. for assistance in their difficulties. And though still short of money themselves the masons, nevertheless, loaned money to various local areas of the carpenters, coopers, plumbers, hatters, basket makers, cotton spinners and coach makers, and also levied themselves to send £100 to the striking miners of Holytown in Scotland.* In one of the most bitter struggles of the economic depression the Holytown miners, who had reached a state of starvation, were still dourly resisting employers who were trying to impose wages and working conditions that were near slavery.

In addition to all this the O.S.M. had responded to an appeal from the London division of the Friendly Society of Operative Bricklayers for a loan of £150. In the late Lancashire Document Strike the bricklayers had suffered a severe drop in their funds and this had been aggravated by investing in a " building speculation we had made in an attempt to improve the conditions of the London members by giving them employment in the winter." This scheme had failed and the £150 was now urgently required to keep the six trustees of the London division out of gaol. James Locket, who was doubling as secretary of the division in addition to being the central secretary of the bricklayers, promised that repayment " may be only a few weeks, at most only a few months." The masons were far from financial security when they received this appeal, but they reminded themselves of the assistance given by the bricklayers during the Houses of Parliament strike and voted that they should receive the loan.

Nearly every building union was severely affected by the economic crisis and, for Harnott, the few months he had been in office were ones of almost continual stress. He

* O.S.M. Returns, January 1848.

had to contend not only with the direct consequences of the crisis but also the reaction it produced among the lodges. Adverse circumstances always seemed to stimulate a rash of sweeping proposals; some of them serious attempts to set the Union on a sounder basis, others like the remedy put forward by Drypool lodge at Hull.

This lodge felt that the problems facing the organisation justified an alteration in the emblem. "In lieu of our present motto on our cards 'In the Lord is all our trust' we propose it be 'Upon Humanity we rely'."

The Drypool members claimed that this was more in keeping with actuality for it was on the members that the Union did rely for its progress. While it was perfectly all right to expect that the 'overruling Father' should extend his blessing to them, it should not be thought that "He alone will support an institution while its members make no efforts."

Harnott attacked the proposition for being so stupid as to suppose the society's progress depended on a motto. Pointing out that a change would entail printing expenses, he concluded by asking the members to consider "whether the motto 'Upon Humanity we rely' will create greater prosperity than 'In the Lord is all our Trust'." His faith in the second motto was supported overwhelmingly by a majority of members!

With his greater personal standing Harnott also began to venture more of his own ideas. He knew the lodges were still hostile to any erosion of their local autonomy and especially in relation to strike action. Nevertheless, he persuaded the Central Committee to send out its own members occasionally to try and bring about an amicable settlement in any of the larger and lengthier disputes that took place. Their missions were so successful that certain lodges proposed that the Central Committee should formally continue this course of action. This immediately aroused hostility from a few lodges who scathingly commented that they could run their own strikes. This was not denied by Harnott. But he did not want lodges to "run" strikes, he said, he wanted them stopped.

In support of the proposition for strike delegates he pointed out that they had ended two important strikes, one at Hull and the other at Britannia Bridge, after they had cost the Union a total of £963. Warning that the lodges would have to accept some form of discipline he added that if only the larger strikes in recent months were taken into consideration, the Union had spent on them " the round sum of £3,096 since the 1st October, 1847, to the 3rd August, 1848! "

Finally a proposition from Bath lodge was carried " that the Central Committee have the power to authorise any lodge in or about the locality in which the strike takes place to send two delegates to investigate the case, and send a correct statement of the affair to the Central Committee; and that any such delegates giving an incorrect account be fined as a majority of the members may decide; and that the Central Committee send any of its members within sixty miles of Liverpool, but no further, except in a case of real necessity."

This proposition was wide enough in its intent to give Harnott and his Committee the control they wanted and for the first time in the Union's history the lodges had, by ballot vote, voluntarily surrendered their autonomy over the conduct of strikes. On a decision of this importance, however, it could hardly be expected that all the lodges would obediently swing into line. The reaction from some of them was typified by the angry dispute which took place between Wigan lodge and the Central Committee over the payment of strike pay to some of their members.

The Wigan masons, like many others throughout the country, had known that their wages might be forced down due to the economic depression. When 200 of them employed on railway work in the town were cut by sixpence per day, they resigned themselves to its acceptance. The main contractor for the job was a man called McCormack. He had, however, leased off a portion of the work to a sub-contractor named Blake who was directly employing about 47 of the men.

Blake followed the main contractor's lead and also cut his men's wages from 5s. to 4s. 6d. per day. Within four weeks, however, McCormack, thinking his men completely supine, attempted the step of bringing down their wages to 4s. per day. This time the masons did not hesitate to come out on strike. They also succeeded in getting the sub-contractor's men to join them, although Blake protested that he had not intended to cut his wages by a further sixpence.

The Central Committee's case on this strike was quite simple. They were willing to pay the men out on strike against McCormack the main contractor, but claimed that Blake's men were not justified in turning out as no imposition had been made on them. Finally the Committee used the new rule to send delegates to Wigan. These confirmed the position as originally reported and also added that the officers of the Wigan lodge were extremely slack in carrying out their official duties.

Sending out delegates in this case inflamed rather than ended the dispute. It might be true that John Gibson, the Wigan secretary, was not nearly so careful with lodge business as he should be, but he was a good writer and one of the masons' most brilliant speakers. With these qualities went a vanity which resulted in his making an acrimonious attack on the delegates who had visited Wigan. He even took the step of by-passing the Returns by sending lengthy circulars round the lodges in which he demanded justice for the strikers—with the threat that if they did not get it the society in Wigan would be extinguished.

The Central Committee were incensed at this attack and placed the matter before the members for a decision and urged that Gibson be penalised for his actions. But resentment against the growing powers of the Committee and the brilliance with which Gibson stated his case resulted, to their surprise, in them being overwhelmingly defeated by 723 to 354. Extremely bitter at this defeat they declared that they would refuse to stand as candidates for Grand Lodge in the next annual elections.

Harnott was just as resentful about the adverse vote but decided on a more diplomatic course. He said that he was prepared to comply with the ballot vote but could not pay out any strike money to Wigan until he received a properly audited statement of the payments made.

This recommenced the quarrel and it was finally decided that two other Central Committee delegates should visit Wigan to inspect the books of the lodge—a course of events for which Harnott had planned. The delegates met with obstruction from Gibson and other Wigan members and this resulted in pages of acrimonious correspondence in the Returns, right throughout the period during which balloting was taking place for a new Grand Lodge. Although having firmly announced its intention to resign Liverpool had been persuaded to again stand election. There was still sufficient enmity and doubt to see them beaten, however, and Birmingham was elected with the narrow majority of 122 votes.

Only a few weeks later the members were given such proof of Gibson's frauds that they voted him guilty in a national ballot. But by then it was too late. In the declining circumstances of the Union Harnott—who had himself been overwhelmingly re-elected by 1,490 votes to his nearest opponent's 66—had also to move office and contend with the breaking in of a new Central Committee.

The O.S.M.'s fortunes had changed drastically. 1847 had been a boom year until the economic crisis, which broke out around October, plunged the masons into a desperate fight to conserve membership and finances. In the year from December 1847 to 1848 membership plummeted from 9,070 to 6,741. By tight control over the finances Harnott had prevented them falling so drastically but now he found circumstances turning increasingly against him. The continuing depression had thrown an unprecedented number of members out of work and expenses for tramps shot up at the beginning of 1849.

The retiring Liverpool Central Committee members underlined the gravity of the situation. Resigning as Grand Lodge after five years " at the helm of affairs " they pointed out the " enormous expenditure " in the first few months of the year and grimly added that: " We are now standing on the verge of a tottering fabric, which if something is not adopted to ameliorate our falling position we shall very soon have the name of the Society numbered with the things that were."*

---

* O.S.M. Returns, 29th March, 1849.

CHAPTER 11

OUTCOME OF A BAD DEBT

EACH succeeding month of 1849 seemed to underline the accuracy of the grim Liverpool prophecy. From having thousands of pounds in its Central Committee coffers, O.S.M. funds began to plunge drastically. The lodges reacted with panic suggestions for reducing debts and conserving membership. There should be no more strikes permitted; strike and tramp benefits should be reduced or completely abolished; entrance money should be cut to 5s. or even 2s. 6d.; these were some of the proposals put forward by certain lodges and just as fiercely resisted by others.

A formal motion that there should be a levy of half a day's wages from members in work, in order to raise central funds, was carried by 106 to 66 votes. It was a flimsy majority, with the total ballot indicating the lack of interest in the Union's affairs and the possible hostile response there would be to such a levy.

General economic conditions in the industry were as grim as the internal affairs of the O.S.M. and the other building unions. In some areas wages were dropping to as low as 3s. 4d. per day. Many employers were seizing the opportunity to reverse improvements that had been gained in extra pay, and the 4 o'clock finish on Saturday. Others found themselves compelled by the pressure of competition to either match the rapacity of their fellows or go bankrupt.

Among the panaceas being urged by the O.S.M. lodges was one from Liverpool George IV that the strike fund should be completely abolished, and replaced by a compulsory emigration fund. Liverpool's reasoning was that if the supply of labour could be balanced with demand there would be no need for strikes.

Emigration as a solution to their problems was not an idea exclusive to the masons. In the general economic depression taking place a large number of unions thought that they could pay for emigration on such a scale as to cancel out the thousands of unemployed men in each trade.

Putting forward its proposition for consideration by other lodges, the Liverpool lodge claimed that " had all the money we had expended in and lost through strikes for the last seven years been devoted to emigration we might have removed 3,000 masons to America, the inexhaustibility of which place will ever be a safe guarantee of plenty."

There was a mixed but generally hostile reception to the idea. The London, Bow lodge, tartly retorted that the scheme was " quite inconsistent with justice and common sense, as those who propound it are the last to go."

The general feeling was that to abolish strikes was to " lie down and let the masters ride rough-shod over us." The Leeds lodge spoke for more than its own members when it wrote: " what benefit would it be to the trade if half of the members were to emigrate at the present day if no protection were afforded to those who were left."

The Liverpool proposition was soundly defeated though it was agreed there should be a voluntary emigration fund for those who wanted this facility.

The tremendous impact on the Union's finances through payment of strike benefit was clearly shown when three elected auditors made a survey of the accounts of all lodges over a three-year period. In their report they showed that by far the largest single amount expended was the sum of £7,375 in turnout pay. Driving this fact home to the members Harnott said that this expenditure " was without parallel in the annals of any other society in existence; each member should notice this fact, with regard for the folly that has been exercised in unprofitable competition with capital."

This report from the auditors sparked off a clash between Liverpool George IVth lodge and the new Central Committee. Within the space of a year Liverpool had lost its position as the seat of government and its proposals on emigration had been soundly defeated in a national ballot. In a spirit of revenge it now tried to show the "short-comings" of the Central Committee since the conduct of national Union affairs had been removed from Liverpool. It attacked the Central Committee for paying "the tremendous sum of £71 10s. 9d." in payment to the members who had been elected to make the audit.

In support of its contentions the lodge submitted an argument occupying four foolscap pages, which it demanded should be printed in the Returns. On behalf of the Central Committee Harnott replied that the complex task of going through a maze of lodge accounts stretching over three years had taken the auditors a total of 15 weeks and the payment was, therefore, not excessive. He also pointed out that Liverpool's statement would cost too much in typesetting for it to be published in the Returns.

Some of the more influential members at Liverpool retaliated by taking money out of lodge funds to pay for the printing of an extremely lengthy circular which they posted direct to all the other lodges of the Union. In this Harnott and the other members of the Committee were attacked as being despots. Within a few weeks the lodges of the Union were engaged in bitter argument and the pages of the Returns were filled with almost nothing but acrimonious recriminations between supporters of Liverpool, the three auditors and the Central Committee.

While Harnott was vainly striving to pacify the protagonists Leicester lodge put forward a proposition which led to increasing bitterness; that Harnott's salary should be reduced from 35s. to 30s. per week.

The entire Union now seemed so frustrated and embittered at being unable to adequately meet the external economic challenge that it was turning inwards to self-destruction. Fortunately, however, one or two of the lodges were completely sickened by the acrimony and they moved formal propositions so that ballot votes could be taken to end the various quarrels taking place. The Leicester suggestion that Harnott should have his wages reduced was defeated by 513 votes to 36.

By 155 to 7 votes a motion was also agreed that discussion on the Liverpool George IVth complaints " should be closed " with a rider that those members who had sent out the circulars attacking the Central Committee should pay for it out of their own pockets and refund the amount to lodge funds. When the Liverpool members refused to do this the lodge was completely suspended from taking part in Union affairs, and its members excluded from all benefits. But the matter did not end there.

A large number of the George IVth members infiltrated into Liverpool Neptune lodge, and used it for putting forward propositions attacking Harnott and once again demanding that his wages be cut. Four times in the same year, in fact, national ballots were held on whether or not there should be a reduction in Harnott's salary. Finally Penzance lodge demanded that the sniping should end and added " we have but one paid servant and he must always be a target to shoot a venomous arrow at."

The struggle within the O.S.M. was a reflection of the jungle-like conditions now existing within the industry as a whole. Competition between contracting firms was fierce, and this inevitably tended to drive down conditions for the operatives.

One of the most glaring examples of the cut-throat atmosphere was the contract for the Great Northern Railways' viaduct at Newark. A large number of firms tried to obtain the job. The highest tender price put in by an established railway contractor was £54,000. There were a number of lower tenders but the firm who finally secured the job did so at the astonishingly low price of £15,000.

This firm was Rennie, Logan and Thompson Ltd. Rennie being the ex-general secretary of the O.S.M. who had petulantly left office because the members refused him an ever increasing salary. His co-director Logan had also played an active part in the Union at one time. Equipped with knowledge on both sides of the fence " they proceeded to try and complete the job in the only way it could be done at such an incredibly low price."

Knowing there was a large number of men unemployed in the region they declared that they would not pay wages on the normal basis. Payment would be entirely by piece. Soon the men in their employ found that however hard they might work they were only earning an average of about 2s. 8d. per day! Refused even an interview with the principals of the firm they finally had to resort to striking in order to obtain an improvement in their conditions. Harnott bitterly attacked the renegades Rennie and Logan who, he said, were not only driving down the conditions of the men but forcing all the other employers to climb down into the same "filthy pit" in which they operated.

He also used this occasion to drive home to the members generally that only by selfless consideration for the future of the Union, and less petulance and acrimony, could it be saved. In February 1851 he again warned that the O.S.M.'s total financial reserves had shrunk to £385 and that the average fortnightly income of around £60 was insufficient to meet even the modest and tightly controlled expenditure being permitted on strikes and tramps. And though final membership figures were not yet available, the Union might find itself with little more than 3,000 paying members which was one-third of what they had numbered only a few years previously.

The only bright spot in the Union's affairs was that, although subject to almost constant and extremely venomous attack from various lodges—especially Liverpool, Manchester and London—the Birmingham Central Committee had retained its position as the seat of government in a contest with Manchester by 406 to 197 votes. Harnott was also re-elected to his position by 732 votes to the nearest candidate's 131. In its desperate plight, therefore, the Union would not have to bear the extra burden of a change in its administration at the top.

But its funds continued to suffer heavy pressure due to increased expenditure on tramp relief which was not sufficiently compensated by the general low level of contributions sent in by lodges who were themselves impoverished. Harnott had always been a great believer in having good financial reserves as a basis of strength for the Union's operations. Now, looking around for ways in which to boost its credit balance, he remembered that the loan of £150 made to the London division of the Friendly Society of Operative Bricklayers in February 1848 had still not been repaid.

He immediately instructed the London Paviors Arms Lodge to contact the London Division of the Bricklayers and " solicit them to fulfill their pledge in returning the loan." The reply the Masons received infuriated Harnott and caused an outburst of anger from the lodges.

" . . . our Society cannot consider that we are indebted to the Masons' Society for the loan that the old Society of Bricklayers borrowed off them; for we, as a society, not being in existence at the time it being borrowed" replied J. Jarvis who signed himself Secretary of the No. 1 Lodge of the London Society of Operative Bricklayers.

Harnott traced James Lockett, now resident in Manchester, who had doubled the positions of London Divisional Secretary of the Friendly Society of Bricklayers and the Union's General Secretary at the time the loan was made. He indignantly asked what Lockett was going to do to honour the loan which had been made in response to a letter signed by him.

Lockett sent an extremely bland reply disclaiming all personal responsibility. The London Division, he explained, had dissolved itself " about the end of the year 1849."*

* O.S.M. Returns, 5th June, 1851.

Reading Lockett's letter—which had been sent in his private capacity—Harnott decided that there had been duplicity by the bricklayers and "the present London Bricklayers Society probably re-established to get clear of former inconveniences."

As a last resort he wrote to the Central Committee of the Friendly Society of Operative Bricklayers, situated at Manchester, appealing to them to honour the debt. The reply was again from Lockett, acting this time in his official role as General Secretary. His letter was twice as long and twice as suavely evasive as his previous one.

Though the Masons' Central Committee confessed themselves at a loss to understand the involved and paradoxical content of Lockett's letter, one thing was crystal clear to them—they were not going to be repaid the £150 and they were convinced that a piece of sharp practice had been put over on them. This was something that soured relationships for a long time afterwards between the O.S.M. and the two quite separate Bricklayers' Unions which now began to develop.

There was, in fact, a great deal of confusion about what actually happened to the London Division of the Friendly Society of Bricklayers at the time its crippling load of debts forced it out of existence to be succeeded by the Union which became known subsequently as the London Order of Bricklayers. Lockett's letter to the Masons indicated that the new organisation had not been formed till after the death of the old society "about the end of the year 1849". But reasonably early records of the London Order definitely claim its foundation date as the 8th April, 1848.

The truth would appear to be that the Lambeth Lodge of the new London Order, which became known as No. 1 Lodge, was formed by members who had deliberately disassociated themselves from the old society which they knew was doomed to extinction. It may well have been that Lockett and others expected that the new lodge would, in due course, automatically link up again with the parent body. If so there was an unexpected twist to the manoeuvres indulged in by the Bricklayers to rid their London division of its debt. For the new London Union, far from reassociating with the Friendly Society of Operative Bricklayers, continued to maintain and develop its separate existence and actually became a bitter opponent in the struggle to build up strength.

It is due, therefore, to the bad debts of the old F.S.O.B. that we owe the birth of the London Order of Operative Bricklayers on the 8th April, 1848. Gradually the parent body from which it had sprung became known as the Manchester Order of Bricklayers.

The anger of the masons at what they felt to be the bricklayers' double dealing had been heightened by their financial embarrassment. But as trade began to pick up again the quarrel and the bitterness died down. Harnott had introduced a new feature into the Fortnightly Returns giving reports of the 'State of Trade' in the areas where the Union was organised. In place of the previous dismal notices about heavy unemployment, reports were coming in that work was much more plentiful than it had been for the last two or three years. Together with Harnott, the Central Committee now became quietly confident that their most pressing problems would soon be over.

They reasoned that more men in work meant a healthier contribution income and a lessening of the heavy expenditure on tramp benefit. But they did not fully take into account the prevalent industrial philosophy of their members. If jobs were scarce the masons were generally prepared to exercise restraint and accept hardships. But a scarcity of labour they legitimately regarded as a basis for advance in improving working conditions and strengthening the Union. The Cardiff masons, for instance, reporting that "trade is good here" emphasised that they had taken advantage of the situation by enforcing a closed shop. "No non-members need apply for work," they added, "a few are out of employ and would rather walk about than ask for work at the Society's jobs."

It was because of this reviving militance throughout the country that the Central Committee soon found that financial expenditure was not so much lessened as re-directed from tramp to strike benefit. Harnott quickly told members that while they could use the present situation to strengthen the Union they were, in fact, in danger of weakening it unless they exercised more caution where strikes were concerned.

The most foolish reasons are given for striking, claimed Harnott, and in the Returns for August 1852 he gave a classic example of what he meant. "A strike has taken place at the central railway station, Birmingham," he reported, "because the foreman discharged two members who objected to give a lift to a member who was put in Coventry for not paying the usual fine for coming to his work on Monday morning with an unclean shirt." Though this strike of 30 masons was settled in favour of the men within a day Harnott warned that "it may have proved a serious affair."

Whatever the financial resources of the Masons' Union the Central Committee realised that every attempt must be made to honour the benefits offered by the Society or they would lose the hardcore of loyal members. In a period where they hoped to expand it was even more essential to offer new recruits benefits which were attractive. And one of the benefits most appreciated by the membership was the accident provision where the rules provided for a general levy to provide a capital sum of £100 for any member who was completely unable to follow his trade due to an accident at work.

The rule stipulated that application for the loan should be sponsored by the branch to which the member belonged, and this must be substantiated by written notice from a registered surgeon. In cases of doubt the Central Committee would send delegates itself to investigate the position. Full details were then printed in the Returns and a ballot vote of the entire membership taken as the final arbiter on whether the benefit should be paid or not. In any one year there were frequent applications for this benefit due to the appallingly high accident level in the industry.

The sum of £100 provided by the masons to its unfortunate members was the only thing which saved them from complete destitution when they were crippled and unable to work at their trade any more. An indication of what this fraternal help meant then in the life of a disabled mason is shown by the letter of thanks written by Edwin Addis.

"It is with great pleasure I take up my pen to communicate a few lines unto you; I am a young man, 26 years of age, I have been a member nearly seven years, during which period I have had good testimonials as to character and punctuality while holding office in your valuable society; I have sustained a great loss, namely, my right arm. I return my cordial thanks to you all for the support which I have obtained. It is my earnest wish, that the younger members of the society may never be absent in rendering entire satisfaction by fulfilling the duties of the society, and promoting its most general benefits and interests. I beg respectfully and sincerely to return you my heartfelt thanks for the kind provision which you have made me, amounting to the sum of £100; my loss indeed is very great but when I look at your kind gift, I almost fancy it compensates me, as it will enable me to procure for myself and family (through economy and industry), an honest livelihood. Gentlemen and Worthy Brothers, I should only trespass upon your valuable time by entering into any detail leading to the loss of my right arm, as you are perfectly aware of the nature of the same. I beg again to return you my unbounded gratitude, wishing that prosperity, welfare, and happiness may always attend the operative masons' society.

I remain, Your obliged and grateful Servant,

EDWIN ADDIS."

When young Addis was granted his benefit the O.S.M. had its own money troubles to bear and the members were still suffering personal privations even though trade had begun to improve. Nevertheless, to pay him his benefit a general levy of 7d. had been accepted by every member in work. The sacrifice entailed to make this fraternal gesture can only be appreciated when it is realised that it meant up to two hours' wages for men in the lowest paid areas—and this when the loss of such an amount was much more significant for the building worker's family than it is today.

CHAPTER 12

THE NINE HOURS' AGITATION BEGINS

THE gradual spread of better trade conditions found the building unions benefiting by increased membership and funds. The great exhibition at Crystal Palace in 1851 also provided more work for the building crafts in London and the men were able to win increases in wages.

It was partly this revival of the building industry, with the emphasis in the London area, which stimulated the rapid development of the London Order of Operative Bricklayers. And it certainly looked as if its influence in the London area and the Home Counties would be very much greater than that of the Friendly Society of Operative Bricklayers which it had replaced.

One effect of the better wage rates being obtained by all of the trades was that their struggle became directed into another avenue—the shortening of the working day. The masons, who were first to take up the new line of policy, made their primary objective the abolition of overtime. Some men were unemployed, they claimed, while others were working overtime equivalent to two days above the normal week. Their first step therefore was to deliver to the employers a notice formally requesting that overtime working should be abolished. Where it had to be operated for special circumstances the Union said the men should be paid at the rate of time and a half.

The success with which this petition met heartened the whole of the building unions. By May 1853 the London masons reported that: " Their labour has been completely successful. There is not one firm in London, so far as the masons are concerned at this date, working overtime! By the force of a well organised moral combination, aided by a course of energetic friendly deputations to the employers, this most baneful system of overtime has been abolished throughout London and its vicinity." *

This progress by the masons did not please everyone. It provoked a sour retort from *The Builder*. "Overtime!" said that worthy journal. "Why, we must all work overtime at one period of our lives, if we would make any advance. That others should prevent it seems to us an infringement of the rights of man, as suicidal as it is unjust."

The London members of the O.S.M. were little concerned about what *The Builder* thought. Their victory on overtime made them eager to further their efforts to shorten the working day. If the employers had caved in quickly on this issue then, they thought, prospects were good for achieving a reduction from 10 to 9 hours per day within the near future.

However, the masons found a determined resistance to any suggestion for reducing hours. For the employers there was a great deal of difference between the two proposals. To abolish overtime had really cost them nothing. There was plenty of labour available and to hire it did not involve a considerable per capita expenditure on fringe benefits as it does today. In fact, it was probably cheaper to hire extra labour than concede the payment of time and a half for overtime.

A shortening of hours, however, was a direct charge on the pocket of the employer who would be expected to pay the same daily wage. And the masters soon made the men aware that the achievement of a shorter working day would not be possible without a bitter struggle.

Rather than a direct contest, therefore, the masons decided to promote their policy by general agitation within

---

* O.S.M. Returns, 14th July, 1853.

the London area. The launching of the Nine Hours Movement, which was to ultimately embrace all of the building unions in the metropolis, took place at a special public meeting held at the Temperance Hall, Westminster, on the 6th May, 1853. The chairman, R. G. Watt, reported it was attended by " upwards of 700 masons and delegates from the other building trades assembled " who unanimously agreed to set up a 12 man committee to plan the work of agitation for a reduced working day.*

" The hours of labour of the Operative Stone Masons," ran their first circular to the Master Builders of London and its vicinity, " whose employment is most unquestionably heavy, laborious and unhealthy, cannot with any degree of justice be compared with the light manual occupations of Shopkeepers and many classes of trade-operatives. It is, therefore, an uncontroverted fact, that our present long hours of hard labour are causing a daily expenditure and prostration of our vital energies, a continual languid state of feelings, and a premature death! This degrading, unreasonable, and unnecessary system is decidedly unprofitable to the employers, and a most fraudulent imposition upon the employed, by depriving them of leisure time, and completely exhausting their physical strength and natural spirits, which are indispensably essential for the much-needed culture of their undeveloped intellectual, artisanic, social, and moral capacities. No undue advantage or untimely proceedings are anticipated by this agitation, but rather the establishment of a more secure and beneficial position for both the employers and employed. Trusting that you will give this truly philanthropic cause a considerate and honourable treatment, becoming your position in society, the native power and dignity of this country, and the intellectual progression of the nineteenth century."

The employers showed themselves far from eager to discuss this request. In fact the masons became convinced that they would rather discuss anything else in

* O.S.M. Returns, May 1853.

preference. Reporting that: "Some few of the builders have advanced 6d. per day (now 5s. 6d.) on the masons' wages," the London Paviors Arms lodge commented: "This move is thought by some to be an attempt to put aside the nine hours' movement. Some of the men have taken the advance while others have refused the golden bait."

The masons perhaps viewed this advance in wages too lightly for, what they almost contemptuously regarded as a bribe to pacify them over working hours, it took the London bricklayers another year to achieve and even then it was only "after twelve weeks battling the 5s. 6d. per day was obtained through the manly efforts of a few men, for not one sixth of the Bricklayers in London were members at that time."*

The pressure for a shorter working day was not relaxed because of the advance in wages and it led to a curious dispute at Sydenham where: "For some time past the nine hours' question has been exciting considerable interest amongst the members who are employed inside the Crystal Palace."

The first positive move was made when a number of decorators applied to the agents of the Crystal Palace Company for a reduction in working hours and amazed the masons by their almost immediate success in "obtaining a diminuation of one hour per day." The reaction of the masons convinced the Company that this award to the decorators would not be tolerated as an isolated example of generosity, "so making a virtue of necessity, the agents of the Crystal Palace Company gave them the boon before they had time to ask for it."†

The pay per day was to remain at 6s. Alarmed at this "capitulation" to the decorators and masons, and the possible consequences among their own employees, the various private contractors with jobs on the Park held a meeting with the Company's agents and angrily demanded

* O.B.S. Trade Circular, 1st April, 1864

† O.S.M. Returns, March 1854.

that the decision be reversed. After two weeks' hesitation the Company gave in and took the extremely provocative step of placarding the site announcing that their men must return to the working of a 10 hour day.

Enraged at the conniving which had led to the Company breaking faith on the new agreement all the men walked off the site and the masons appealed through the Fortnightly Returns for official backing from the O.S.M. But even before the ballot vote was declared on this appeal the dispute had apparently ended. The men accepted a return to the 10 hours day on the strength of having obtained an increase from 9d. to 1s. per hour for all overtime. Their total gain therefore amounted to 3d. per hour when working overtime, and this in itself seemed worthless if the masons' claim were true that all overtime had been eliminated in London and its vicinity.

But the masons at Sydenham had, they claimed, not terminated their dispute but merely suspended it awaiting the result of the vote on their original application for official backing. If the majority of members decided for them receiving strike pay they would immediately resume the contest for a nine hour day. When the vote was finally declared however the membership had decided against them by 294 to 248 votes. Certainly the adverse majority was a small one but, compared with the normal approval of strike action for desirable aims, it was very significant of opinion throughout the provinces.

In many areas, including Halifax, Tamworth and Rochdale, the masons were then fighting to increase their daily pay from 4s. to 4s. 6d. At Mansfield it was only after strike action that wages had been pushed up from the very low rate of 3s. 4d. to 3s. 8d. per day. To these members any funds available for backing disputes should be used to eliminate low rates of wages rather than to support "luxuries", such as a reduction in hours, for men already fortunate to be earning 6s. per day. Even in the large provincial centres where the O.S.M. was strong enough to obtain wages of 5s. and 5s. 6d. the members were still hostile to the London appeal, for it was a hard struggle to retain any advantages they had secured. The most they themselves had been able to achieve in shorter hours was the four o'clock finish on a Saturday. Not surprisingly they regarded the Sydenham masons as attempting to push up their conditions to an exceedingly high level at the expense of others much less fortunate.

No small part was played by the Central Committee of the O.S.M. in swaying the vote against the Sydenham application. Its members came out against official strike backing because " In our opinion the nine hours' movement should become a question for the Legislature, the same as the ten hours' bill was for the manufacturing districts."

Harnott, as secretary of the Union, also had two major reasons for being unenthusiastic about fighting the nine hours' claim in London. Firstly, he felt that if there was any priority for drawing on the masons' hard pressed funds it must be given to the lodges attempting to enforce town trade agreements. These were an advance on individual shop or site conditions, and they were also an indication of the extent to which the organisations of masters and men were each beginning to coalesce. In the ten years between 1850-60 there was a steady adoption of town agreements, often only after hard fought strikes, covering general conditions on working hours, winter and summer wages, apprenticeship, walking time and refreshment breaks. Harnott recognised in this trend the shaping of some form of joint consultative machinery, however primitive, which should be encouraged in the interests of the industry as a whole.

The second reason for his objection to entering a possibly protracted fight in London was the increasing manipulation of the common law to severely punish men pursuing trade union objectives. It might be necessary, in the near future, to spend money in fighting this growing evil.

Since the repeal of the Combination Acts in 1824 it was no longer an offence to belong to a union. But this did not mean that it was safe to actively carry out trade union decisions. For the employers and ruling class generally, indignant at the repeal of the Combination Acts, soon found other laws which they could use to suppress trade union activities. The main line of action by these people was to instigate proceedings accusing the men of "conspiracy". And to the magistrates and judges of this period, products of and sympathetic to their class, it was usually sufficient to show that trade unionists had commonly entered into decisions about their wages for them to be severely punished for alleged conspiracy of illegal combination.

Strike pickets were also in danger of sentence to hard labour if employers took action against them for " unlawful intimidation or threats " to blacklegs. Use of the common law in this way was rapidly leading to the farcical situation where men were acknowledged as free to belong to a union but liable to lose their freedom if they attempted to pursue the logical consequences of combining together.

One case that caused bitter resentment throughout the O.S.M., and revealed the mentality of the judiciary towards trade unions, took place in the summer of 1856 and concerned three masons who had been acting as strike pickets at Cardiff. They were tried at Glamorganshire Assizes on a charge of riot and assault—the assault amounted to little more than cursing the blacklegs who had taken the place of strikers.

The judge, Sir Charles Crompton, made an opening statement which really served to convict the defendants even before evidence was taken. His observations to the jury on what constituted unlawful acts were so all embracing that it was obvious the men would be found guilty on one point or another. On the general question of conspiracy, he said:

" A conspiracy or combination—a combination or agreement of that kind between two or more parties amounts in point of law to a conspiracy, and a conspiracy of a most serious nature."*

* O.S.M. Returns, 24th July, 1856.

Dealing with the fact that the masons had obviously been acting together as pickets, the judge added: " Any persons so gathered together to the number of three or more, and causing alarm and terror, to the Queen's subjects, by creating a disturbance—such gathering together constitutes a riot."

Any possibility that the men might have escaped the charge of assault, because it was rather weak, was covered by Sir Charles who hastened to say that there need be no physical violence necessary for a conviction.

" There must be something " he told the jury, " to show that they are acting in common concert, gathered together to prevent others from working and even though no actual blows passed, any gathering together for that purpose will constitute either a riot or an unlawful assembly."

Although a good defence was made on behalf of the men the judge again used his summing up speech to hammer home his original points and it was no surprise when the jury brought in a verdict of guilty. Sir Charles then wasted no time in sentencing the masons to " be imprisoned for three calendar months, with hard labour."

A constant succession of these cases, concerning members of all unions, resulted in the various trades concentrating their efforts on trying to obtain a clarification of the law relating to combinations. For over five years pleas were made in the legislature for an amendment to the Acts in an attempt to stop the ruthless sentences being passed under it. On Tuesday, 18th April, 1859, these efforts were rewarded with some success when Royal assent was given to the Molestation of Workmen Act. The main substance of this Act was to give greater protection to pickets on union duties. " The extension of liberty guaranteed " commented Harnott, " is of the utmost importance to the whole of the working class."

The protection turned out to be more theoretical than real for the courts sought and found other means of repression. For the moment, however, the masons, bricklayers and other trades felt free to concentrate their attention on other problems. And one of the most pressing and dangerous of these was a general sharpening of the struggle between employers and men over the shorter hours demand.

When the London masons had been rather frigidly refused strike backing by their union for an attempt to reduce the working day to nine hours, they decided to redirect their efforts into petitioning employers for a Saturday half holiday. To this demand the masters affected a contemptuous indifference though they were really becoming increasingly concerned at the growing pressure in London and throughout the country generally for shorter hours. The agitation of the London building workers, in fact, was beginning to draw a response from the provinces and there was a growing awareness on both sides that a challenge must come—and in the not-too-distant future. In facing that challenge the employers recognised that, united only on a local basis, they would be at a serious disadvantage compared with the nationally organised unions of the men.

As a preliminary to the struggle, therefore, they formed "the National Association of Master Builders" at the beginning of 1858. This Association was confined to the Midlands and the North in its early stages. In trying to extend its organisation the masters took a lesson from the trade unions and followed the tactic of sending delegates to visit other towns in an attempt to persuade masters to join the Association.

"The movement commenced at Liverpool" reported Harnott to the masons, "and meetings have been held in various large towns throughout the kingdom. The Liverpool masters consulted those of Manchester and the result was that they resolved to send delegates to various towns. This has been done, and associations have been formed in Bolton, Halifax, Nottingham, Birmingham, Sheffield and Huddersfield."*

* O.S.M. Returns, 29th April, 1858.

Feeling secure within the new Association the masters now felt confident of delivering a challenge to the men and did so by an arrogant notification to all their employees that, after 1st May, they were ending the day wage system and would thereafter pay only by the hour. This, they assured each other, would completely kill the shorter working day agitation because any reduction in hours would now entail a loss in total wages by the men.

The bitter hostility this proposal drew from the unions almost equalled that which had been aroused previously in Lancashire when the notorious 'Document' had been presented. The men felt that payment by the hour would have much the same crushing effect on every advance they had ever gained. Under it they could, for instance, be hired and fired by the hour instead of by the day. During bad weather they would have to foot the bill if they could be employed on and off from hour to hour. Also lost to them would be the full day's pay for the short Saturday and only the actual hours worked would be paid for. And, if there was no longer to be an agreed length of working day, then obviously there would be no 'overtime' and all hours would be paid for at the same rate.

The most feared consequence of all was the possibility that a number of men might attempt to push up their wages by working as many hours as possible. They would also probably jettison all the working regulations which had been fought for by the unions and this could lead to them being completely crippled as effective fighting units.

The masters had chosen what they considered an advantageous time in which to present their notice of termination of payment by the day. All the building unions had been involved in a continual succession of local strikes and even the masons, the most powerfully organised, were financially anaemic due to struggles by various lodges to enforce town agreements. But Harnott knew, whatever the weakness of the Union, the battle on payment by the hour was one that they must fight and win. If the masters succeed, he warned his members, " depend upon it we shall place ourselves at the will of every employer who chooses to trample upon us . . . let us set at defiance those tyrants and task masters who seek to lower us to serfdom . . . prepare for a determined resistance against the introduction of this hour system, and then you will be serving yourselves, and confer a blessing on the offspring who succeed you."*

On the morning of 1st May, the building workers in Liverpool, Bolton, Halifax, Huddersfield, Thornton, Croston, Henderton, Nottingham, Sheffield and Manchester tramped to the yards to find their employers insisting that they could only start work on acceptance of payment by the hour. And, to a man, they marched back out of the gates and warned that there would be no return to work except on a continuation of the traditional practice of payment by the day.

So complete was the unity of the men that it astonished the masters who felt that they had selected the time, and the issue, which should have brought about an easy defeat of the unions. Now they apprehensively met and discussed the possibilities of having to face a bitter and prolonged contest which they themselves had brought about. And, in the face of determined resistance by the men, the ties of their much vaunted Association soon proved not strong enough to prevent their almost complete collapse.

Within a few days the battle was largely over. In all of the towns under dispute, with the exception of Newcastle and Huddersfield the masters had capitulated and the men were back at work on a day wage basis. By the 17th of the month even those employers had given way and " victory was complete " jubilantly claimed the unions.

There were some members, however, who viewed the ' victory ' with a rather jaundiced eye. If victory lay with anyone they felt it could be more appropriately

* O.S.M. Returns, 15th April, 1858.

claimed by the employers. For they had very neatly forestalled the struggle for shorter hours by forcing a dispute over hourly payment of wages. The unions had fought a battle merely to retain the status quo. It was against this background that the London drive for shorter hours rapidly reached an almost similar climax.

CHAPTER 13

ON STRIKE FOR A YEAR

THE first 'joint prayer' asking the London employers for a reduction in hours was presented by delegates of the carpenters, the stonemasons and the bricklayers towards the end of 1858. As the other trades began to associate themselves with the standing conference of building unions which had been set up to achieve the nine-hour day, a feeling of confidence began to sweep through the men. And on the 19th March, 1859, George Potter the conference secretary sent a demand on their behalf to the employers brusquely demanding a 'yes or no' answer on the shorter working day.

"Supported as our claim is by the public press" he wrote, "acknowledged favourably by the Association of Architects, advocated by the pulpit, and their own energetic and persevering efforts cannot fail to call forth your entire approval."*

But the employers were not moved to approval simply because of the impressive list of supporters claimed by the unions. They emphatically rejected the petition on the grounds that: "much inconvenience would result from the discontinuance of work at so early an hour as half past four,† involving as it would the stoppage of all machinery, plant and cattle and labour at that early hour."

This reply convinced the men that achievement of the shorter day would not—at least as yet—be simply a matter

* O.S.M. Returns, 14th April, 1859.

† The normal starting time was six in the morning.

of peaceful persuasion and negotiation. They therefore had the choice of making a challenge by striking, or of carrying on their propaganda agitation until the employers became more amicable. It was on deciding between these alternatives that a division became apparent between the unions.

Of the three major unions involved the carpenters and bricklayers showed themselves willing to take militant action. The masons, however, were in a difficult position in taking a clear stand. For, of all the trades involved in the agitation, they were the only ones who formed part of a really extensive national body. Unlike the autonomous London organisations they had to accept the discipline imposed by the O.S.M.'s rules and, as previous national ballots had turned down their request for official strike backing on the nine-hours' question, they knew they would be regarded as acting 'illegally' if they came out on strike.

Faced with this indecision between the unions the nine-hours' conference took the only realistic course open to it—to continue petitioning by the method of selecting certain large building employers. And it was following this peaceful course of action which sparked off the major dispute of 1859.

The conference had chosen by ballot four firms where the petitions should be presented and one of these was Messrs. Trollope.* The firm's reply to the men was to sack the masons who had taken a leading part in the delegation. The immediate result of this was a total withdrawal of labour from the job and, throughout London, the rest of the employers and men were tensely aware that a major conflict was now almost unavoidable.

It was the employers who first moved into action. Taking a lesson from their northern colleagues they decided to short-circuit any strike for shorter hours by enforcing a lock-out of their men. On the 6th August, 1859, they shut their yards and threw a total of nearly

* *History of Trade Unions: The Webbs*, page 229.

25,000 men out of work. The masters reasoned that this action would adequately demonstrate their enmity to the nine-hours' demand and would also knock the heart out of the more militant trades.

For nearly six weeks the yards were silent; then the employers decided that their 'lesson' had been effectively taught to the men. All jobs, they announced, would again be open on the 12th September to those wishing work. But there was a qualification on their offer of employment. They had so overestimated the effect of the lock-out, in fact, that they attempted to drive home their anticipated victory by declaring that no man would be started unless he first of all signed the detested anti-union 'Document'.

But this move actually strengthened rather than weakened the determination of the men—who were already heartened by the welcome if unexpected support they had received from the press and general public. Although a few men went back and accepted the 'badge of slavery' the majority refused to humble themselves.

Reporting that Cubitts had been successful in obtaining some labour *The Times* of the 13th September added that "no skilled masons, however, presented themselves for employment. . . . The absence of artisans in this department, which was generally remarked yesterday, not at Messrs. Cubitts only, but generally at the master builders' works, is attributed to the wealthy and well organised society to which they belong, and which has ramifications extending from a central point over the whole Kingdom."

The united front of the London masons, however, was due more to their own militant spirit rather than the enthusiastic backing of their Union. The dispute had, in fact, only emphasised the ambiguity of their position in the eyes of the other O.S.M. lodges. In making their fresh plea for strike pay the London members claimed they were not fighting to further the nine-hour movement but in opposition to the 'Document' which "could be a death blow to our invaluable union."

This application drew accusations from the Central Committee and a number of lodges that this was only juggling with words and that the London masons were defiantly turning their faces against previous ballots rejecting support for them on shorter hours. To try and make their actions 'legal' on the grounds that the 'Document' had been presented to them was nothing more than pure sophistry. "What was the cause of this precious memorandum being introduced?" caustically commented the Central Committee. "Why, the Nine Hours' Agitation which the London artisans wished to thrust upon their employers."*

Nevertheless, added the Committee, we must oppose the 'Document' wherever the employers attempt to introduce it. Though they felt that strike rules could not be extended to the London masons, therefore, they backed a successful Bristol proposal that a levy of 1s. per member be imposed as the basis of a fund for supporting their fight against the 'Document'.

This did not mean, however, that the London masons were officially committed to fighting out the dispute, and the growing division between them and the other trades was accelerated by an unusual letter from a man called C. Henry Pomeroy. Pomeroy was regarded as a "confidential representative of the contracting firm of Messrs. Myers", and his letter was directed to Richard Harnott of the Masons. Criticising the actions of the 'agitators' behind the nine-hour movement, Pomeroy claimed that introduction of the 'Document' was "the aggression of the one which has brought forth the indignation of the other."† Referring to a previous building dispute which had been finally settled by discussions between Harnott and Pomeroy's boss, George Myers, he appealed to Harnott to take a lead in settling the Document dispute by "using your best influence as I have before stated, to bring about amicable concessions by all parties concerned."

---

* O.S.M. Returns, 18th August, 1859.

† O.S.M. Returns, 15th September, 1859.

To the O.S.M.'s Central Committee this letter appeared to offer a way out of a struggle about which they were distinctly lukewarm, and which had now been dragging on for nearly two months. They therefore delegated Harnott to go up from Bristol (where the Grand Lodge now was) and negotiate for peace through Myers. News of this move did not excite any sympathetic feelings from the other unions, particularly the bricklayers who were in an extremely militant mood. Why sue for peace, they said, when the general sympathy that lay with the men was shown by the unprecedented sum of £23,000 which had been contributed from all sources to their support. The London masons were also affronted that Harnott should presume to interfere in the strike, and a number of them decided to lay in wait for him at Paddington Station.

In front of the astonished Pomeroy, who had gone to meet him, they thrust Harnott into a cab and forcibly took him to a room at the Sun Tavern in Lambeth. To prevent his escape two of them slept in the same room with him—"some say in the same bed—lest he should hold any unauthorised communication with the enemy", reported a rather scandalised *Times*.*

But Harnott managed to reason his way out and promptly called a general meeting of the London masons. At this meeting he won approval for his attempt to settle the dispute on the proposed compromise that the men should drop the shorter hours' claim on condition that the employers withdrew the 'Document'. This news of the masons' willingness to treat with the masters created uproar among the other unions attached to the nine-hours' conference. Though men had now been steadily trickling back to work as the dispute lengthened, there was an estimated 7,000 men still adamantly opposed to the 'Document'. But a negotiated return to work by the masons would take 2,000 of this number—and from the only union which had a real basis of financial and organisational strength. On the decision of the O.S.M., in fact, largely depended the outcome of the whole dispute.

* O.S.M. Returns 15th September, 1859.

It was the masters themselves who blocked any possibility of a solution through Harnott's efforts. To his overtures they replied that " they considered the difficulties in the way of withdrawing the ' Declaration ', taken as it was by nearly 8,000 men, were insuperable."* And though a small number of the masters signed an undertaking to withdraw the ' Document ' (" releasing probably upwards of a 1,000 men from the trammels of bondage "), Harnott had to return to Bristol and confess his inability to arrange a complete cessation of hostilities.

There was an immediately aggressive reaction from the Central Committee and the members of the Masons' organisation. They had been prepared to temporise with the employers but, if they would rather fight, then there would be a fight—but the men would not accept the ' Document'. By an overwhelming majority it was agreed to levy every member an eighth of a day's wage, each week, and this poured £200 per week into the strike fund of the London district.

In this the masons were fortunate. The bricklayers and others were suffering desperate poverty, which had increased as the bitter winter months brought no prospect of a general return to work. At the beginning of 1860, however, the conflict began to resolve itself. Here and there a firm withdrew the 'Document' while, in other places, the men drifted back to work as their capacity to hold out came to an end.

But it was not until the 7th February, 1860—over six months from the start of the dispute—that the employers finally announced a general withdrawal of the ' Document'. There was no great jubilation, however, from the unions at this ' victory '. The struggle had been too bitter and exhausting. The meaningful declaration by the masters in terminating the battle also revealed the cost at which it had been fought.

" The objects contemplated by the declaration having been accomplished, its further formal administration is

* O.S.M. Returns, 15th September, 1859.

unnecessary,"* they claimed. This was, of course, a piece of wishful thinking. The unions were in a weak state but they certainly had not been killed off. One of the astonishing events of that period, in fact, was their remarkable and speedy recovery from the 'Document' battle, in which the masons alone had spent £5½ thousand.

This recovery was largely due to booming trade conditions in the building industry generally. Within a few months, therefore, the employers were intensely irritated to hear that the men were again preparing an agitation for the nine-hour day.

This time, however, there was a radical difference in the way the unions approached the employers. George Potter's conference had lost its authority as the co-ordinating organisation. The masons had seceded from it during the lock-out, and the plasterers had left at the close of the 'Document' battle. When the bricklayers also determined to withdraw it left the painters and carpenters, who were unable to form an executive.

The unions therefore reached the peculiar position where they agreed upon memorials for the nine-hour day being presented to the employers at the beginning of March 1861 —but "all independent of each other." Even if the employers had not been aggressively spoiling for a fight, they could not have passed up this chance to administer a 'final blow' to the unions when they knew that disunity prevented them making an effective challenge.

To the March petitions, therefore, they retaliated by declaring that hourly wages would replace payment by the day. Like the northern builders, in their unsuccessful attempt to impose hourly wages some few years previously, the London employers reckoned that the shorter working day agitation could be killed completely if they were successful in imposing payment by the hour.

Led by the firms of Kelk, Lucas, Smith and Axford they informed the men that after the 23rd March, day wages would stop and be supplanted by payment at the

---

* O.S.M. Returns, 2nd February, 1860.

rate of 7d. per hour. Not one of the unions was unaware of the significance of this declaration, or in any doubt that its effect would be far reaching on the conditions they had built up by years of costly struggle. Yet their enthusiasm had so outrun their reviving strength that there was only a brief spark of defiance before an almost completely pathetic collapse. With the exception of the masons and the bricklayers the trades were just incapable of any protracted fight, and had to suffer the humiliation of working the new hourly wage system under 'protest'.

" The bricklayers and the masons march under the same banner " declared Harnott in a statement that, if necessary, the two unions would fight alone. Their reply to the employers' challenge was to demand a 'compromise.' This was to be an agreed wage of 6s. per 10 hours for five days, and 3s. for Saturday, which would mean finishing at 12 noon. If successful this would be a gain of a half holiday on Saturday for the men. But the employers were too confident of their strength to even discuss this claim and met it with a contemptuous indifference. There was no alternative for the masons and bricklayers but to move into action alone. The other trades decided that they would continue to work under protest while contributing to the fund set-up for the strikers.

For a few weeks it even seemed that this was a good move. Strike finances were kept good, and it looked as if the bricklayers and masons could stop out for ever if necessary. The obvious flaw in the plan, however, was that most of the masters were able to continue operations of a kind simply because they had men at work—even if under 'protest.' The employers generally were not being inconvenienced and they could hold out at least as long as the strikers, simply because there was no economic pressure on them to make terms.

A fight which never looked like being successful became even more hopeless, in July, when the masons discovered that some bricklayers were using subterfuge to return to work for employers who were almost at the point of having to close their yards. In an angry mood Harnott reported.

" The bricklayers have allowed some of their body to sub-contract work under the builder, these second-hand employers being permitted to use their discretion how they make their payments for work done under them. The subs are well aware of their position with the men, and thus submit to the compromise of 6s. per day, of five days of 10 hours, and 3s. for Saturday, ceasing work at 12 o'clock. This underhanded way of getting out of the hobble seems to take with the men, and thus the principal party (the builder) is left to evade the grand point, while, on the other hand, the joiners, carpenters, plasterers, plumbers, and etc. in the firm, are still at work under the obnoxious hour system—which is ingeniously termed 'protest.' Thus the master builder is almost entirely released from his difficulties which leaves him to contend alone with the masonry branch."*

The position of the masons became even worse when the bricklayers officially wound up their strike committee and withdrew completely from the struggle in November. The London Order of Bricklayers claimed that all its strikers had either resumed work under the compromise or in firms where day wages were still being paid. There was, therefore, no more cause for them to strike.

All of the circumstances now seemed to emphasise the completely hopeless prospects for the masons. But these proud and stubborn men refused to recognise even the possibility of defeat. At a large public meeting sponsored by the London Trades Council, which had not long been established, their spokesman, Thomas Connolley of the South London lodge, claimed that even though the other trades were lukewarm in their support " we mean to win with or without their aid." In a fighting speech typical of the O.S.M., he declared: " Having once taken up a position, retreat is a word unknown in the masons' dictionary."

And rather than retreat the masons decided to advance. To put pressure on the employers Harnott ordered a

* O.S.M. Returns, 4th July, 1861.

withdrawal of labour in every provincial yard belonging to the London masters against whom they were fighting. At the very best, however, this was only of marginal help in the struggle and was more than offset by the strike pay necessary for the extra turnouts.

The winter months at the turn of the year brought appalling hardships for the men and their families. Even then they refused to concede victory to the employers. " Once comfortable homes have been broken up " announced a grim Connolley, " but we are not dispirited, on the contrary we see, and at no great distance, victory beaming upon us. Thank God, although our homes have been destroyed, the materials for re-erecting them still exist."

The spirit of the London masons was matched by an astonishing and almost suicidal, determination by Harnott and his Executive to fight the battle to a finish. In face of growing discontent from lodges who declared the contest hopeless and likely to lead the Union to bankruptcy, the Executive announced that it would not think of deserting its " brave army in London." In a poetic reply to the grumblers they declared:

" Defeat to masons is unknown,
For Labour's cause they fight;
It would be madness then, we say,
To close the London strike."*

But the growing pressure against continuing such a hopeless struggle was too great to be beaten down, even by someone who possessed the immense authority that Harnott had in the O.S.M. The Halifax lodge forced a national ballot vote on its proposition that the strike be finished on the 7th June, and the men to return to work on the best conditions they could get. The masons had been battling for over a year in London, and neither they nor Harnott liked to swallow the sour taste of defeat,

* O.S.M. Returns, 27th March, 1862.

but a majority vote for the Halifax proposition forced him to instruct: " the members who have heroically braved the greatest strike on record in the history of the society " to withdraw from the contest.

Their defeat however was by no means absolute. The confusion in the different methods of working in London testified to that. In some yards they had forced the employers to accept the compromise. In others the masters had not even taken up the challenge and had continued payment by the day. And this confusion on hours and wages was reflected right throughout the country. But the London strike was a major turning point in the struggle against payment by the hour. Although the building unions fought rearguard actions against it all over the country, it gradually spread during subsequent years until it became universal.

CHAPTER 14

DEATH OF A GENERAL

ONE union which, surprisingly, gained substantial benefits from the metropolitan battle on payment by the hour was the London Order of Bricklayers. The clash had aroused such a militant spirit in the bricklayers in London and the home provinces that the Union found its membership increasing faster than at any period since its foundation in 1848. Even more valuable as a source of strength was the number of previously autonomous local lodges of bricklayers which decided to link up with the main body.

"We have begun to extend all over the country" reported the Executive in November 1861, "having added no less than nine new lodges in provincial towns, and ten or twelve more are preparing to follow in the same direction."

More remarkable than the increase in membership was the report by the Union's secretary, Edwin Coulson, that funds had actually increased during the strike. "Notwithstanding the severe and protracted struggle we have had resisting the hour system of payment, the funds have steadily improved and the increase on the quarter ending March is £99 11s. 8½d."*

In Coulson, who had taken over the secretaryship from Henry Turff, the London Order had a man whose robust energy and concentration of purpose were well suited to

* London O.B.S. Report, March 1862.

the aggressive drive being undertaken to extend the Union throughout the entire country.

Coulson had a broad, powerful body topped by a full face set in grim, determined lines. His near baldness was compensated by a short stubby beard, which ran underneath his jaw like the tough bristles of a scrubbing brush. His total appearance was an accurate testimony to the crude strength of the man, and the determination with which he pressed the interests of the London Bricklayers. If it proved necessary, in the line of duty, he was not averse to occasional physical violence to carry out his objectives.

After the prudent withdrawal of his Union from the London dispute in November 1861, he had taken swift advantage of the favourable conditions for developing the London Order. The old concept of a metropolitan based unit was completely thrown overboard, and Coulson personally thrust far out into the provinces to open new lodges. This was an activity which was bound to lead to inevitable conflict with the Manchester Order of Bricklayers—and conflict of a serious kind.

When the old Friendly Society of Bricklayers had originally lost the London section in 1848 there had been more relief than regret. A millstone of debt had been removed as the responsibility of the central executive, and it was complacently assumed that there would be a return to the fold by London in course of time. Even when all hope of this had diminished there was no great concern so long as the London Order remained safely confined in the far south. But, with the aggressive organising campaign of Coulson and his executive, the Manchester Order became seriously concerned at the real possibility of the wayward offspring forcing the parent body completely out of existence.

George Housely, now secretary of the Manchester Order, was an unimaginative man whose poor capabilities were reflected in the exceedingly dull pages of his Monthly Report. Unable to match the organising ability of Coulson, the only retaliation he could think of was to deny the validity of the London Union's membership card. Whenever a member of the London Order journeyed for a job in an area where the Manchester men were well established, Housely condoned his local lodges forcing the men into his own Union before allowing them to work.

He declared that the London Order should not venture into districts where the Manchester bricklayers already had organisation. Coulson merely retorted: " We contend that the men of any district should choose for themselves." And although Charles Shearman, a prominent member of the London Order's General Council, protested at Coulson's buccaneering attitude it was obvious that he had general support for what was virtually a declaration of all-out war.

Rebuffed by Coulson, the Manchester men retaliated by even more vicious attacks on London members coming to work in their areas, treating them, in fact, as badly as if they were blacklegs. Coulson's reply to this was much more effective and to the point. He proceeded to fling a ring of London Order lodges right round Manchester and through to the North as far up as Edinburgh and Motherwell in Scotland.

By June 1868 the membership and financial reports of the two unions showed that the Manchester Order was rapidly losing the struggle for supremacy. With 4,822 members in 93 lodges, Housely reported that total financial balances of the Union came to just over £2,934.

The London Order had less members—3,409—but they were organised in 96 lodges, and their monetary assets were much higher at £4,384. The antagonism between the two unions now reached the stage of unrestrained conflict, and this led to a sordid climax during the outbreak of a fierce battle between the building unions and the Northern employers—who made an attempt to enforce payment by the hour and compulsory arbitration.

The hourly wage proposal almost automatically stimulated hostility from the men and it was inevitable that there would be a battle when the General Builders' Association (a rapidly growing organisation of the masters, though still confined mainly to the Midlands and the North) also threw down the gauntlet on compulsory arbitration. On this particular issue, though, there was a serious division within the trade union movement itself. Some of the more 'sophisticated' leaders regarded strikes as crude, costly and antiquated means of settling disputes with employers. Even though they appreciated that men appointed as arbitrators in disputes would inevitably be those possessed of 'high rank and position'—and therefore most likely to favour the employer—they still felt that any loss through this would be more than compensated by not having to expend large sums on strikes.

But some of the trades, especially the masons, had contemptuously rejected the necessity for 'outsiders' to adjudicate on disputes between them and the masters. Now they were all faced with a declaration from the General Builders' Association that, in 29 different towns, a change was to be made to hourly wage payments and should any dispute arise in future "no strike or lock-out shall take place." Instead the masters and the men were to amicably discuss the problem. Failing an agreement between themselves it should be referred to "a disinterested party, whose decision shall be final and binding upon all parties."*

When they received official notice from the masters stating that these changes were to be made in the working rules the men went over to the offensive. On the 10th April, 1869, a large number walked out of the yards and declared there would be no return until the notices from the Association were withdrawn. Among the strikers were members of the Manchester Order of Bricklayers. The Union, however, was in a far from sound state financially and was really in no position to continue a long fight. And it was at this moment that Edwin Coulson and his Executive Council, in their blind antagonism to the Manchester Order, allowed themselves to become party to one of the lowest episodes in trade union history.

* O.S.M. Returns, 4th March, 1869.

One of the members of the London Union—and well known for his activities—was a man called Henry Markely. Markely had a shifty, vindictive nature which found an outlet in his being a leading protagonist in the fight between the two bricklayers' unions. For some time he had urged that the battle should be carried right into the enemy's camp by allowing him to open a London Order lodge in Manchester itself.

In the extensive Manchester dispute over hourly wages and arbitration he now saw a way of satisfying his hatred of the other union at some monetary advantage to himself. He again wrote to Coulson and asked for permission to open a lodge in Manchester. Coulson and his Executive Council must have known that this was virtually a stab in the back of the Manchester Order members out on the streets yet they gave permission for Markely to proceed. And even though the employers had now sharpened the struggle by locking out all the men who would not yield to them, Markely went ahead with the opening of a London Order lodge and established himself as secretary.

But this was only the first part of his plans. He now contacted the employers and was secretly appointed by them as a sort of double agent in obtaining alternative labour supplies. In this role he advertised throughout the metropolitan area that there was plenty of work available in Manchester for members of the London Order. There was a subsequent in-rush of some of the worst elements in the Union—Coulson even assisting in sending one batch North—who quite happily took up the work of the locked-out members of the Manchester organisation. They were nothing more than blacklegs. They were less perhaps in that they worked under the cloak of respectability given them by their membership cards of the London Order.

Now fighting desperately on two fronts, George Housely sent an urgent appeal to the London Trades Council requesting that they arbitrate on this latest, and most serious, clash between the two unions. A meeting was therefore arranged between representatives of the two

Orders and the Trades Council which took place in Sheffield on the 9th and 10th July.

From this joint conference the Manchester Order obtained its major objective of getting the London bricklayers to agree that its members should be withdrawn from all of the black sites. But this point was gained at a price which was both humiliating and indicative of the growing inferiority of Housely's Union. For Coulson forced home his claim that he should be allowed to start lodges anywhere in the country. And, even more astonishing, he joined with the London Trades Council representatives in pressing an agreement on the Manchester men which virtually made them concede the fight against arbitration. It read:

"That in the interests of both employers and workmen, this meeting recommend that the dispute existing in the Bricklaying trade of Manchester should be settled by the following mode:—That a Board of Conciliation be appointed of an equal number of employers and men, and that a chairman be elected who shall be acceptable to both parties; and that the decision of the Board shall be binding upon both employers and men."*

Not only was this decision to capitulate forced on the Manchester Order but Edwin Coulson and George Odger, secretary of the London Trades Council, arranged to visit Manchester to meet the employers and make sure that arbitration was put into effect. Once again, however, they found themselves blocked by Henry Markely, who refused to withdraw his blacklegs or accept the decision of the tripartite meeting. "There is no good feelings between the two societies" he insisted, "and I mean war to the knife." He also admitted his secret agreement to act as an agent for the employers and stated that he meant to carry it out.

At this Coulson and Odger became surprisingly faint-hearted about their mission. "We then felt it our duty to proceed no further in the matter and we regret to have

* London O.B.S. Trade Circular, 1st August, 1869.

been brought into contact with a man so utterly void of respect for the class to which he belongs," they reported.*

There were some members of the London Bricklayers however who had been disgusted by Coulson's conduct of the Markely affair. Led by George Howell, a number of the London lodges forced a general meeting to debate the disgraceful episode which had taken place in their name. To the delegates Coulson first tried to minimise his own guilt then, seeing the grim reception being given to his statement, threw himself on their mercy. "Let those who are without faults cast the first stone," he pleaded. "And surely my past conduct is worthy of some consideration and respect."

His plea was in vain. The delegates went on to pass a motion: "That this meeting thoroughly condemns the conduct of the General Secretary, E. Coulson." His humiliation was complete when Howell also successfully moved that a copy of the condemnatory resolution be sent to the Manchester Bricklayers' Executive.

This was of little consolation, however, to the Manchester Order. Housely and his executive had been completely demoralised by the hard bargaining at the meeting with the London Bricklayers and the Trades Council. The failure to achieve arbitration proved the last straw for their men, almost beaten to their knees, and the Union was forced to accept unconditional surrender. In their monthly report ending 30th September, 1869, they announced their complete collapse in the terse message that: "The lockout at Manchester is now terminated, the men having resumed work on the employers' terms."†

With the defeat of the bricklayers, only one trade was now left to contest the field with the employers—the Stonemasons. The struggle had, in fact, resolved itself into the familiar pattern of recent disputes on payment by the hour. With the more amenable employers and the weaker unions withdrawn from the battle, the most

* London O.B.S. Trade Circular, 1st September, 1869.

† London O.B.S. Trade Circular, 1st December, 1869.

reactionary masters and the stonemasons fought it out to the end. There was, however, one outstanding difference this time—the masons were not just displaying a stubborn determination to commit industrial suicide rather than surrender.

Already they had made such an impact on the supposed united front of the Masters' Association that, in 27 of the 29 towns under dispute, they had forced the masters to accept defeat.* Only in Liverpool and Manchester, the Association's strongholds, were a number of employers holding out. Far from pursuing a hopeless objective, therefore, the masons were conducting more of a mopping-up operation in an attempt to achieve total victory. It was because they felt confident of inflicting this complete defeat that they continued to fight, even without the other trades.

But the winter of 1869 came and only a slight advance had been made by the Union. As the months wore on into the spring it was obvious that the struggle had been fought at great cost to both sides. The O.S.M.'s reserves of nearly £12½ thousand were almost gone. In Manchester three employers had been declared bankrupt. Yet there was still a small hard core of men and masters who remained deadlocked in both cities.

And it was nearly April before the first signs of a weakening resolve came—in the ranks of the Liverpool masons. They now felt no hope of beating the few remaining employers who were holding out. In any case they had only about 34 men still on the strike roll. On the 18th April, 1870, the Liverpool committee therefore gave up the struggle and advised these men to seek employment on the best conditions they could get.

In Manchester the men must also have realised the inevitability of their withdrawal from the dispute. Yet another month passed before they could bring themselves to face this fact. It was the 21st May before they gave

* O.S.M. Returns, 14th October, 1869.

their remaining 66 strikers the order to cease hostilities. By this time they had been out for over 13 months in one of the longest and most severe battles in the history of the O.S.M. It was also the last in which they would have the guidance and determination of Richard Harnott behind them.

For too many years he had been carrying the burden of one of Britain's largest and most extensive unions entirely on his own shoulders. When he was first elected in 1847 the O.S.M. had about 6,000 members and was only beginning to stabilise its various benefits. By early 1867 the membership and work had trebled and Harnott was so hard pressed that even he—who hated admitting defeat and had enough of the autocrat in him to like working independently—had to appeal to the Union for an assistant.

The promptness with which the members responded to this appeal, without the usual parsimonious quibbling, showed a general and sincere awareness that too much was being demanded of Harnott, physically and mentally. In July 1867 William Graham had been elected as the first assistant secretary to him. But by then it was too late. Harnott had been overworking for many years and his poor health already showed the inevitable consequences.

The long drawn-out strikes over payment by the hour had also given him great anxiety because of their possible repercussions on the stability of the O.S.M., with whose fortunes he had completely identified himself. Then he suffered a personal tragedy which led almost directly to his own end. His son fell seriously ill. Though Harnott spent every penny he had to try and save him, he died of consumption.

Harnott's spirit was now broken as well as his health. Still he determinedly continued to work. On Tuesday, 6th February, 1872, he went to the office as usual, but looked so ill that James Dyer, now his assistant secretary, tried to persuade him to go home. Harnott refused, and the grim old man sat doggedly at his desk until six in the evening. After he left, the alarmed Dyer went straight to Harnott's son-in-law and pleaded with him that they should both go to the surgeon and find out just how bad Harnott was. They went at 11 o'clock the same evening.

" He is very ill indeed " they were told. " He ought not to go to business any more; he is completely done for; he is suffering from disease of the brain and disease of the kidneys; he has dropsy set in and he has had a paralytic stroke, and God only knows how soon he may have another."*

The warning was too late. Just after five the next morning his wife woke to find him dead, his left side contracted by another paralytic stroke. Aged 65 Harnott had led the masons for 25 of those years. In that time he had built a reputation which was widely known in Britain and throughout the world wherever British masons had emigrated and carried their trade union traditions and memories with them. To his own Union members he had been their admired and revered 'commander on the battlefield of labour.' And when they buried him it was as he had been in life—a General commanding one of the most militant and exclusive regiments in Labour's army.

Through the streets to the Salford Cemetery a slow marching brass band led the way playing the Dead March in Saul. Harnott's coffin was borne in a hearse drawn by four black horses. Immediately behind walked a mason carrying a black velvet cushion on which rested a mason's mallet and chisel.

And behind the mourning coaches walked over half-a-thousand masons; marching with their leader for the last time.

---

* O.S.M. Returns, 25th April, 1872.

CHAPTER 15

CONFIDENCE—BEFORE THE FALL

TEN of the most dramatic years in the history of the trade union movement are those between 1870 and 1880. It is a decade which opened with the unions achieving great advances in working conditions and a considerable strengthening of their organisations. It closed with a disastrous depression in which they had to struggle desperately for their very survival.

Their first successes were achieved in Parliament—a place which had more frequently been used to suppress rather than support them. Among a number of acts won during the first few years after 1870, the Trade Union Act of 1871 was one of the most important. To a great extent it removed the taint of 'illegality' from the unions: they were now able to take greater measures to protect their property and funds against fraud by members or branches.

The passing of this Act, with its other beneficial clauses, was a major victory for the movement and excitedly celebrated as such. With their new-found respectability the unions experienced an inflow of members from workers who had previously held aloof. The O.S.M. auditors exuberantly reported "a considerable increase in the number of members, both to the Trade and Trade and Sick Fund; also several additions have been made to the number of lodges." In fact 1872 saw an increase of nearly 3,000 members* and 24 lodges, which made their

* The masons actually recruited 5,000 during the year but, like the bricklayers and other unions, they suffered from lapsing membership ust like the unions of today.

highest total so far of 301 lodges. Even the link with Ireland was re-established and lodges opened in Waterford and Sligo.

Both unions of bricklayers also had a considerable increase in membership, though on a more modest scale than the larger and more extensive masons' organisation. Coulson reported an increase of 576 members and a reserve fund of £4,936 which was " the largest sum in the history of the society."

Between January and December 1872 the Manchester Order membership rose from 4,320 to 5,835. The central reserve fund of only £884, however, indicated one major difference between the London and Manchester unions. Even when Manchester was numerically superior to the London Order its more loosely knit and archaic structure was revealed by its financial inferiority.

The increased strength in organisation was accompanied by valuable advances in wages and conditions, partly due to the very buoyant economic climate. In fact, the unions achieved such success during the first few years of the decade that the members and their leaders were confident that the golden era of trade unionism had begun.

The most significant of these early gains was a general improvement in wages and hours. And the renewed agitation by building operatives for the nine-hour day was also a reflection of the new militancy sweeping through the workers all over the country. Even in Canada and America a new spirit was abroad and reports were coming to Britain that the men there were also " agitating, and going in for the nine hours."*

In London, long the central arena of conflict on shorter hours, the masons again made the first move in January 1872 when they served " six months' notice that on the 1st of July we should require a reduction in the hours of labour from 56½ to 51 hours per week, and an increase of wages of one penny per hour."† This demand was

* London Order Trade Circular, May 1872.

† O.S.M. Returns, 20th June, 1872.

subsequently summarised as a battle cry by all the unions as a demand for " nine hours and ninepence per hour."

The reaction of the employers was curiously mixed. Of course they were hostile to the claim, but there was also a bitter resignation prevalent among many of them. For they were acutely aware that economic conditions were to the men's advantage. Throughout the country they could also see other employers capitulating to similar demands. Gone too were any illusions that they had successfully forestalled the shorter working day claim when they won the battle to establish hourly wages. What the employers had regarded as a major obstacle, in fact, had been surmounted by the men through the simple expedient of asking for a higher hourly rate to compensate for the shorter day.

They were further shaken on the 1st March when the carpenters and joiners also put in a claim for ' nine and nine,' with the 1st July as the deadline—the same as the masons. And though the carpenters and joiners were later in presenting their ' memorial ' they were more militant in their desire to back it with strike action. They therefore convened a huge meeting in St. James' Hall, at which the enthusiasm was so great that they precipitated the expiry date of their own notice by deciding to strike two selected firms on the 1st June. Interpreting the strikes against these two firms as an indication of what was to come for themselves, a number of the London masters united and retaliated with a lock-out on the 19th June.

But they were without the support of the great body of employers who had little taste for a long clash on the issue—especially when economic conditions favoured the men. Out of about 1,000 employers in London, in fact, 250 had threatened the lock-out but only 60 had actually shut the gates of their yards on the 19th June.* The rest of the masters simply waited and watched, hoping that some definite result would be reached before general expiry of the masons' and carpenters' demands on the 1st July.

* O.S.M. Returns, 20th June, 1872.

The partial lock-out had forced other unions into the struggle alongside the carpenters and they took it up eagerly —especially the London Order of Bricklayers—feeling that it was a wonderfully opportune moment for a decisive and favourable result. But it was just at this moment, when the trades were uniting for action, that there was a breakaway settlement by the masons. This was all the more surprising because the O.S.M. had abruptly rejected a previous proposal by the employers to invite the Earl of Derby and the Marquis of Salisbury to act as arbiters on the matter.

Instead the masons had called a mass meeting of the London members a fortnight after the beginning of the lock-out. A resolution was passed there agreeing that a deputation should meet the employers " and if possible make such arrangements that would terminate the dispute." At a subsequent six-hour meeting with the employers the deputation got: " what we consider a very fair compromise—the 51-hour week being virtually secured. The 52½-hour week worked during 40 weeks of the year is compensated for by 47 hours per week worked in the 12 winter weeks. Our real compromise was made in the wages, we having accepted 8½d. in lieu of the 9d. per hour as required by the memorial. We fought hard for the 9d. but only succeeded in obtaining a partial promise for the other halfpenny next spring, should the state of trade warrant it."*

The other trades were angered at this settlement by the masons particularly because the chances looked good for a speedy victory against the 60 employers enforcing the lock-out. In a report to the bricklayers Coulson commented that: " The Masons' Society, after making a pretended show of their desire to co-operate with the other trades, afterwards covertly met the Masters' Committee, and entered into an agreement."

Henry Broadhurst, then chairman of the London masons, retorted that no obligation had rested on them

* O.S.M. Returns, 4th July, 1872.

to act in concert with anyone. He claimed the carpenters had taken strike action without consulting them and added that, anyway, "the other trades had shown little real anxiety in the matter until they were locked out." Irrespective of Broadhurst's argument the rest of the trades resented the masons abandoning the dispute in which they were still engaged. They felt that it was a reversal of all the traditions of men who had previously proved themselves tenacious to the end.

A major reason for the non-militance of the O.S.M. on this occasion was undoubtedly the leadership of Henry Broadhurst. A uniquely talented man, he was to become general secretary of the Trades Union Congress, a Member of Parliament and the first working man to hold government office. Early in his career he displayed a more subtle and politically expedient approach to industrial problems which the masons had usually settled by trials of strength. After the death of Harnott the Grand Lodge had moved to London with James Dyer the newly elected secretary. Competent but colourless is a brief but reasonably accurate description of Dyer's character, and it was a combination of these incidents which led to Broadhurst achieving the considerable influence he had over the affairs of the Union.

Having settled the agreement with Broadhurst and the other O.S.M. delegates the employers now announced that: "They would carry out the terms they had made with the masons upon all branches of the building trades." The bricklayers especially were furious over this arbitrary attitude by the employers and showed it by immediately striking three building firms. Generally, however, neither of the two sides wanted a prolonged dispute. The employers had no desire for a trial of strength and most of the unions were ready to make a speedy compromise if it gained them a considerable advance without having to foot costly strike bills. By the beginning of August, therefore, the other trades had separately made agreements with the employers and the bricklayers found themselves alone. Coulson finally reported to his members that "as the other branches of the building trade had made terms with the employers, the Council considered it a wasteful expense to carry on the contest."*

On Friday, 30th August, their representatives met the Central Association of Master Builders and agreed to accept 8½d. per hour with a system of hours that differed from the masons' earlier settlement in only one respect, the bricklayers were to work 48 hours per week during the 12 winter weeks as against 47 for the masons. In effect the masons had secured a better deal than the bricklayers, or the other trades, in that they worked 12 hours per year less.

Even though the unions had failed to obtain the complete nine-and-nine demand, they had still secured a major advance when contrasted with previous extended struggles in which they had achieved almost nothing except near extinction of their organisations. And this advance had been won with only a proportion of the trades in dispute for a relatively few weeks.

Obviously the ease with which they successfully contested the employers on this occasion was a sign of their growing strength allied to good economic conditions. Now that they were able to demonstrate the advantages they were able to secure for their members a new flood of recruits came in and membership began to climb rapidly. By 1877 both bricklayers' societies and the masons had touched a level of membership and finance higher than at any previous time in their history. George Housely, of the Manchester Bricklayers, was able to report that they numbered 7,775 members by the end of 1877, and had a reserve fund of £5,549.

The progress of the London Order was even more spectacular. In the annual report for 1877 Coulson wrote: "It is with much pleasure I inform you that our Society has more members and money than it ever had in any previous year." He had good reason to be pleased. At December 1877 membership had climbed to 6,749 and

* London Order Trade Circular, September 1872.

"The worth of the Society is now £16,717 7s. 8d. or £2 9s. 6d. per member."

In wealth the London Order even rivalled the Operative Stonemasons, who were still spending a great deal on strikes. But in membership no building union was the equal of the O.S.M. At the end of 1877 they had reached a peak of 27,110 members. Only two other unions in Britain could claim to be stronger—the Engineers and the Durham Miners.

It was at the crest of this great wave of advance; when confidence was high, that there came a sudden and catastrophic fall. Within twelve months the situation had changed drastically for the masons and nearly every other union in the country. Between 1877 and 1878 a severe economic depression began which swept through industry like a hurricane. When it had finally passed many broken union structures lay among the debris.

In the building industry almost every organisation found itself plunged from the heights of influence to fighting rearguard action against cuts in wages and extension of hours. Employers who had sanctimoniously preached the virtues of moderation to the unions when power lay with them, now ruthlessly cut back the conditions of their men.

No building union suffered a heavier blow than the masons. It was all the greater because, in their unbounded confidence, they had attempted too much and were completely helpless to save themselves when the crisis came. Still moving forward at the beginning of 1877, the London masons had decided to challenge their employers for a shortening of the summer working weeks from 52½ to 50 hours. In addition they wanted an increase in pay of one penny per hour. In line with past practice they gave the employers six months' notice of their claim, and this was to terminate on Saturday, 28th July, 1877.

This time, however, the employers were not so amenable to the claim. When the notice terminated 65 firms gave the increase and the men went into work on the Monday at these yards. But 1,700 masons were out on strike against the rest of the employers who intended not to give an inch. Even so the men had no great fears about the outcome. " We think it will only be a short dispute, as trade is very good, and we believe the members of the Master Builders' Association are only waiting for one or two of their firms to give way, and then the dispute will soon be settled."*

For a time this prophecy of an easy victory seemed accurate. More builders conceded the claim. Then the first signs of a recession were felt and the employers immediately stiffened their resistance. The coming of winter was an added disadvantage for the men and made the possibility of a quick victory now very remote.

By the end of January 1878 the struggle had lasted six months and the central funds of the masons had almost been completely drained of the £16,000 held in reserve. Under no illusions about the possible outcome of such a widespread strike in the rapidly developing depression the Central Committee appealed to the membership to bring it to an end. They emphasised that if it were not halted the Union would soon be bankrupt. The members, however, seemed to have regained their old fighting spirit and were still not prepared to heed the warnings of possible economic disaster. By 2,761 to 1,925 votes they defeated the Central Committee proposals for calling off the strike.

And it was not until the 18th March, when the slump was driving hundreds of foreign masons to London as blacklegs, that the O.S.M. finally admitted defeat. By then the Union was completely penniless. Dyer, its secretary, was reduced to pleading for personal loans—even a few pounds was accepted gratefully—to keep the O.S.M. from sinking. But the full impact of the depression was yet to come. When it had reached its height and brought trade almost to a halt, the O.S.M. was completely unable to protect its members from the attacks of the employers.

The extensive Union benefits that had been built up during the boom years, and had proved so attractive in

---

* O.S.M. Returns, 26th July, 1877.

recruiting new members, now proved a millstone dragging the O.S.M. further into the abyss. Dyer was distraught and impotent. If only we had the money spent on the abortive London strike, he wrote helplessly, " we should not be necessitated to insert miserable comments and begging appeals and yet be without the means of paying our sick and burying our dead."*

By November 1880 membership had slumped by nearly half to 14,299 and the O.S.M. was £2,358 in debt. It was only then the members seemed to realise that the Central Committee's warning had been only too true, and they stirred themselves sufficiently to appoint a rules revision committee in the hope of putting the Union on a more sound foundation. But the time for saving the great power and influence of the O.S.M. was completely gone. Only slowly did it eventually reach financial stability and a moderate membership. Never again did it touch its peak of 27,000. In the future lay only a junior role for the men who had once been the proud spearhead of the building unions, and who for centuries before then had been the supreme aristocrats of British artisans.

The Manchester Order of Bricklayers also suffered severely. Their numerical strength fell to 3,200 and their funds were frittered away in a succession of futile strikes. George Housely was completely unable to halt the decline. His pathetic inability of self-expression left him an almost mutely despairing witness of the Union's misfortunes at a time when a clear and impassioned lead would have at least contained the losses. So poverty stricken was the Manchester Order that Ashton-under-Lyne lodge suggested quarterly instead of monthly audits " by which we may hope to save £25 per year."

One organisation which again did not suffer the general fate was the London Order of Bricklayers. Their stability during this crisis was almost incredible. At a time when (as the Webbs wrote) " the depression of 1879 swept many hundreds of trade societies into oblivion," the London Order only dropped by 600 members to 5,700.

* O.S.M. Returns, 9th January, 1879.

And its total financial assets actually increased to an all time high of £23,537! Far from being despondent about the future their expansionist attitude was shown by a decision to go ahead and build their own headquarters at Southwark Bridge Road.

There were two major reasons for the remarkable stability of the London Bricklayers. Firstly, and most important, was that their head office remained fixed in London instead of being shunted all round the country like the masons. This gave them the opportunity of building a really efficient administrative structure. The members of the Executive also remained fairly static and gained greater experience.

The second reason was that, in Coulson, they had a far more outstanding and dynamic chief official than either Dyer of the masons or Housely of the Manchester bricklayers. He and his Executive commanded far more respect from their members and consequently exercised much greater control over them during the economic disaster.

Coulson's character had also been undergoing transformation. The crude aggressiveness of his earlier years had gradually given way to a more reasoned and persuasive attitude. Though there was still a great deal of rivalry between the two orders of bricklayers, the fault now lay mainly with the Manchester men as far as the continual petty bickering was concerned. Coulson and his Executive could see very much further than these trivial internecine quarrels. Their policies were, in fact, as advanced as any union within the building industry.

At the height of the general crisis they were already clear-sighted enough to realise that only through greater unity could building workers protect and advance their conditions. When the National Association of Master Builders of Great Britain threatened that they were going to reduce wages "through the depression of trade," Coulson and his Executive decided to invite all the other unions to a joint meeting "with the view of arranging a plan for a mutual federation to enable any Trade Union to effectively resist the aggressive action of the employers."*

This invitation met with some success, and the meeting took place at the offices of the London Order on 27th February, 1879. 31 delegates were present representing the two orders of bricklayers, masons, the national and metropolitan unions of plasterers, carpenters and joiners, and the painters. Enthusiasm for the proposal was high and a committee of eleven, with Coulson as chairman, was appointed to arrive at the best method of implementing a unanimous resolution that:

" This meeting believes that, in view of the aggressiveness shown by the National Federation of Employers, it is desirable to form a National Federation of Building Operatives; and this meeting further pledges itself to use every means in its power to attain this desirable object."†

On the 20th July, 1880, a further meeting was held and the delegates agreed on a proposed draft of rules which they were to put to a ballot of their members for acceptance or rejection. Already however, enthusiasm for the project was dying and this meeting had not been so well attended. In his Annual Report, produced later in the year, Coulson commented that " definite replies have not been given by any society, except the Bricklayers, and their votes were—for, 1,377, against, 729. The severe depression of trade, no doubt, has kept this subject in abeyance."

Most of the unions were, in fact, now fighting for their existence. This almost exclusively preoccupied their attention and the immediate prospects of federation gradually died. It was simply another, and not particularly lamented, victim of the depression. The same depression which had nearly annihilated the masons while leading to the almost overnight emergence of the London Bricklayers as the powerful new leaders of the trowel trade unions.

---

* London Order Trade Circular, February 1879.

† London Order Trade Circular, March 1879. This is the first formal beginning to the developments which ultimately lead to the N.F.B.T.O. in 1918.

CHAPTER 16

THE NEW SPIRIT

THE depression was a hard and costly lesson for the operatives. They now knew that a loose collection of lodges held together by a slender central thread was not sufficient to withstand a serious challenge. A great deal of their cherished autonomy would have to be sacrificed by lodges if they wanted a really united and powerful union.

The masons, who had received the greatest blow of all, started their recovery when the Central Committee at Sheffield urged that a general revision of rules should take place. " A Revising Committee, with the experience of the last two years," they confidently declared, " will compile us a Rule Book such as our Society, nor any other, ever possessed."

A rules revision committee of nine members was subsequently elected by the whole of the membership and immediately amended the sick and superannuation schemes so that finances were again established on a firmer basis. But the most far-sighted alterations in rules were those related to the administration of the Union. A General Council was to be elected and " That Council to elect nine of their body as an Executive Committee, to be the governing body for twelve months. We think this will be a great improvement, and by giving them more powers it will prevent us from running into many dangers which hitherto have injured us."*

* O.S.M. Returns, 7th July, 1881.

This new executive was given much greater control over disputes than the lodges would ever have tolerated in the past. And, in addition to this, the members even conceded their annual right to move the Central Committee about the country like a pawn on a chess board. The Executive Office was to " remain in one town so long as it retains the confidence of the Society."

1883 was the year in which the new 'fixed office' was to be established and nominations were invited from lodges wishing to compete for this honour. In February of that year the result was announced: London was an overwhelming first with 866 votes and Sheffield, which was then the central lodge, came second with 194. James Dyer, however, was not to make the return journey to London. Dyer, who had been secretary of the O.S.M. for 11 years, had recently not been in very good health. In April he caught a bad cold and went to bed for a few days. After an apparent recovery he had a complete relapse and, on Wednesday, 21st April, Dyer died of broncho-pneumonia. He was only 48 years of age.

The revival of the Union's fortunes and the transfer to London were to be the responsibility of William Hancock who was elected general secretary in Dyer's place. And it was he who opened the new central office at 4 Stamford Street, Blackfriars.

While the O.S.M. began its struggle to regain strength the London Bricklayers meantime had shrugged off their very slight setback in membership. Membership increased: not spectacularly, but the end of each year showed a slightly mounting figure. And a big boost for the London Order came with the opening of their new offices at 48 Southwark Bridge Road on Saturday, 26th May, 1883. Rejecting private contractors, the offices had been built by the direct labour of O.B.S. members at a cost of £6,415, which included £2,204 for the land.

Speaking from the platform in their new and gaily decorated main hall, Coulson proudly enumerated the main features of the building. " With an imposing red brick frontage, the structure contains a fine hall for meetings, having a superficial area of 1,800 square feet, capable of accommodating over 400 persons, and tastefully fitted up, the ceiling being of polished pitch pine. In the basement is an apartment in which 400 persons could meet; and on the first floor are commodious committee rooms, the General Secretary's and clerks' office, and all the conveniences necessary to the transaction of the business of a great trades union."

Coulson's boast of his "great trades union" was well justified. Together with its new premises and capital of £27,593 the London O.B.S. had 128 branches, with 6,000 members in them. Breakaway unions have had generally little success in the building industry or any other and the London Order, which ultimately came to dominate the trowel trades, must be unique as one of the most successful breakaways in trade union history. By comparison the parent body, now the Manchester Order, was in a pitiful plight.

If anything had been learned from the aftermath of the economic crisis the lessons were not put into effect. Housely and his Executive remained helpless—and almost impassive—as their Union gradually crumbled beneath them.

Only a few lodges indicated interest in the decline of the organisation and the most vociferous of these was the Belfast lodge. But even its anxiety was not matched by far-reaching proposals to help the Union. The lodge's single recommendation was that the drain on the funds should be halted by cutting out tramp relief for a year "as something *must* be done to keep our society in existence." Nowhere in the Union's reports was there any indication that the lodges had any conception of radical changes to save their organisation. Not a suggestion was made for the establishing of a sounder structure on the lines of the London O.B.S. or the reorganised masons.

The absolute depth of shortsighted bungling was reached when the Executive took £500 out of the anæmic but vital trade fund in order to prop-up the completely depleted accident and burial fund. This did stimulate a proposal from the Nottingham lodge for a vote of censure to be passed on the Executive for their criminal juggling with the funds. On this occasion Housely showed one of his rare flashes of anger with the savage retort that: " It will take a stronger authority than the Nottingham Lodge to induce the Council to take a vote or spend the society's money in voting papers, on such trash as is written in this letter."*

Housely's main contribution to the dilemma facing the Union was to voluntarily cut his own salary, by 5s. per week in 1880, £1 per week in 1881 and 10s. per week in 1885.† But this was no more than a token of his personal despair and of no great practical assistance to the fortunes of the Union. Membership continued to fall and touched rock bottom with a really severe blow in October of 1886.

" Some Lodges have seceded from our society, because of our difficulties and the suspension for a time of our benefits " reported Housely. " The names of these lodges are Warrington, Hull, Loughborough, Rugby, Middlewich, Redcar, Ballymena, Dundee and Spenny Moor." When the remaining membership came to be counted it totalled only 1,284.

There was one inevitable outcome to all this. The frustration of the members began to centre increasingly on their chief officer and the Executive Committee. It came to a head in 1889 with a letter from the Leicester lodge complaining about the decimated state of the Union. Housely's salary should be cut, claimed Leicester, and the expense allowances for Executive Committee members likewise. " If something is not done we shall soon cease to exist as a society " the lodge concluded, and demanded that there should be a vote on their proposal.

Housely inserted the letter in the Report complete with all its original spelling mistakes in order to belittle the lodge. He even added a footnote that: " The Council have had, from time to time, some strange compositions

---

* Manchester Unity Report, 26th February, 1885.

† Manchester Unity Report, 27th May, 1886.

to deal with; but for ignorance and impudence, this epistle goes far beyond anything they ever had to deal with."*

The other lodges did not think the Leicester propositions so 'strange' and they let Housely and the Executive know it. There was finally only one way in which the position could be resolved. In 1890 the members voted to move the head office to a new town and this had the desired effect of forcing Housely's resignation. Only one lodge, Rotherham, wrote urging that it be not accepted. And this was more than offset by a curt insertion from Nottingham that they had held a special meeting to consider Housely's resignation and "It was unanimously resolved that we, as a Lodge, accept it."

The rebuff to Housely, after 24 years as General Secretary, was given bitter point when the members elected the Nottingham lodge secretary, George H. Clarke, in his place. In the subsequent vote for a new central lodge Stockport beat Birmingham into second place.

George Clarke, who had gained experience as an able and active member of the Nottingham United Building Trades, now had the unenviable task of moving the head office of a beaten organisation to Stockport and trying to recover strength with the doubtful aid of a fresh and completely inexperienced Executive Council. At the end of 1890 his Union's total membership was still only 1,683, and there was a balance at the bank of £577.

The continued decline of the Manchester Order was even more noticeable because the other building unions were now beginning to recover membership due to the slight improvement in trade. The masons, for instance, had increased to 12,538 by 1890 and were continuing an upward trend. All debts had been paid off and there was a central reserve of £4,311. The number of lodges was, at 304, almost as great as at their peak.† Hancock the General Secretary confidently wrote that, with the gradual

* Manchester Unity Report, 26th December, 1889.

† O.S.M. Returns, 5th February, 1891.

thaw in trade, the Union would completely recover its old power as the supreme building organisation.

But this title was now beyond the grasp of the O.S.M. The progress of the London Order of Bricklayers was spectacular contrasted with the other two societies. By 1890 it even had a slight superiority to the masons in membership—12,740. Its financial reserves were incontestably supreme. Liquid assets of the central funds and lodges came to £33,235. Adding the capital value of head office brought total assets to nearly £41,000.

Nor had this saving been achieved by a ruthless stamping out of all trade disputes. Steady progress had been maintained during the past few years and, knowing the upturn in trade would present lodges with greater opportunities for action the O.B.S. auditors asked for an extra levy to boost the trade fund " deeming it desirable that ample funds should be ready for any emergency."

In the same Annual Report Edwin Coulson indicated that: " At the end of June next I shall be ready to place my work in other hands, as I find the constant strain and anxiety of office is more than my health will allow me to do." Though he was then only 63 years of age he had been General Secretary of the London Order for nearly 31 of them. The whole of his prime years of existence, in fact, had been given to a determined and exhausting building up of his Union. Few men had, like him, fashioned a handful of impoverished lodges with a few hundred members into a powerful national organisation.

Yet it was his very success which brought him grief. Coulson was a fighter and agitator; characteristics which were invaluable when the London Order was struggling to establish itself, but he was no great administrator. The larger and more complex the Union grew the more obvious became his inadequacies. Nor did he lack enemies to point out his deficiencies.

It was, therefore, in a very frigid atmosphere that he moved towards retirement. Then he had a personal blow which even took away the anticipated pleasure of a few years of peace. In May 1891, just one month before he retired, his wife died suddenly. She had suffered from asthma for some time and, wrote a saddened Coulson: " The anxiety and worry of moving to a new home, with the hope of having a few more years together in peace and happiness may have hastened her death."

There was no respite for Coulson. The newly elected secretary, John Batchelor, took over and the Executive Council carried on as if he had never existed. No written tributes were paid him. A half-hearted attempt was made by a few of the Committee to organise a testimonial, but this raised only the miserable amount of £20 7s. 10d. The Committee subtracted 17s. 4d. for expenses and posted the remaining £19 10s. 6d., without ceremony, to Coulson.

The Executive Council noted all this but made no attempt to give any grant at all from central funds. In fact, Coulson's only ' reward ' from the Executive Council was a censorious resolution passed in August—which completely ignored his worries during the last few months of office—" That this Council strongly condemn Bro. E. Coulson for having allowed the business of the General Office to get in arrears thereby causing a quantity of extra work for the present Executive Council."

It was a bitter end to his career. Whatever his faults he had given a great personal contribution to the success of the London Order that no other individual could match. Now this was all forgotten in the petty spite of the moment. Coulson retired to Cambridge, but he was now a broken man and he only lived another two years. Of his death there was only a peremptory note in the London Order's Monthly Report. Nor did the Union make any effort to do him honour at his funeral.

With his death the last of the old triumvirate of the masons' and bricklayers' officials were gone. Harnott and Housely had been his contemporaries: men who had been brought up to regard unions as mainly fighting organisations and who might have been disconcerted by the growing emphasis on friendly benefits and the tighter and more complex administrations being adopted.

The London Order, for instance, now made a speciality of central control over lodges that would have created rebellion only a few years previously. The slightest whisper of mismanagement of branch funds and the secretary was ordered to attend the Executive Council, together with his branch books. Defaulters were pursued mercilessly and prosecuted in the courts. Even defaulters on the run had little chance of escaping for the London Order treated all its branches as if they were detective agencies. They were told to keep an eye out for these men and report them to the police.

To assist them in this task John Batchelor had a special column in the Monthly Report headed " HUE AND CRY " in which detailed and far from complimentary descriptions were given of defaulters. Joseph Murray, who disappeared with the York branch funds was described:

> " height about 5 ft., clean shaved, with straight nose, fair and inclined to be freckled, one eye peculiar to the other, bow legged, walks with a waddle-step, dressed old-fashioned with a square coat and generally both hands in his pockets, wears a large old-fashioned hat always too large for him, and always chewing tobacco."*

With this appearance poor Joseph didn't stand a chance of avoiding detection. In fact he must have had a golden tongue to have gained access to the members' money in the first place!

The new men in charge of the unions and their members also had new objectives. Organisationally they were now accepting the idea of closer association. Even if a national federation of building unions was still some years away, the 1890's saw a rapid growth of local building trades federations throughout the country.

Industrially too the sights were raised. There was widespread agitation throughout the trade unions for the

---

* London Order Monthly Report, September 1893.

eight-hour day. It was, in fact, in fighting for this particular objective that the building unions found themselves driven closer together in London. A move which led finally to collective bargaining between the federated unions and the employers began with a bold attempt by the carpenters and joiners in 1891 to win the eight-hour day with a compensatory wage of 10d. per hour.

In May their union brought three shops out on strike in support of these objectives. The Central Master Builders' Association responded with a lock-out of carpenters and joiners in 179 firms. In June the union broadened the conflict when it retaliated by striking another 60 firms*. This struggle was to drag on for over six months and was confined to the carpenters and joiners with the other trades levying themselves to help strike funds. With both sides finally almost exhausted it was agreed to accept arbitration. The arbiter gave an award which resulted in a reduction of hours to an average of 50 per week, but with no compensatory increase in wages.

The other building unions were far from pleased at this settlement and refused to accept it as applying to their own members. The London Bricklayers called it an "unjust award" and carried a regular notice in their Monthly Report stating that "the Arbitrators award in the late Carpenters' dispute does not apply to bricklayers." Branches were told to take immediate action against any employer who attempted to bring the bricklayers within its terms.

The carpenters' struggle, however, taught the trades that only by a united front could they exert any real influence. The employers too were rapidly becoming associated to the extent that they felt a general agreement was far better than sectional trade rules. The result was that two meetings were held, on the 10th and 23rd June, 1892, at which the various trades met the Employers' Association over their claim for a "common code of working rules" embodying shorter hours and a rise in pay.

---

* *Our Society's History*, page 137.

The employers did not want a fight in the middle of the summer with business beginning to boom. Nor did they want a repetition of the disastrous dispute with the carpenters. The unions, therefore, won a bloodless victory. A common code of rules was agreed to come into operation on the first Monday of November 1892. Wages for craftsmen were to be increased to 9½d. per hour and working hours were arranged so that they were altered on four occasions throughout the year.

For 38 weeks of summer the men worked 50 hours per week. During the first three weeks of winter (officially commencing on the first Monday in November) there was to be a 47-hour week. The middle eight weeks of winter was at 44½ hours, and then the men went back to 47 hours for the last three weeks of the winter period.* Over the year these hours averaged out at just under 49 per week. The normal day, however, was over eight hours as it was agreed that the men should finish at 12 noon on Saturday throughout the year.

One fact which may have influenced the employers to make concessions was the new spirit of unity among the operatives. For some time in London there had been a Building Trades Committee at which the trades had a rather loose contact with one another to discuss common problems. Desire for a much closer knit organisation, however, reached fruition when delegates from the various organisations met at the head office of the London Bricklayers and formed the London Building Trades Federation on the 31st May, 1892—only a few days before the showdown with the employers.†

Throughout the country the same thing was happening in all the major towns as the building unions began to establish joint town working rules. Obviously, to police these and thrash out their own proposals to put to the employers, they needed a common forum which the local federation provided.

---

* O.S.M. Returns, October 1892.

† London Order Monthly Reports, January/July 1892.

The new spirit, however, was not merely confined to the local level. When the Manchester Order of Bricklayers at last brought their rules up to date in 1893 the London Order immediately made overtures on amalgamation between the two societies " now they have arranged their new rules on somewhat similar lines to ours."* This and later offers, however, were antagonistically rejected by the Manchester Bricklayers who regarded them as invitations to be swallowed rather than a proposed unity of equals.

But the general atmosphere was one in which there was a gradual thawing of the rigid barriers between unions. Journals were becoming filled with letters and resolutions from branches pressing for federation or amalgamation. There were great obstacles to amalgamation, however. In the early rudimentary days the conservatism of lodges was the main stumbling block. Now that the unions had been established for some years there was an increasing number of full-time officials with strong vested interests. Various funds and benefits had also been established which would prove difficult to harmonise. Because of these reasons the only immediate general prospect was federation.

This situation not only applied to the building trades but to the entire union field. Failing amalgamation it was agreed that federation was the next best objective. The pressure became so strong that a scheme was ultimately prepared by the Trades Union Congress for a General Federation of Trade Unions in 1898. All the organisations affiliated to Congress were asked to vote on whether or not they would join such a federation. The prospects for success seemed reasonably good. The delegates to the Trades Union Congress at which the decision was taken had been enthusiastic. But when the detailed proposals went before the unions they were only endorsed by a few organisations. In the building industry general support had been much less than lukewarm.

In a national ballot by the O.S.M. the proposal to join the general federation was heavily defeated with only 17

* London Order Trade Circular, April 1893.

members voting in favour. The London Bricklayers also turned it down by 2,572 votes to 1,416. The Manchester Bricklayers refused to participate—" tailors, shoemakers, cotton spinners, etc., cannot learn us our business "—by 1,336 to 834 votes.

From these developments it was obvious that, while federation was a live discussion point within the building unions, they would only approach it on an industrial basis.

CHAPTER 17

GRIM START TO A NEW CENTURY

NOT only the operatives were being driven towards closer unity; the employers also had taken up the idea of federation. For them, however, it was proving much simpler to achieve. They had few of the sectional interests, and hardly any of the demarcation problems, which divided the men. And as the individual craft master rapidly gave way to the general builder their interests grew even more similar.

The employers were also apprehensive about the advance of the unions towards closer association, and felt that inevitably a challenge must come from this development. Among the bolder spirits there was even a feeling that the best way to crush the unions was by striking first. By 1899 the employers had soundly established a National Association of Master Builders of Great Britain and Ireland and they felt the time had arrived to make their challenge for complete control of the industry.

In March that year the employers within the Association began hostilities by locking out their plasterers on the grounds that their Union was indulging in restrictive practices. They then followed this move with the most impertinent and arrogant letter to the other trades that the masters have ever penned.

" This association ask the whole of the building trades operatives' unions for a definite assurance that they have no sympathy with, and will not support in any way, the National Association of Operative Plasterers in the present dispute, and if such assurance is not forthcoming from all of them by the 6th May next, the question and terms of a general lock-out shall be settled at a meeting of this association."*

This letter was simply a request for betrayal of the plasterers by the other trades. The unions showed their contempt by openly sending money to aid the locked-out members of the National Association of Operative Plasterers. Those who deigned to reply to the employers sent curt notes refusing any assurance whatsoever.

The union leaders also held two conferences to frame a united policy with which to meet the employers' attack. The second of these was at Manchester in May. 16 delegates representing all of the major building unions attended.† (The delegate from the Gas Workers and General Labourers at the meeting was J. R. Clynes. He subsequently became an M.P., Cabinet Minister and Leader of the Parliamentary Labour Party). They learned that their refusal to desert the plasterers had infuriated the employers. There was now also a 25 per cent lock-out of all building workers in Yorkshire, where the masters were generally in favour of a much tougher line with the men.

Though the union officials at the conference were infuriated at this aggressive step by the employers they felt anger had to be tempered with prudence. For they recognised that with the masters now associated nationally, and themselves virtually so, any direct challenge might precipitate the first ever extensive national battle between themselves and the masters. And, apart from a general reluctance to face up to such a wide conflict, they were also engaged on internecine warfare over some of the new techniques coming into the industry.

The plasterers, in particular, were showing to the other unions a little of the aggressiveness about which the employers were complaining. They were at that moment locked in hostilities with the bricklayers over who should

* London Order Trade Circular, May 1899.

† Manchester Unity Quarterly Report, 24th June, 1899.

do cement floors. At Nottingham the quarrel erupted into such a public scandal that the Trades Union Congress had even intervened and tried to talk sense into the antagonists.

Deller, the Plasterers' General Secretary, accused the bricklayers of being graspers and said they were engaged in "an unholy attack on his members." This prompted the vicious reply from George Clarke of the Manchester Order that the bricklayers were merely defending themselves against plasterers "whose lust of conquest and greed of power has very nearly begun to stink in the nostrils of the men in the building trade."*

Little wonder that the unions sadly, but wisely, concluded that their energies were too scattered to take on the might of the employers just at that time. Instead they requested a joint meeting with the Employers' Association and promised to draft a scheme of national conciliation for discussion. This scheme, in effect, was to set up a national joint council which would "adjust by conciliatory means all questions relating to hours of labour, rates of wages and working rules generally."†

The constitution suggested was, on a great number of points, similar to that of the present National Joint Council for the Building Industry. It was finally agreed that these proposals be discussed at a meeting between national representatives of the major unions and employers on 27th July, 1899. At that meeting agreement was reached to proceed with the formation of a conciliation board almost entirely along the lines of the draft put forward by the unions. It looked, for a short time, as if both men and masters were poised for a really progressive and major advance in industrial relationships.

Then the employers astonished the operatives with a move deliberately designed to frustrate the decision they had so recently taken. "It is not expedient to proceed with the formation of a National Board of Conciliation

---

* Manchester Unity Quarterly Report, 30th December, 1899.

† London Order Trade Circular, July 1899.

at present," they wrote, " unless a monetary guarantee be given on both sides for the carrying out of the decision of the Conciliation Board."

The mere suggestion that a system of " fines " might be imposed on those breaking conciliation decisions was enough to condemn the whole project in the eyes of the union leaders. The employers, in fact, must have known that the men would react in the way they did. For they were well aware that one of the burning topics throughout the entire trade union movement was the outcome of a strike by workers on the Taff Vale Railway Company, where the employers had commenced a suit against the Amalgamated Society of Railway Servants for losses incurred during the dispute.

The power to withdraw labour was the ultimate and only real weapon the unions had. In practice it meant that, in struggling for advance, the men were prepared to suffer hardship in the hope that enough loss would be involved for the employer to make him more sympathetic to their claims. On the negative side the strike threat was offered to employers who tried to reduce wages or worsen conditions. If the laws were altered so that unions could be made to pay for losses caused through withdrawal of labour then they would, in effect, always be striking against their own interests.

The building unions in rejecting the employers' proposals for a guarantee fund were simply refusing to voluntarily place themselves at this disadvantage when defending their members. The conciliation board, therefore, was stillborn but the demarcation disputes between the various unions were not completely ill winds which blew no one any good. They at least drove the two bricklayers' unions to an appreciation that similar problems confronted them.

The London Order in particular felt that amalgamation of the Scottish, Irish and the two English societies was now necessary. The Manchester Order was also in an amalgamation mood but they were more restricted about its scope. They were prepared to take over the smaller Irish society but not to be swallowed by the London Order.

Over a period of some months a confusion of meetings and proposals took place, with the trend towards amalgamation proceeding almost in an atmosphere of horse trading. This confusion was increased by the fact that no clearly defined national society existed in any country. In England and Wales there was the great split between the London and Manchester Orders.

Then the Manchester Order already had six branches in Ireland, with the three largest being Londonderry, Bangor and Coleraine. It also had a ' branch ' at Glasgow in Scotland which claimed only one member.* The London Order was much stronger in Scotland, having branches in Edinburgh, Falkirk, Glasgow, Kilmarnock and Dundee, with an aggregate of 395 members.

The Irish Society of Bricklayers consisted simply of the two branches at Belfast and Londonderry, while the Scottish Society had its kingpin in the Glasgow branch but was not very widespread. Proposals for amalgamation, therefore, was not so much a coming together of differing national societies as an attempt to unravel the tangled skein of organisation which had developed.

When the Manchester Bricklayers subsequently made their hostility clear to the London Order by refusing even to take a vote on amalgamation with them, Batchelor and his executive went ahead with their discussions on fusion with Ireland. Agreement was finally reached and Belfast and Londonderry branches transferred their 452 members to the London Order on the 1st January, 1902.

Three months later the Scottish Bricklayers brought their nine branches and 968 members within the fold of the London Order. With a total of over 38,000 members and assets of £112,000 it was now immeasurably superior to either the Manchester Order of Bricklayers or the Operative Stonemasons' Society.

And the superiority of the Union lay not only in size but in the foresight of its executive council and the abilities

* Manchester Unity Quarterly Report, 31st March, 1900.

of its General Secretary, John Batchelor. Batchelor was a peppery individual, almost as aggressive as Coulson was before him. The similarity of temperament had, in fact, led to constant clashes between the two men in the past. But Batchelor was able to temper his harshness with much greater reasoning powers. It was mainly due to his persuasiveness, in fact, that the Scottish and Irish societies had entered the London Order. It was a decision by the House of Lords, however, which really revealed how very much more progressive he was in thought and action than many of his trade union colleagues.

The Taff Vale railway case had been slowly fought through the courts until it reached the House of Lords. To the astonishment of the trade union movement, which had felt itself reasonably secure behind the Trade Union Act of 1871, the law lords of 1901 ruled in favour of the Taff Railway Company and awarded £23,000 damages against the Amalgamated Society of Railway Servants. There was an outburst of indignation and consternation throughout the unions. Once more their rights on picketing and directing members in dispute were so dubious as to involve the possibilities of heavy penalties.

Batchelor also felt outraged by the decision and took immediate and positive steps to fight back. He called specially summoned meetings of every branch in the London Order to discuss the implications of the Taff Vale judgement. Included in his suggestions was the point of completely isolating the purely friendly benefit finances from the trade section. This would ensure that the friendly benefits would not suffer in any case for damages brought against the Union over a trade dispute.

He also gave detailed instructions on how picketing and strike action should proceed so that the Union would not be openly exposed to prosecution. " In cases where objection is taken to material manufactured or supplied by any firm " he advised, " it is competent for members as individuals to leave the work rather than use it, but it is illegal for a delegate or officer to order them to do so."

Batchelor also recognised that the Taff Vale judgement was not merely an isolated act against the unions, but part of a continuous process engaged in by employers and people of their class. Whenever they felt the unions to have an industrial advantage they would not hesitate to use their immense political power against them. And in this they were greatly assisted by the many union leaders and members who voluntarily confined their fight to the industrial field because "politics and religion should not be discussed by unions."

It was these union leaders who had held aloof from the first attempts to obtain independent Labour representatives in the House of Commons. The same people had also ignored the special meeting held in 1900 at the Memorial Hall, Farringdon Street in London, where a group of more politically advanced unions had come together to lay the foundations of the Labour Party.

And they would have foolishly continued fighting with their political hand self-tied behind their backs if the Taff Vale judgement had not hammered home the stupidity of doing so. By their actions the Taff Vale Railway Company, and the House of Lords, unwittingly had become the greatest recruiting agents for the new and still very weak Labour Party.

The London Order of Bricklayers now decided to enter the political field. Batchelor put forward a scheme to set up a permanent fund to fight for Labour representation in Parliament and the members responded with a majority vote providing for one shilling per head to be levied annually.

Affiliation to the Labour Representation Committee (the name by which the Labour Party was known until 1906) by a trade union did not necessarily mean that its members had been converted to supporting socialism, but simply that they felt trade union objectives had to be pursued in the political arena. The debate which took place between the members of the Operative Stonemasons' Society revealed quite clearly the differing attitudes that trade unionists had to political representation. The

O.S.M. itself was quite politically advanced, having for some years been paying loss of wages and contributing to election expenses for local candidates. When the invitation came from Ramsay MacDonald, Secretary of the Labour Representation Committee, that they should affiliate nationally, the Ipswich, Battersea, Croydon and Liverpool branches formally proposed affiliation in the Fortnightly Returns.

Their statements in support of the proposition, however, were purely on the point of safeguarding their immediate trade interests. The Croydon branch said that: "As practical masons we often work on large contracts executed for the Government. Are the conditions on such jobs anything like fair?" Croydon, and doubtlessly other branches, obviously looked upon the House of Commons as a higher industrial joint consultative body rather than the doorway to a completely new conception of society.

The word socialism was, in fact, mentioned only by the Truro lodge which put forward an opposition amendment that the Society should not affiliate to the Labour Representation Committee. "This, we suppose" said the lodge "is another new fangle beginning with the New Century. . . . A good old Trade Unionist and a Liberal would not like to support a Jingo Joe, and Khaki Unionist, neither would he a Socialist, who has done more to cripple the Liberal cause and has no respect for Trade Unionism, only to use their funds."*

In a national ballot by the masons, affiliation to the Labour Party was carried against the Truro amendment by the not very substantial majority of 498 to 390 votes. And included in the majority would be many members not voting for socialist legislation but merely for the opportunity of forwarding the Union's own narrow interests. These men were not basically opposed to the prevailing economic or social conditions and they failed to appreciate the need for radical change even when it was

* O.S.M. Returns, 29th November, 1900.

gradually demonstrated to them that society was fundamentally unstable.

For, brought in with the new century, was the first faltering in trade and the shadow of a fresh economic recession. In building the impact was sharper than that felt by other industries because the first cuts made by industrialists were in heavy fixed capital investment. The building unions were soon engaged in desperate attempts to prevent employers cutting back wages and conditions, and this time under the restrictions of the Taff Vale judgement. By 1903 the recession had become widespread and unemployment was so heavy that union membership began to fall drastically. Even the London Order of Bricklayers, which had comfortably weathered the last crisis, found membership plummeting each year until it had fallen by 7,000 to a total of 31,000 in 1906.

The masons had dropped to 14,000 members while the Manchester Order of Bricklayers, with just over 2,400, was a mere shadow of the union it had once been. Nor did there seem a great deal of hope for its future. The cautious and unenterprising attitude of its Executive was more than matched by the reactionary spirit of its members. They seemed completely blind to even the most object lesson.

In 1906, for instance, the grim circumstances in which the trade unions were now struggling were greatly relieved through a magnificent victory achieved by the Parliamentary Labour Party. It forced through the Trades Disputes Act which had the effect of reversing the Taff Vale judgement. It was a classic example of the benefits of political action to the trade union movement. Yet, when it was once more proposed that the Manchester Order affiliate to the Labour Party the members again defeated the proposition by 746 to 574 votes. And some of the lodges in the biggest towns with the highest unemployment—Liverpool, Leeds, Nottingham, Birmingham and Birkenhead—voted almost solidly against political affiliation.

As the depression continued the position of several of the unions reached a point where the members began clamouring for revisions of rules. The London Order of Bricklayers, however, felt that this was a policy of despair and something much more radical was required to save the situation. The Union was now losing an average of 2,000 members a year and its executive declared that only by a positive policy of amalgamation was there a hope of conserving the strength of the building trades—and forming a united front against the attacks of the employers. Batchelor immediately began approaches to the other unions to get action on amalgamation but was only able to draw a response from the Manchester Bricklayers, whose membership had now slumped to 1,760. This time George Clarke and his Executive reluctantly agreed to take a vote on amalgamation; but Clarke at the same time almost guaranteed its defeat when he introduced the matter in a hostile and almost fatalistic fashion.

" The two societies " he wrote " stand at present in the same position as two ships that have come into collision; both are equally badly damaged and in danger of sinking. The captain of one vessel shouts across to the other to come aboard his ship and bring his crew with him, but the answer is: ' No! you seem in no better position than I am and if I am to sink I will go down on the ship that has carried me up to now.' "

It was a poor analogy. True the London Order had felt the full ravages of the depression and was reduced to about 23,000 members. But that number, plus its financial assets of £63,000, made the Manchester Order a cockleshell by comparison. But Clarke's members dutifully rejected amalgamation by 822 to 269 votes, and appeared almost fanatically prepared for a hero's death going down with their own sinking ship rather than survival on a lifebelt thrown by the London Order.

The Stonemasons' Union was perhaps even more reactionary in that it quite peremptorily rejected the invitation by Batchelor to discuss amalgamation. The continuing depression had reduced it to 8,000 members and seemed to have effected a paralysis of the minds of most of them. They became almost morbidly oppressed with their own immediate problems to the exclusion of nearly everything else. Branch officers continually complained that only a few members attended meetings or were prepared to work for the organisation.

In national ballots the low proportion of members voting reached an almost ridiculous level. In 1910, for example, Birkenhead proposed that the head office should be uprooted from London and once again sent circulating round the country. The General Secretary, William Hancock, had by this time announced his intention to resign due to age and his Assistant, William Williams, had been elected in his place. If ever the Society required stability it was just then. Yet the Birkenhead proposition was carried by the frail margin of 174 to 159 votes; about four per cent of the members had troubled to take part in this most important decision.

A few months later the head office was transferred to Manchester and the new General Secretary had to start life with an inexperienced executive. Williams, however, was a better official than Hancock had been. He was more advanced politically, for instance, and his first step was to completely alter the shape and contents of the Fortnightly Returns and encourage letters on political and economic subjects. In addition he reviewed the Returns back to the days of Angus McGregor and used quotations from them to " stimulate a keener interest and higher sense of pride in our organisation."

In his efforts to do this Williams was also helped by a gradual revival in trade. In 1909 the level of employment touched its lowest point and gradually began to rise again. Even so, in 1910, there was still an average of between ten and sixteen per cent of building workers unemployed throughout the country. And when the trade unions came to consider their position over the last ten years they found the whole of their efforts had been exerted simply in an effort to retain what they had already won by the end of the previous century. At Ashford, in Kent, building craftsmen were still working 56½ hours per week in the summer and 53½ in the winter for a wage which averaged out to £1 13s. 5½d. per week.

In general, hourly wage rates varied between 6d. to London's high rate of 10½d.—about the same as they were in 1900. But over the period a real decrease in living standards had taken place, because the cost of food and other necessities of life had been gradually increasing. There was no doubt that ten years from the start of the 20th Century building workers' conditions were worse than they had been at the beginning.

CHAPTER 18

THE AMALGAMATION CRUSADE

MEN of vision within the trade union movement have often found themselves bitterly frustrated—almost to the point of cynicism—by the paradox of extreme conservatism within a movement professedly striving towards a new and ennobling conception of society. Progress and change, instead of being the product of far-seeing minds, have too often resulted from fear or in response to economic pressures which have shown up glaring weaknesses in organisation. A movement which should have acted with foresight, courage and boldness in pursuing its objectives has often been more like a dull, lumbering ox responding only to the goading pin-pricks of external circumstances.

John Batchelor and his executive could justifiably be called men of vision who became depressed at the inability of the building unions to advance with the times. Even the ten years of depression seemed insufficient to jolt the leadership generally out of their apathy and conservatism. Though there was a growing feeling among the ordinary members that only a united building union could weather economic depressions, or withstand the strengthening employers' associations, the leaders seemed oblivious of this developing mood.

Batchelor felt that moves towards amalgamation or consolidation of the trades, as he termed it, would always be frustrated if discussions were confined between the various trade union officials. After all, these men represented the most vested interests in retaining sectionalised unions. They would always seek to rationalise their hostility to consolidation if they felt their personal power and prestige at stake. Ironical though it might be, they had a stake in preserving the very demarcation squabbles and internecine feuding which were weakening their organisations.

If this obstacle of officialdom could not be removed, thought Batchelor, there was only one alternative; it had to be by-passed. Although he knew that it would bring him the hostility of other union leaders Batchelor announced that the London Bricklayers would take the lead in going direct to " the individual members of each trade through their branches, instead of as before relying on the general officers."

In an uncompromising attack on vested interests he added: " Workmen's wages are not so high that their money should be wasted in payment of an excessive number of officials, and by consolidation less officials, either branch or general, would be required, office rents would be reduced, and there should be a considerable reduction in expenditure on these accounts."*

As part of this new drive the London Order of Bricklayers sponsored a provisional committee for consolidation of the trade unions in the building industry. Also playing a leading part in its activities was the chairman of the Union's Executive Committee, George Hicks of the Battersea branch. Hicks and Batchelor were to form a powerful team in boosting the activities of the provisional committee, and Batchelor also helped by putting the head office of the London Bricklayers at the disposal of its members. Hicks and other leaders of the new ' progressive organisation ' went round the country speaking at meetings of building workers encouraging them to press their own officials to talk amalgamation. Possessing great speaking ability, George Hicks had a robust physique and mind to go with it. Whatever idea he took up he was prepared to bulldoze through to the end.

* O.B.S. Annual Report, 1910.

Now that the provisional committee possessed the necessary machine they had to decide on the direction they were going to drive. At a meeting in the bricklayers' hall it was decided that they should push for amalgamation of all the building trades through the auspices of the Trades Union Congress. The reason for this was that a motion had already been passed at the 1910 conference of the T.U.C. instructing the Parliamentary Committee to contact all affiliated unions and obtain their opinions on "amalgamation by industries."

The provisional committee for consolidating the building trades decided that it was necessary to have a more definite proposition committing the Parliamentary Committee to action, and they sought this objective by getting the London Order of Bricklayers to place a motion on the T.U.C. Agenda for 1911 which read: "That this Congress, recognising the increased power of the capitalists in closing up their ranks and their adoption of improved methods, deplores the lack of similar consolidation among the workers. It urges, therefore, that the Parliamentary Committee take steps to call conferences of the different industries, with a view of amalgamating the several Trade Unions connected with each industry."

At Congress the motion was carried unanimously. Like many other T.U.C. resolutions, however, it was in danger of being treated more as a theoretical statement of principle rather than a practical vehicle for moving the trade unions forward. The Parliamentary Committee members were obviously in an unhappy position. They had little real power to do anything, and they also recognised that union representatives saw no contradiction in paying enthusiastic lip service to an ideal at conference which they were prepared to block in actual practice.

The London Bricklayers and the provisional committee, therefore, saw that adoption of their Congress motion was only the start of the struggle. If the Parliamentary Committee could not move then they would have to take the initiative. A few months after Congress, therefore, a leaflet was published headed "Operative Bricklayers

Society Consolidation Committee." The Union's colours were firmly nailed to the mast-head by a sub-title which uncompromisingly declared: " **Object.**—One Union for the Building Industry."

Among the signatories to the leaflet were included the most prominent and influential members of the Union: Harry Adams, Jimmy Lane, Jack Wills, George Hicks and John Batchelor. The leaflet put forward a pungent argument in favour of one union and concluded with this section on its possible administration.

" **INTERNAL**

Internal organisation should be of such a character as to allow of the fullest freedom for the various trades to discuss and promote the advance of their sectional interests in line with the general policy of the whole organisation.

Sectional strikes should be reduced to the lowest possible margin consistent with the maintenance of a *fighting* organisation. When a district or a national stoppage is decided on, all sections should be prepared with claims for improved conditions. One of the immediately pressing needs is the abolition of long agreements, and the unifying of the time set for their expiration, so that concerted action is possible for the industry all over the country.

We have thus briefly enumerated some of the advantages to be gained from an amalgamation of existing trade unions; we therefore suggest the following as the Name, the Object, and the Immediate Functions the organisation should take:—

Name.—The Building Workers' Industrial Union.

Object.—To unite the present building trades' unions into one union, embracing the whole of the wage workers engaged therein; with a view to building a union which, in conjunction with other industrial unions, will ultimately form the framework of the machinery to control and regulate production in the interests of the entire community.

Immediate Functions.—1st: To maintain a fighting organisation, working to improve the material conditions of the workers engaged in the building industry; to take joint action with other similar unions in the furtherance of the interests of the workers nationally and internationally, believing that the interests of all wage workers are identical.

2nd: The systematic organisation of propaganda among the workers, upon the necessity of becoming organised on the industrial field, upon the basis of class instead of craft. Organise by industry as workers, instead of by sections as craftsmen.

Financial.—1st: For trade purposes, a uniform scale of contributions and benefits.

2nd: The amalgamation of the friendly side benefits into a separate account."

With this new programme, and the whole weight of the London Bricklayers behind it, the consolidation movement went ahead on a genuine upsurge of enthusiasm among the rank and file of every building union. Joint meetings were held throughout the country to which flocked building operatives anxious to achieve unity with one another. Other years in trade union history may have had their amalgamation drives but none have ever compared with this one in the genuine fervour it aroused in the ordinary member. The whole campaign, in fact, took on the character of a crusade. Intended to convince the union leadership of the need for unity it succeeded far beyond that objective. Even the employers were acutely aware—and apprehensive—of this new militant spirit sweeping through the country.

Reporting a special meeting of the masters in London the *Evening Times* for the 22nd November, 1911, commented that: "The proceedings were private, but the result is known. The employers represented firms and companies in London and its vicinity, and they formed the London and District Employers' Federation, with the object of defending themselves against the Socialistic Labour movement and the offensive strike operations. This is the first step in a scheme for uniting the industrial employers throughout the country in a great Federation, and is a reply to the recent trend of action among the workers, who desire to bring about a general federation of the Trade Unions in order to be in a better position to war with capital."

The climax of the consolidation campaign was reached when it pressurised the T.U.C. Parliamentary Committee into holding two special conferences on amalgamation, on the 18th April and the 23rd May, 1912. At the second of these in Manchester, 15 delegates attended representing all the major unions but one; the General Union of Carpenters and Joiners. Their secretary, W. Matkin, wrote that his Executive had decided against sending a delegate because they felt "that the first step towards closer unity would be brought about by first amalgamating kindred associations."

Ignoring this warning straw in the wind the meeting went ahead and adopted a scheme which, apart from a few minor amendments, was almost exactly the statement contained in the first leaflet issued by the London Bricklayers Consolidation Committee. At a resumed meeting of these unions, on the 21st June, they took an important decision to instruct the Parliamentary Committee to take a vote of each building union on the broad proposals for amalgamation.

By 22nd October, 1912, this ballot had been completed in every union. Over 117,000 papers had been issued and 43,697 members of all the unions had voted. Though this meant 76,000 papers had not been returned it was nearly a 40 per cent vote, and good compared with normal union ballots. Every single organisation had reported a majority in favour. The aggregate total being 31,541 for amalgamation and 12,156 against.

But the most vital vote was still to be taken. Members might favour a broadly expressed ideal of closer unity but became very much more cautious once details were set down about the disposal of various benefits. If the officials had their vested interests, the ordinary member usually had his planted firmly in the benefit section of his union. And it was in striving to reconcile almost completely opposed interests that the support for amalgamation began to break up. Even at the conference in December, which was to formulate greater details for submission to a further ballot, the first signs of friction were apparent.

Jack Wills represented the London Bricklayers at the conference and his report to the Executive of the Union was, in effect, a sad pointer to the inevitable end. He had attended the conference, he said, " as the only representative of our society, and consequently had to bear the brunt of the opposition to the draft rules submitted by our committee. No other society had prepared anything for discussion, and, with slight alterations they were eventually adopted by one vote."

The finalised ballot proposals for the new union were drawn up in two parts which had the effect of completely separating the trade purposes from the friendly benefits. The greatest conflict came over the position of officials who would be redundant. Finally a paragraph was agreed that:

" Provision shall be made by the new organisation for the employment of the officers of the Trade Unions forming the new organisation for a period of three years, at not less than the pay received and the conditions enjoyed at the date of inauguration. In the event of any officer or member of the staff of any of the unions not accepting the position assigned to him he shall be suitably compensated."

It was this provision, almost as much as the confusion over friendly benefits, which planted the rock on which the ideal of amalgamation finally foundered. The members of the London Bricklayers were especially incensed because the first call to action by John Batchelor had been based on the reduction of officials and costly administration. Now they were being asked to perpetuate both.

Even strong supporters of amalgamation, like Tom Hayward of the Bristol branch, wavered in face of what they took to be a negation of the whole principle.

" This compensation to officials is a thorn in my side," he wrote in the Bricklayers' Monthly Circular. " I ask myself why compensate them when I and my fellows of the rank and file have been grovelling about all our lives seeking here and there to use the only commodity we have for sale, our labour power, half starved, struggling to pay our contributions the whole of our lives, sometimes letting our children go to school shoeless rather than run out of our union? Who will talk of compensating us, when the officials have had a surety of a salary; surety of a job for so long? They have to stand aside for the new order of things."

In the ballot on the detailed proposal for amalgamation the members were asked to vote separately on parts 1 and 11—the second relating to friendly benefits. When the vote was announced by the Parliamentary Committee of the T.U.C. on the 21st July, 1913, it revealed the hopelessness of being able to proceed. The confusion and disappointment among members was revealed by the much lower total poll. The members of the Painters, Plumbers, Plasterers, Electrical Workers, Slaters and Tilers, and the General Union of Carpenters and Joiners had voted against both sections.

Even the London Order of Bricklayers had rejected part 11 and carried part 1 by only a small majority, 2,416 votes to 1,775. The only unions voting in favour of both sections were the three labourers' unions, the Manchester Order of Bricklayers and a small painters' society which was really an autonomous lodge with 50 members.

Although the Stonemasons had voted in favour of both sections by a small majority, their Executive Council told the T.U.C. that the vote had been disqualified because of the abysmally low poll.

The great opportunity for welding all the unions into one had gone. Even so, the consolidation committee refused to admit total defeat and attempted to carry through amalgamations between the small societies which had voted in favour of the proposals. But even the political and economic climate was against them and gradually overshadowed their efforts. Britain was drifting towards war with Germany, and in the building industry major industrial warfare looked like breaking out at any moment.

Better trade conditions had revived the militant spirit of the men. Sporadic strikes were taking place throughout the country, and very often without the sanction of their executives. One of the major reasons for these disputes was the determination of union members that 'nons' must join the ranks. The men were also becoming impatient with control over working rules by conciliation boards. They believed that the strike weapon was much more effective in achieving advances when economic conditions were in their favour.

Demarcation disputes also became more frequent and were fought even more bitterly because they had the full weight of the unions' executive councils behind them. The London Bricklayers had several wrangles in Scotland and England over masons laying bricks, and both unions of bricklayers were again fighting with the plasterers over the laying of partition walls with breeze blocks. The most extensive dispute on this particular demarcation issue took place at the building of the Adelphi Hotel in Liverpool.

When the plasterers began laying internal walls with breeze blocks all the bricklayers walked off the job in protest. A meeting of the local conciliation board was hurriedly called to patch up the dispute before it developed into anything more serious, and a decision was made to refer the case to full arbitration pending which all building with breeze blocks should be suspended. Next day, however, the plasterers walked into the job and promptly broke the agreement. Out again came every bricklayer on the Adelphi site.

Against all reason the employers refused to enforce the interim conciliation decision and quite peremptorily told the bricklayers that, if there was not an unqualified return to work, they would lock out the bricklayers on all the other jobs in the town. Though this seems a completely unjustified attitude it reveals the extremely incendiary state that general relations had reached when the employers at Liverpool, Birkenhead, Seaforth and Garstang actually locked out their bricklayers because the men again refused to back down on the Adelphi job.

This lock-out lasted for over 2½ months until an arbitration award was made in favour of the work being exclusively the right of bricklayers.

But it was in London, more than anywhere else, that the sites were proving a constant battleground as union members tried to chase nons from organised jobs. And this activity was mainly confined to the London Order of Bricklayers. The full-time secretary of the Union's Metropolitan District Committee was Harry Adams, a young firebrand of 31, who keenly felt that militant trade unionism could only be sustained by constantly practising militancy on the sites.

It was the work of Adams and the members of the London Bricklayers which particularly angered the employers in the London Master Builders' Association (L.M.B.A.). They claimed that every strike against a non-unionist was a direct breach of the Working Rule Agreement that "there should be no discrimination between Union and non-Union labour." On the 23rd December, 1913, therefore, the L.M.B.A. summoned representatives of all the unions to a meeting at which they demanded that the executives should punish members who were taking unofficial strike action in defiance of this rule.

Harry Adams and Jimmy Lane, who was chairman of the Metropolitan District Committee of the Bricklayers, attended this meeting as representatives of the Union. And to Harry Adams the employers put the direct question asking what action the London Order was prepared to take in disciplining unofficial strikers. When Adams refused to give any undertaking the employers passed a resolution ordering him and Lane to withdraw from the meeting. This angered the plasterers and crane-drivers representatives who left with them in protest.

After they had gone the meeting continued and the masters decided that an ultimatum must be given. They issued this in a five point memorandum sent to each union. Taken together these points formed a document impossible in its demands, and completely insulting to the mentality of the entire trade union leadership. Each executive was asked to ensure:

"1. The return to work of all men to jobs where strikes exist immediately after the holidays.

"2. That a guaranteed trust fund should be formed by deposits by both sides, to be available for the purpose of paying penalties for strikes or lock-outs in violation of the working rules.

"3. That a statement in writing be sent to this association that your society deprecates the strikes without the matters in dispute being brought before the Conciliation Boards, and that you will undertake to penalise your individual members in case of the non-observance of the rules.

"4. That an undertaking be given that no attempt will be made on any of the jobs of members of this association to carry out card inspections.

"5. That a reply be in the hands of this association on or before the 5th of January, stating as to whether or not your Executive Committee accepts the principle involved in the foregoing proposals."

There were unions whose leaders had been slightly resentful about the 'too aggressive' attempts of the London Bricklayers to force the pace on jobs, but the arrogant memorandum from the employers was the very thing required to make them equally militant. The masters found a solidly united opposition to their demands. It is also highly probable that no one would have been more surprised than the employers if the unions had capitulated. Their real object was to precipitate a fight, at the worse time of the year for the men, when they felt that they could administer a short sharp lesson, leading to much stricter discipline on the sites.

On the 7th January, therefore, the employers within the L.M.B.A. carried out the second stage of their plan by announcing that, as the unions had rejected their proposals, they no longer regarded any of the working rule agreements as being in force. They followed this announcement almost immediately with the presentation to each worker in London of an agreement for individual signature. This 'agreement' began with a plaintive preamble about the difficulties the L.M.B.A. had with unions which, it claimed, were unable to control their members. All agreements, it concluded, must now be on an individual basis. Workmen were asked to sign a contract which was, in effect, a slight variation of the old 'Document'.

The men were no longer required to avow that they were non-unionists, but that they would work peaceably with nons and not use strikes to force other operatives to join the unions. This contract also committed the signatory to the penalty of 20s. if he broke it. The closing date for signing was the 24th January, 1914. Any man failing to assent by then would be considered as having resigned from the job by 12 noon on that date.

The unions now realised that the employers were adamant about forcing the issue and they made preparations to meet the challenge of this new 'Document'. The London Bricklayers immediately levied every member 1s. per week in anticipation of a long dispute, and also transferred £3,000 to the London area accounts ready for the fray. And to let the employers know that the bricklayers would never discipline their members as demanded, old John Batchelor threw down the gauntlet in an appeal to his members for a united fight.

"Now then, brothers; forward to the front. The challenge has been thrown down, and we have to vindicate our position. Some of our members refused to work with non-unionists, and came out against them. The builders demanded we should order them back to work. Our Committee declined the proposal, leaving members their hard won liberty of action which we, as a trade, have held intact for over 50 years. Shall we retain that liberty won for us by those who have gone before . . . or shall we submit to be dictated to by those who hold the purse . . . . I know your reply will be—NO! ”

There was never any doubt about the willingness of the men to meet the challenge from the employers. On the morning of 24th January, nearly 20,000 London building workers were locked out by the masters in the L.M.B.A. because they had refused to sign the ‘Document’. And one of the most bitter and widespread conflicts ever seen in the industry had begun.

CHAPTER 19

IN DEFENCE OF LIBERTY

THE London lock-out of 1914 was the most dramatic building dispute that had taken place within the 20th Century. Other later battles with the employers might be fought on a wider front, but none of them was to witness the intense depth of suffering, sacrifice and courage displayed by the London men and their families.

The employers, who had precipitated the conflict, were the ones most surprised at the fervour and unity shown by the men. After nearly two months of being out on the streets hardly any union member had defected. Unlike previous disputes on the 'Document' the masters' hopes of a crack in the ranks of the men were almost completely unrealised. They were not so confident now of an early victory in a battle whose strategy had been dictated by them. Instead they were being forced to recognise that they would have to treat with the operatives of whom they had been so contemptuous.

They therefore approached the officials of the unions in dispute and invited them to meet under the auspices of the National Building Trades Conciliation Board "for the purpose of considering and suggesting means of obtaining the observance of trade agreements." Negotiations took place during March and April and the outcome was a number of proposals which, in fact, were the first stages of a reluctant retraction by the employers' association of its previous dogmatic attitude.

The men were asked to return to work on a promise that the 'Document' would be withdrawn; monetary guarantees for 'penalties' were not to be demanded, and ticket inspections were no longer expressly forbidden although they should not take place if an employer objected.

As payment for these concessions the union officials were asked to obtain obedience to working rules to the "utmost extent of their disciplinary powers embodied in their constitutions." But the point which drew the greatest opposition from the men on strike was the continued insistence by the masters that all matters in dispute should be brought before the Conciliation Boards, which was another way of saying that the right to strike against non-unionists would not be tolerated. But this was the main principle for which the men were now voluntarily suffering. And it was no surprise that, when the joint proposals from union leaders and employers were put to a ballot of the strikers, they were contemptuously rejected by a large majority. The men were prepared to continue their dispute rather than close it at a stage where the employers would be left possessing greater disciplinary control than before the lock-out had commenced.

At this point it became obvious that some of the union executives and their London membership were not entirely in sympathy with one another. The London Order of Operative Bricklayers might prosecute the struggle with every penny they had, but other union leaders wanted to try and settle it on what they considered reasonable terms. They found, however, that this was not to be an easy task. The fight for unfettered rights to promote union organisation had been started by the ordinary members at site level and, even though they were now suffering from the effects of the prolonged dispute, they were still remaining firm in defence of an ideal which has not always been endorsed by the trade union movement—the right to establish a closed shop.

And their rejection of the first compromise put to them by their officials and employers was no isolated gesture. For, when another 'final' set of terms was offered by the employers and agreed by the union officials in May, they were just as decisively refused by the men when again put to the vote. The reason for their rejection was still the same. The masters had withdrawn even further from their original stand but they were adamant that strikes against non-unionists should be prohibited.

With the failure of their second attempt to draw the dispute to a close a note of desperation now entered into negotiations between union leaders and representatives of the L.M.B.A. Frustrated at their inability to crush the men, the masters threatened that they would appeal to their colleagues right throughout the country to enforce a national lock-out if the London operatives refused to go back to work.

This threat added to the fears of officials belonging to some of the weaker unions who felt that the continual strike levies being imposed might lead to a 'run-out' by their provincial members. In addition to this the trade union movement had its own internal problems to contend with. Jack Wills, who had been a leading light in the consolidation movement set up by the London bricklayers, had become extremely cynical about the prospects of amalgamation between the unions. It was rumoured that he and a number of influential trade union members were considering the formation of an industrial building union which might draw members away from the traditional organisations.

In the Midlands too, the quarrel between the Manchester and the London Bricklayers had become more complex with the formation of a breakaway bricklayers' union which called itself the Bricklayers' Trade and Provident Society —it became more commonly known as the Sheffield Society.

Little wonder that the officials felt they needed industrial peace to turn their full energies into the wars within their own ranks. They would, in fact, have been prepared to concede ground to the London builders if they could have settled a dispute which was now a source of great embarrassment to them—especially with the threat that they might have to face an extension of the lock-out throughout the whole of the country.

A series of meetings took place, therefore, between them and the employers in the hope of drawing up a set of proposals which would this time be approved by the men. And the draft agreed was certainly an almost complete withdrawal by the masters of all their demands. In addition to retraction of the 'Document' the right to ticket inspections on the job was granted—although it was not to be done within actual working hours. Instead of a completely hostile opposition to the idea of men fighting non-unionists it was also agreed they would now have the right to protest against employment of anyone they found particularly 'objectionable'. There was to be no victimisation of the men who had taken a leading part in the dispute.

But, still unpalatable to the men, was the insistence on conciliation boards as supreme arbiters on disputes, and the employers' refusal to give a general code of working rules. Nevertheless, those who had drawn up the agreement felt that men who had been striking for nearly six months would be more amicably disposed to having the battle concluded on terms which were reasonably face-saving to both sides.

After all, when the dispute started the operatives had just come through the very lean years of the depression period. They had no financial reserves to fall back on. Now, after nearly twenty-six weeks out of work, they and their families were starving and destitute. The furniture and homes of some of them had gone.

Families were being evicted for non-payment of rent and there was little sympathy for them from official relief organisations. When application was made to Poor Law Committees for some starving child to be given food, it was sometimes refused a piece of bread and a bowl of soup if its father happened to be "one of those trade union agitators who are striking against their masters."

If ever men had almost unbearable pressure upon them to concede a struggle it was the London building workers in 1914. In rags themselves they also had to bear the anguish of seeing their children bewildered and suffering privation for principles they were too young to understand. But these conditions, which might logically have been expected to degrade them and weaken their resolve, strengthened their determination to defy employers who were trying to starve them into submission.

And when the third set of proposals was put before the striking metropolitan operatives they again astonished their leaders, and the masters, with an aggregate vote rejecting the terms. They were prepared to continue their desperate struggle rather than surrender the slightest liberty to pursue their trade union objectives as they thought fit.

But cracks were developing in the previously united front. The Stonemasons' Union, in which there were serious internal divisions over the continuance of the London dispute, had recorded a slight majority of their members in favour of accepting the third compromise. They decided to go ahead and make a sectional agreement with the masters for their members to return to work. At this there was an angry public protest by officials of the other trade unions, and an outburst of vehement indignation from the other men on strike.

But there was no doubt that some of the leaders were extremely hypocritical in their attacks on the masons and this was revealed in a letter from William Williams, Secretary of the O.S.M., when he wrote to the other unions notifying them of the decision by his General Council to end the dispute. His Council felt that the limit of concessions had been reached from the employers, he said, and thought they should go ahead and settle, especially . . . "as it was agreed by the various E.C.'s that failing acceptance of the terms submitted to the ballot that pressure should be placed upon the men to end the dispute by withdrawing support after a certain date."

Williams had, in fact, revealed that the fear of some of the trade union leaders was so great they were prepared to use financial pressure to force their members back to work. Under cover, various attempts were now made to obtain sectional agreements to end the dispute and a general feeling of suspicion began to develop between the unions. John Batchelor, Secretary of the London Bricklayers, was extremely caustic about the timidity and apprehension of his trade union colleagues and he began to realise that his members were now facing an almost hopeless struggle to maintain their position.

Then the employers really created panic among the union officials by their announcement that a national ballot of building masters showed they were prepared to impose a country-wide lock-out commencing on the 15th August if the London operatives refused to capitulate. Unions now sought desperately to end the stalemate before the imposition of a national lock-out which would involve 500,000 men. But the grave possibility of the first ever country-wide conflict developing in the building industry was ended by the commencement of a much greater one—on the 4th August Great Britain declared war on Germany.

An immediate attempt was made to close strikes throughout the entire country in every industry. The executive councils of the various building unions moved in to take complete charge of the London dispute. About a week after the announcement of war they had agreed to their members returning to work on the basis of the third set of proposals formulated with the employers.

But by then thousands of building operatives in London had voluntarily suffered for seven months in defence of their union principles. Harry Adams, at the centre of the conflict said: "The hardship was terrible; men lost their homes and saw their families go hungry and yet would not give in. And in the midst of all the suffering and misery was a spirit of comradeship and unity which completely lifted us above it. Many of those men who were soon to give their very lives in France fighting for 'liberty' had already exhausted themselves in a seven months battle to preserve it in England."

CHAPTER 20

THE GREATEST TROWEL TRADES UNION

AT least one building union historian has painted the Great War years almost like a stark black and white scene: stagnation on the home front throwing into sharp relief the pace and fighting of the trenches.* This is a false picture. In a war it is obvious that a whole nation—not only its military force—is galvanised into action. Traditional attitudes are jolted and vested interests become less tenacious.

Add to this the gradual growth of employment, the need for much greater mobility in the labour force, and it is obvious that real opportunities existed for unions with vision and capable leadership. Not all organisations possessed these attributes or were capable of grasping the advantages given them. Nevertheless the period of the 1914-18 war saw the building unions moving faster and with greater purpose than in almost any other four years of their history.

Discounting any advantages that might have accrued in individual societies, the creation of a soundly based federation would still rank as an outstanding achievement of the war years. And this remains true even if the move towards federation was partly to weaken the drive for all-out amalgamation.

---

*In his *Builders' History*, page 434, Raymond Postgate says: "The effect of peace upon the building trades unions was like spring upon an icebound river. The obstacles which wartime inertia had let remain were rapidly removed and quick movement followed."

Just a few days after the war began, officials of the established unions had received a shock when it was announced that Jack Wills and a few other leading ' consolidationists ' had formed a new organisation on an industrial basis. Named the Building Workers Industrial Union (B.W.I.U.) its formation owed much to the despair of its founders of ever achieving one union by a process of gradual amalgamation.

Whatever the reasons, or justification for them, there was no doubt about the antagonism the new union drew from leaders of the old. Even John Batchelor of the London Bricklayers—the one organisation almost completely preoccupied with the aim of consolidation—treated it as an act of outright betrayal in face of the enemy. Writing about the close of the London lock-out he told his members: " The battle was won, but it is regrettable to find at the moment of victory that a few of our members and of other Societies were so lost to their duty as to endeavour to start a rival society to, as they no doubt fondly hoped, complete the disintegration the builders had started."

Castigating Jack Wills for having played a leading part in the formation of the B.W.I.U. Batchelor added: " But I firmly believe the attempt is due to fail, and it will be a sorry time for him in that case to find that he has lost the respect of the men with whom he was so long associated."

The London Bricklayers were not alone in their hostility to the men leading the new union. Wills and his comrades found every other union official ranged against them. In fact the most notable achievement of the new organisation was that it drove the others into a much closer association with one another! On the 25th February, 1915, representatives of the various societies met at the Cross Keys Hotel in Theobald's Road, London, and formed the National Association Building Trades Council (N.A.B.T.C.). Although it was later to evolve into an invaluable organisation with a positive approach to the problems of the industry, at its inauguration the National

Association was really only a loose collection of executives with the primary aim of associating on a narrow front against the threat of opposition.

The major resolution passed at the first meeting was simply a throwing down of the gauntlet to Wills and his union. " We recommend to the E.C.s of this affiliated Society," it ran, " the necessity of refusing to recognise the cards of membership of newly formed unions which are in conflict with this council and if necessary, to be prepared to support each other's members sustaining in this action."

Batchelor and his Executive Council might also be bitter about the B.W.I.U. but at least they recognised, as some of the others in the National Association failed to do, that it was born out of frustration at the failure to achieve amalgamation through orthodox processes. They therefore decided that activity on this front was the best antidote to the new industrial organisation. On behalf of his Executive, therefore, Batchelor wrote to John Gregory, Secretary of the Manchester Bricklayers, urging that there should be renewed attempts to provide one union for bricklayers: " I do not think there is any need for me to write anything on the desirabilty of the whole of the bricklayers being enrolled in one organisation, but I will say this, that whilst we are divided we are weaker than we should be united, and the division gives a certain class of men the opportunity of playing one off against the other."

This time the Manchester Order's executive was more disposed to talk amalgamation. Their membership had shrunk to about 1,500 and their finances were in an extremely poor state with some of the benefits showing an almost continual loss. They were also grimly aware that the London Order was almost completely getting the best of the organisational fight between them. But within the membership generally there still remained a solid core of anti-amalgamationists who, although professing the finest of trade union sentiments, would apparently rather commit organisational suicide than associate with the

London men. And nowhere was their schizophrenic attitude revealed more clearly than in the voting confusion which consequently took place to decide whether or not amalgamation talks should be held. The Leeds lodge moved that the Council enter into negotiations and publish full reports of proposed conditions so that members could make a final decision on the issue.

A completely contrary motion from the Liverpool lodge flatly demanded "that the Council attend no Conferences re amalgamation without the vote of the country."

The Executive of the Manchester Order made no attempt to clarify these motions in order to put one clear-cut proposition before the members. Instead they blithely issued voting papers carrying each motion in its original form. Members caught the mood of the game and happily responded with a thumping majority for each one. This then produced the understatement from the Executive that the voting had placed "the Council in an awkward position as to knowing whether we have the vote of the majority of our members to enter into negotiations with the O.B.S. to discuss amalgamation . . . therefore the Council are going to take another vote."

This time, with a definite proposal for amalgamation talks before the membership, there was no great majority for the motion. By 677 to 597 votes it was agreed to allow the council to meet the London Order. But prospects looked bleak. Even before any offers had been made, or terms negotiated, almost 46 per cent of those voting had rejected the idea of amalgamation in any form whatsoever.

When the meetings took place in July and November 1915, between both Orders, some hard bargaining went on. But at no time did it seem likely that there would be any result to justify the energy spent. Not only were the Manchester Order's anti-amalgamation lodges constantly sniping at their representatives to the negotiations, but the on-site rivalry between the two unions had, if anything increased.

When John Blount, an executive member of the Manchester Order went into the Coventry area to do a bit of organising he complained that a London Order member had deliberately organised opposition to him. "He wrote to his E.C.," reported Blount, "and told them I had come to open the M.U.O.B. and organise the district and that they must send down the best man they could get in opposition to me, as I should make headway, so they appointed Coppock & Co."

'Coppock & Co.' was the title by which the Manchester men far from affectionately referred to young Dick Coppock, an organiser for the London Bricklayers. Of a compact and powerful physique Coppock was the nearest thing to an organising machine that the London Order had. He possessed an impassioned oratory that could sway men and a keen, thinking brain with which to direct the great energy he displayed running about all over the Midlands for his Union. And all this was built on a vast self-confidence that made him quite unworried about any odds that might be against him. Faced with another trouble spot old John Batchelor, who fully recognised all these qualities, would dispatch 'Coppock & Co.' to deal with it.

Coppock's answer to Blount was to organise a huge meeting for Coventry building operatives at which he appealed to bricklayers to give their allegiance to the London Bricklayers' Society. Faced with this kind of in-fighting on the jobs and in the towns it was inevitable that the acrimony carried through to top level discussions —especially when John Blount was an influential member of the Manchester Order's Executive Council. And, in fact, it was he who successfully moved that the only condition upon which they should agree amalgamation was that the London Order "accept our liabilities, and that our members should be placed in the exact position in the new Society as they are in this Society."

This was too much for the L.O.B.S. to swallow, even in the interests of unity. Batchelor claimed that his Union was worth much more per member than the Manchester Order. But, " if they were prepared to pay the sum of £1 1s. 5¾d. per member to make it equal to their amount per member his council was prepared to put M.U.O.B.S. members in the same position as their members at once on Amalgamation."

In addition to this qualification the London Bricklayers also flatly refused to guarantee John Gregory a job in the proposed larger union or to allow special places on their General Council to M.U.O.B.S. representatives: " They may stand their election for the Executive in the same way as other members but no more than this can be allowed."

After reviewing these conditions it was not surprising that the Manchester Order's Executive found that they " could not see their way to advise members to amalgamate on such terms." To the Seaforth lodge, one of the leading anti-amalgamation lodges, this was the opportunity to move in smartly with a motion " that we will not accept the unsatisfactory conditions that the O.B.S. is prepared to receive us on Amalgamation, and that we take no vote of the country, or negotiate with the O.B.S. re amalgamation."

General feeling within the Manchester Union was that the financial disparity between them and the O.B.S. should not have mattered. Even though they realised that, to give them the same footing in the London Bricklayers would have meant their position being subsidised, they thought this should have been accepted. They stubbornly claimed that if the London Bricklayers wanted them in, they should be prepared to pay the price. And because it was now plain that the O.B.S. was not prepared to pay this price for amalgamation, the Seaforth motion was carried overwhelmingly by 862 to 100. The prospects of early amalgamation had once again been killed.

But there were members who still persistently pressed the idea in the columns of their union journals. Developments within the industry were also driving officials to joint action on a number of fronts. The problems facing them were common ones for their members and the solutions would bring equal benefits. The events of the war were also bringing an awareness that the future would demand a much closer relation between them than in the past. Separate trade agreements, they agreed, were to be swept away and general working rules brought in to cover all the operatives. By this time too the National Association Building Trades Council had discarded its purely defensive role—the Building Workers Industrial Union had proved not to be such a great bogey after all—and was concentrating on formulating policies to meet conditions when the war finished.

Special attention was given to apprenticeship and training, and to a proposal from Mr. Malcolm Sparkes that there should be the formation of a Building Industrial Parliament. Malcolm Sparkes was a building employer with much more radical principles than normal among his colleagues. He felt that such a Parliament would be a vast improvement on the old Conciliation Boards and the National Demarcation Scheme which had been set up at the outset of the war to prevent demarcation disputes crippling production. He visualised representatives from both employers and men meeting in an atmosphere of goodwill and harmony for the advancement and benefit of the entire industry.

There was no doubt that Sparkes, if naive, was intensely sincere in his desires to achieve a much closer relationship between both sides in the industry. The sacrifice he had witnessed in the London lock-out had made a deep impression upon him: " The terrible futility of that struggle, followed immediately by the still more terrible European war, have given me food for some of the hardest thinking I have ever done." The union officials who listened to Sparkes when he spoke to the N.A.B.T.C. decided that they were prepared to conduct further discussions with the employers on the setting up of such a Parliament. And if such an organisation were created they agreed to select their quota of twenty representatives.

Again this was a decision which revealed their increasing dependence upon one another and the urgent need for a much closer link to be forged than they had on the present N.A.B.T.C. And the first step towards this objective was taken by the Amalgamated Society of Carpenters and Joiners when it convened a meeting of interested societies to discuss its proposals for a National Building Trades Federation.

Following this preliminary meeting the idea was put before the N.A.B.T.C. in the hope that it would be formally adopted by the wider representation on this body. On the 17th and 18th October, 1916, the National Association met at the Bee Hotel in Liverpool and the major item on the agenda was the formation of a federation. After a very full discussion it was unanimously resolved:

> "That a special meeting of the Council be held to meet the members of the General Council of the Amalgamated Society of Carpenters and Joiners to discuss the proposal of the formation of a National Federation."

The almost universal enthusiasm for the idea of federation seemed strange—especially when it was being fervently propounded by societies who had proved themselves clearly hostile to amalgamation. But this was the whole point: while all the unions recognised the urgent need for closer unity most of them were not prepared to sacrifice their individual identity to achieve it. Federation, they thought, would give them the best of both worlds.

In presenting the final scheme for the new organisation the chairman and secretary of the N.A.B.T.C. openly acknowledged this feeling. "The many attempts at amalgamation in the building trades have hitherto proved abortive," they wrote, "and we feel that the best method to achieve amalgamation is a closer connection, with partial financial responsibilities, which we believe will be a step towards the full amalgamation of all unions in the building trade."

On the 5th February, 1918, the N.A.B.T.C. met for the last time. After winding up the outstanding business of the National Association it was formally resolved that "This building trades council be, and the same is hereby, dissolved from this date, and those societies who have voted in favour of the federation scheme are hereby formed as the National Federation of Building Trades Operatives."

It was one of the finest decisions that the operatives had taken in their long history. Unlike the short-lived Operative Builders Union of 1832-34 the unions supporting the N.F.B.T.O. were much more soundly based themselves and able to maintain their newly created organisation.

Almost immediately the Federation swung into action with a campaign for the 44-hour week. Composite branches were also set up throughout the country and assisted greatly in overcoming the problems of organising rural districts. Previously this had proved difficult because very often there were not sufficient tradesmen of any one kind to justify the setting up of branches. The composite branches overcame this because every class of operative was joined together in order to form a workable unit. But the really outstanding success of the Federation, in the very first years of its existence, was the help it gave in creating the widest amalgamation between unions that had yet been known.

Between 1916 and 1918 there had been constant interchange of opinion over amalgamation, especially between the trowel trades. The London Bricklayers had again approached the Manchester Order but without success. And for a short time it looked as if all the talk about unity was merely a show of activity destined to achieve nothing at all. Then, with the Armistice, the position suddenly clarified. The London Bricklayers made definite steps towards taking over the Sheffield Society. Only 300 members strong, it had proved more of an irritant than a menace to the other two bricklayers' unions.

Nevertheless this news produced the reaction in the Manchester Order that it would require to be strengthened or it would be swamped. Still antagonistic to the London Order, however, the Manchester men decided to approach the Operative Stonemasons on amalgamation. Their decision was influenced by the fact that the Operative

Stonemasons were, like themselves, much weaker than the London Bricklayers and less able to completely swallow them and submerge their interests.

The O.S.M. and the M.U.O.B. had, in fact, lost the opportunity of the war years for recruiting members and strengthening their position generally. Fuller employment should have helped to preserve their benefit funds and, with conciliation boards settling most grievances, strike expenditure was a fraction of that in the immediate pre-war year.

Yet the Manchester Order had only managed to increase membership slightly during the four years of the war; from 1,544 to 2,020. Their financial position had hardly improved at all and in this they were the same as the masons. The masons had allowed their contributions to remain low and subsequently had greatly lowered their worth per member.

The only one of the trio which had exploited all the circumstances of the war was the L.O.B.S. At the beginning of hostilities membership had dipped to 26,363 but, by 1918, it had again risen to 34,441. The next year it moved well beyond 40,000 and, completely excluding all property, the financial assets of the Union had touched £50,000.

The foresight of the Executive Council had also kept pace with membership and finances. They were intent on creating a completely modernised union. Within a few months of the end of the war they had finalised plans for nine divisions to be created throughout the country, each of which would have a full-time divisional organiser. Even more of a radical departure from the past was their new system of electing an executive council from the whole of the Union. It had always been a source of grievance to provincial members that complete executives should be chosen from Grand Lodge or a confined area. Now the London Bricklayers made arrangements for its first really national executive when it devised rules providing for the election of one representative from each of the nine divisions.

When John Batchelor and his Council heard that the Manchester Order had turned from them to the Masons to discuss amalgamation he immediately wrote to Bill Bradshaw, Secretary of the National Federation of Building Trades Operatives, asking that the Federation try to widen the amalgamation talks. And on the 16th July, 1919, the Federation convened a conference in Manchester at which all the important trowel trades and others were represented. The finest speech at this meeting was made by T. Boardman of the Manchester Bricklayers, who had always believed, even in face of antagonism from his own colleagues, that one day they would have to unite with the London Order.

In an impassioned appeal for greater unity he ended by "congratulating the Federation in doing what he regarded as the finest thing it had ever done by calling a conference that afternoon." Turning to his own Union representatives, and to the London Bricklayers, he appealed to them to forget their prejudices and support his motion that all the trowel trades unions should pledge themselves to "promote amalgamation at the earliest possible moment." To Boardman's great pleasure, and the satisfaction of the unions represented at the conference, the motion was carried without dissent.

Five societies immediately made preparations for balloting their members on the proposal that they should fuse together. These were the London Operative Bricklayers' Society, the Operative Stonemasons' Society, the Manchester Unity Operative Bricklayers' Society, the National Association of Operative Plasterers and the Street Masons and Paviors.

In the preliminary ballot the Manchester Bricklayers and the Operative Stonemasons obtained an overwhelming vote in favour. The other three societies had also obtained large majorities but had fallen short of the aggregate 50 per cent vote necessary for the Registrar. The London Bricklayers went ahead with a further vote in which they obtained an overwhelming majority for amalgamation. The Plasterers and the Street Masons, however, dropped out of the negotiations and made no further attempt to proceed. But the other three unions were now committed by the overwhelming desires of their membership and talks between them continued until, by 1920, final agreement had been reached on how to overcome the financial disparity between them and on the basis of the new trade and friendly benefit sections.

The goal for which old John Batchelor had personally struggled so long was within reach at last. But he was not to have the satisfaction of being the chief officer of his Union to the end of its separate existence. The Armistice had become the signal for election battles on the trade union front. When John Batchelor again came to the membership for re-election in 1919—the year in which he was presented with his 50 years' membership award—he found himself faced by four other contestants for the post, the two strongest being George Hicks and Dick Coppock. In the first ballot the result was:—

Batchelor	3,661
Hicks	3,497
Coppock	1,960

The other two contestants had only a few hundred votes between them. Then, because the rules demanded an exhaustive ballot for the general secretaryship, a run-off vote was held between Batchelor and Hicks. In this second ballot George Hicks collected nearly all of those given to the other candidates and soundly beat Batchelor. Of course John Batchelor was an old man by this time and, as he said himself without rancour: "It was probably a good thing for the members to relieve me of this high responsibility." But there was a great deal of sentiment for the man who had done so much for the Union and, unlike the shabby treatment meted out to his predecessor Edwin Coulson, Batchelor was given a collected benefit of £450 and appointed as a 'consultant' at £150 a year. This meant at least that he would be a participant in the discussions between the three unions bent on amalgamation.

The way was also smoothed for the final stages by the Sheffield Society being absorbed into the London Bricklayers at the beginning of 1920. To ensure that officials would present no obstacles to the plans it was agreed that William Williams and John Gregory be placed on the staff of the new organisation at a salary of £450 per year. George Hicks had already bulldozed his own executive council, in March 1920, into increasing his annual salary from £300 to £600 at one move. The settlement for Williams and Gregory was also a tacit understanding that he would be given a clear run by them for the General Secretaryship of the new union.

When this ballot was held there were 14 other contestants against him for the job, but none of them so well known or with such organised support. In the first vote he had an overwhelming majority over all other candidates; polling 17,419 votes to 1,016 for the next highest, George Wyver, a member of the Masons' Union.

On the 1st January, 1921, the Amalgamated Union of Building Trade Workers was formally brought into being. With its creation the bricklayers were once again united after the split which had taken place in 1848. And they were now linked to the Masons, men who had for so long held a proud place in the history of the building industry and still possessed traditions which would be a valuable contribution to the stability and progress of the new organisation. With an estimated membership of 75,000, and total assets worth nearly £105,000, the Amalgamated Union of Building Trade Workers was the greatest trowel trades union that had ever been seen in the country.

CHAPTER 21

INTO NATIONAL CONFLICT

THE birth of the A.U.B.T.W. was not merely one isolated, progressive event of the immediate post-war years. Amalgamations were taking place in other trades. The whole climate of the industry was an exciting one which brought developments that were usually to the benefit of the men. If any one month could reveal a glimpse of the achievements during this period—objectives for which the unions had been struggling for years—it was May of 1920.

That month alone saw the introduction of the 44-hour week and the establishment of the National Wages and Conditions Council for the building industry.

The 44-hour week was celebrated by the unions as their greatest gain. Monetary increases could be nullified through rising prices but, they thought, the 44-hour week was a firm possession they could not lose. And, considering the tremendous battles of the past, it was incredible that the shorter working week was won in a bloodless victory—especially when it represented a considerable decrease in hours for some areas.

At the end of the Great War there was still an amazing disparity in wages and hours between various localities throughout the country. A table published by the Manchester Bricklayers in September 1918, showed that their best area was Liverpool. In that city bricklayers were working an average week of 46½ hours in the summer, reducing to 44 and then down to 41½ in the winter. Their rate of wages was 1s. 6d. per hour.

At the other end of the scale the men in Scunthorpe had to work an average of 55 hours per week all the year round for just over 1s. 1d. an hour. For these men the 44 hour week was an unqualified blessing.

The first step towards the achievement was made by the National Federation of Building Trades Operatives which sent round a circular asking all affiliated organisations if they were in favour of the claim being made. This was purely a rhetorical question intended to assemble a show of strength for the benefit of the employers. When every union had given the expected affirmation the General Secretary of the Federation, Bill Bradshaw, then tabled the demand to the Employers' Federation. From the employers the Federation received a blunt refusal.

The next move was reference of the contested claim to the National Board of Conciliation. And here again it was simply another meeting of much the same employers and unions—resulting in anticipated stalemate. In fact at this particular meeting in July 1919, four different proposals on hours were debated and on each one " the voting resulted in a tie."

Finally the meeting was adjourned to September the employers stating: " that the operatives, having taken a vote of their members, appear to be unable to accept anything less than the demand indicated by the vote; but the employers had not so far tested the feeling of their members in that way, and it was therefore suggested that the further consideration of this matter be deferred to enable that to be done."

At the resumed meeting of the Board the employers opened by announcing that their vote had shown their colleagues as solidly against shorter hours as the operatives were in favour. Logically the issue now looked as if it could only be settled by a trial of strength. But surprisingly the meeting continued to debate the matter; again seemingly reached deadlock, and then once more continued the discussion.

Finally, after some hours of acrimony apparently leading nowhere, the operatives made a stand by moving the motion: " That the 44 hour week come into operation as from the 1st May, 1920."

A delaying amendment by the employers was lost and then, when the original motion was put before the meeting, the union representatives were both astonished and delighted when two employers crossed their votes to support them. The 44 hour week had been won—the first major achievement ever to have been gained without a long struggle on the sites.

And when the shorter week came into operation it was alongside the creation of the National Wages and Conditions Council. It was this Council which was to set down the pattern for the industry in its joint consultative machinery. True there were two other organisations in existence then which might have been expected to exercise an influence on the industry and, to some extent, cut across the Council's work.

Malcolm Sparkes's scheme for a Grand Parliament of masters and men had been accepted and commenced its work in 1918. But it was too much like Parliament to adequately give specific guidance to a complex industry. The over-full Council of 132 members also seemed to take some very fine decisions in principle which were allowed to remain at that stage.

The other body in the industry was the National Conciliation Board which, set up in 1908, followed the creation of local conciliation boards four years earlier. The Board did exercise a considerable influence on wages and conditions, with its greatest award undoubtedly being the 44 hour week. But generally it worked too slowly to give satisfaction and could only effect changes in a piecemeal fashion.

With the creation of the National Wages and Conditions Council both the Builders Parliament and the Conciliation Boards gradually became obsolete.

Under the Wages and Conditions Council, for the first time, wages were to be decided on a national basis. Operatives were to be paid according to the particular graded area in which they worked. There were 17 grades in all with Grade 'A', the 'Standard Rate', being 2s. 4d. per hour.

To try and eliminate wage disputes the Council also evolved a scheme which provided for the automatic adjustment of wages, linked to the cost-of-living index. This became known as the Sliding Scale Agreement.

With its adoption, together with the other advances they had made, the operatives thought that a new future lay before them. Some, in fact, believed their achievements might improve conditions so much that the trade union movement would be weakened. The general concern on this matter was apparently so great that George Hicks hastened to reassure A.U.B.T.W. stalwarts with a special message.

"Whilst it may be argued that our organisations are kept alive by the uncertainty of wages," he wrote, "and by the adoption of a sliding scale the incentive is weakened, we want to state that in maintaining the 44-hour week, in resisting wholesale dilution, in fighting piecework and payment by results, and in the complete stamping out of systematic overtime, etc., there is plenty of scope for the energies of our members."

It was the expression of a mood peculiar to the operatives for the first time in the history of their unions; that such gains had been made the basis of their existence—discontent by workers over wages and conditions—might be swept away. They genuinely thought they were poised on the verge of a great future. Within months, however, they were to learn that they had been tottering on the edge of an economic abyss.

The impetus of the war was gone. Unemployment began to rise as quickly as the cost-of-living index went down. Only a few months after his 'reassurance' to members that all their troubles were not yet over, George Hicks sent out what he called "the most unpleasant circular letter it has been my duty to communicate to branches."

At a meeting of the Wages and Conditions Council, he informed them the unions had been forced to submit to a reduction of 2d. per hour as from the 16th May, 1921. And with it was a threat of even worse to come. It had been impossible, in view of the general economic collapse, to prevent this reduction, George Hicks told his members. Only after long argument had they been able to prevent a reduction of 3d. per hour and the loss of their cherished 44-hour week. " All things considered, distasteful as it was, and is, we felt by accepting we were making the best of a bad job."

This first shock was merely the beginning. The bitter rearguard struggles of the building unions, against the attacks of the employers, were now being echoed throughout the entire country as miners and other workers fought to prevent poverty and degradation being inflicted upon them as their ' reward ' for winning the war. But they were almost powerless to resist the onslaught of the employers who were now taking retribution for the concessions wrung from them in better times.

In the building industry the continuing fall in wages was an accurate barometer of the grim economic climate. Less than three months after the cut of 2d. per hour, wages went down by another 1d. on the 1st August. A month later the employers had taken another ½d. The wage rate was finally so eroded that, by the 1st June, 1922, it had fallen by a total of 8d. from the original Grade ' A ' rate of 2s. 4d.

A fully qualified building craftsman on the Standard Rate now had a wage of 1s. 8d. per hour; within the space of two years therefore the rate had been slashed by nearly 29 per cent. And never had wages risen so quickly for the men as they now fell in favour of their masters. (It was not for 26 years—January 1946—that the standard rate of wages again reached and passed the 2s. 4d. level of 1920.)

Yet there was no question of the trade union negotiators complacently accepting these reductions. At every stage they had bitterly resisted the employers. But they were becoming aware that, with the slump making the employers ruthlessly confident of their supremacy in negotiations, the only thing that would restrain their attacks was an all-out battle. This course of action soon appeared inevitable when the employers, in January of 1923, made an incredible demand that wages be further reduced by 20 per cent and that hours be increased to 47 a week. Their case was simply that " economic conditions force us to do this."

At the Wages and Conditions Council where the employers tabled these demands they were rejected out of hand by the unions. Such proposals were in violation of the sliding scale agreement they retorted. Throughout February further acrimonious joint meetings were held until, finally, the employers threw down a demand which they threateningly called " the price of peace." The men must accept a reduction of 2d. per hour on the Grade 'A' rate, with proportionate reductions in other grades, for a period of twelve months. If the unions agreed to this then the 44-hour week could remain in force until March 1924, when it would again be reconsidered.

Reporting the impasse to members of the unions affiliated to the Federation, Dick Coppock, who had recently been appointed secretary on the death of Bill Bradshaw, added that the employers threatened to pursue their original proposals for a 20 per cent cut in wages and an increase in hours if the reduction of 2d. was rejected by the men.

" This statement is not made to overawe you," wrote Coppock, " but to give you a truthful account of the employers' present attitude of mind . . . Your representatives have warned them of reprisals that would come when economic conditions are in the operatives' favour. The employers say in reply 'Well, we shall have to meet that when the time arrives'."

At the end of the N.F.B.T.O. statement was a ballot paper. Members were asked to vote either for the acceptance of the 2d. reduction or that they were against it and "fully prepared to accept the consequences of rejection either by strike or lock-out." When the votes were counted the aggregate of all the unions showed officials the support they could expect if they chose to make a challenge: 42,606 men were prepared to have wages cut by 2d., but 183,558 would rather fight it out with the employers. In the A.U.B.T.W. the majority against the employers' offer was 25,432 to 7,108. The militant spirit that ran right through the Union was also shown in a resolution sent from the administrative staff at head office to the Executive Council.

"This meeting of the staff fraternity of the A.U.B.T.W. wholeheartedly supports the building trade workers in their resistance to the attacks of the employers and decides to impose upon its members a levy for the purpose of financially supporting such resistance . . . The Staff further requests that they may be informed of any other form of assistance they can render to help the victory of the building trade workers."

Now that they were confident of the support of their members the union officials bluntly demanded that wages remained as they were, and that no further reductions take place except in accordance with the constitution of the Council. Again there was deadlock between the two sides. Then the thwarted employers made a decision which was almost equal to throwing over the entire negotiating machinery. They informed all their men that from the 14th April, 1923, they would only employ them at a reduced rate of 2d. per hour and on the basis of a 47 hour week in the summer.

It was, quite bluntly, a lock-out threat to all those who insisted on working for union negotiated conditions. Faced with this prospect of a national conflict the N.F.B.T.O. set up a consultative organisation with the Trades Union Congress General Council and Labour M.P.s. The Federation was assured of support for the vital principle of retaining the shorter working week. Within the A.U.B.T.W. and all the other unions the machinery for administering a national strike was set into motion.

Then, only two days before the deadline the leader of the Labour Party, Ramsay MacDonald, stepped in with a last minute suggestion for a joint meeting between the chief representatives of the employers and the unions. He arranged for George Hicks and Dick Coppock, president and secretary of the Federation, to meet their opposite numbers from the employers in a private room at the House of Commons. After a discussion lasting until late at night the employers' representatives finally consented to withdraw the lock-out notices and submit the dispute to arbitration. On their demands for a longer working week they agreed that, first of all, a ballot vote should be held in the various regions to find the reactions to this proposal.

By the 15th May the arbitrator, Sir Hugh Fraser, had announced his findings—to become generally known in the industry as the Fraser Award. Craftsmen in the higher graded areas were to have their wages cut by 1d. an hour, with the exception of London which was only reduced by ½d. an hour to allow for the fact that the metropolis had always enjoyed a higher wage rate in the past.

The lower graded areas were also only to be cut by ½d. an hour and all wage rates, the unions were promised, were to remain static until January 1924. And, most important, the employers were only to reduce wages in the future in accordance with the cost-of-living sliding scale and not on account of bad trade or excessive unemployment.

" As a product of negotiation the settlement is eminently sound," reported George Hicks to A.U.B.T.W. members. " The only argument that can be lodged against it is that of war at all costs, and no industry is at the present moment and within the limits of cold reason, in a position to wage war without counting the cost. The simple fact is that a lock-out or strike under existing circumstances could have no other result than compromise sooner or later, provoked by impoverished funds and the impetus of want and misery . . . . . compared with the economic position of other industries the building trades have not felt the full brunt of the capitalistic attack and are therefore stronger. This may be nothing much to boast about, but is a plain fact which indicates at least that the rout of the labour force has been partially arrested."

It was true that building operatives were not being degraded so far or so fast as miners and men in other industries. But drawing comparisons was slight consolation to men who had expected the aftermath of the war to be a much better life for themselves and their families. They had found the reverse to be true. Unemployment, with its grim companions poverty and hunger, stalked the streets of every town and city. Men found that, with all the experience and craft concentrated in their hands and brains, they might as well have been born deaf, blind and without any faculties whatsoever. Society apparently had no use for their services.

George Hicks therefore was attacked by branches which objected to his painting a picture showing them as holding a privileged position. They pointedly accused him of supplying ammunition which would be fired at them by the employers in due course. They were not so far wrong in their suspicions for, after only a few weeks, the employers returned to the attack on hours. They insisted that they could no longer sustain a position where building workers were being paid higher wages, and working a shorter week, than any other major industry.

The unions reminded the employers of the agreement that hours should be decided regionally. They had balloted their members to find them all solidly against any alteration to the 44-hour week. The reaction of the employers to this, in spite of vigorous protests from union officials, was to write to the arbitrator, Sir Hugh Fraser, and ask him to intervene. And though the unions continued their protests to Sir Hugh he "observed that the terms of reference had been fulfilled and he had no other option than to hear the case."

In August he gave his second major award for the industry. From the 17th September hours were to be 46½ per week in the summer and 44 the rest of the year.

But, in any town or district where agreement could be jointly obtained, the 44-hour week could be continued.

This award was the signal for a renewal outburst of anger from branches of the A.U.B.T.W. and demands that Union negotiators should resign because they had capitulated to arbitration. A large number of branches also expressed their frustration by extremist proposals for the Union to withdraw from membership of the N.F.B.T.O., and the Wages and Conditions Council. Rather than accept what they called the humiliating arbitration awards they wanted to conduct guerilla warfare on their own.

In other unions much the same spirit was being shown. Nor would it be correct to think that, on this issue, the membership was divorced in sympathy from their leaders. Only an awareness of their economically weak position made union negotiators grit their teeth and accept the conditions thrust on them by the employers. But they were determined on a course of reprisals when the time came, and this proved to be only a few months after the hours' arbitration.

Conditions gradually began to improve throughout the country and the cost-of-living index ended its long slide and started to climb again. On the 1st February, 1924, an increase of ½d. was made in wages under the sliding scale agreement. This was the moment for which the unions had been waiting. With building labour now becoming scarce they decided to challenge the employers at the game they had played in the past—varying the wage rates to suit general economic conditions. On the 29th February they tabled a demand at a special meeting of the Wages and Conditions Council for rates to go up by another 2d. per hour.

Now it was the employers who had to try and exercise a restraining hand. They agreed that a greater volume of building work was now available but claimed that this was due to their policy of forcing down labour costs. Any increase in wages, they claimed, would only lead to a fall of public confidence in the industry. They rounded off their defence by producing statistics to show the allegedly serious effect on costs that an extra 2d. per hour would produce. The ½d. the operatives had received under the sliding scale was all they were prepared to concede.

For three months both sides met and argued over the claim but neither would give way. Then the union negotiators said they would advise their members to accept a 1d. increase if the employers were prepared to give this. The employers countered this compromise with the offer of a ½d. on the wage rates, plus a promise to investigate the possibilities of compensatory payment for time lost through bad weather.

The unions reluctantly agreed to take this offer to a national ballot of their members though they held out little hope that it would be accepted. They were correct in their assumptions. An overwhelming vote instructed them to try and negotiate better terms, failing which the men were prepared to strike. One effect of this vote was to convince the employers that the men were now prepared for industrial war and, though they still refused to budge from their offer of ½d., they now promised to review the sliding scale and effect an improvement in it which "would eventually give an improved status of 1d. per hour."

On this further promise the unions once again balloted their members and this time received a majority in favour of a settlement on these lines. The aggregate result was 69,080 in favour with 41,547 against. But the temper of A.U.B.T.W. members could be judged by the narrower margin in favour of the offer: 9,095 for the settlement and 7,179 against.

For a moment it looked as if a national clash had once again been averted. Then the Employers' Federation attempted to push the bargain a little too hard. Now that the unions had agreed to the tentative terms offered, they said, the settlement could be effected once one or two other matters had been cleared up. These extra conditions turned out to be an insistence that unions stamp out "indiscipline" over working rules, and that a current dispute by Liverpool operatives should be forcibly closed by the Executives. When these demands were angrily refused the employers broke off all negotiations and threatened a national lock-out on the 5th July to " enforce discipline and the observance of agreed working rules."

But this time the employers found their bluff was to be called. The unions had been deadly serious about their strike threat. At meetings on the 24th and 25th June the organisations affiliated to the N.F.B.T.O. unanimously agreed that " having received an ultimatum from the employers we readily accept the challenge." Throughout the country members were instructed that a national strike on the 5th July was to be the answer to the masters' demands. Where employers, or public authorities building houses, conceded the agreed terms of the 16th June settlement, then work could continue. Where these terms were not given the men were to withdraw their labour and they would be given full strike backing.

On the 5th July the masters and the men met in the first, and only, national strike confined to the building industry. It was a struggle which could hardly be explained on the facts of the negotiations that had just taken place. For much greater awards had been conceded by the employers—the original 44-hour week for example —without striking. Now the men were forced out on the streets by the employers apparently because there had been slight breaches of discipline aganst the working rules.

It was George Hicks who put the matter in clearer perspective when he dismissed the employers " prattling " about lack of discipline and the Liverpool dispute as rubbish. " Two reasons for the employers' attitude come to the front on examination," he said. The first was the refusal of many men to work longer than the 44-hour week irrespective of the recent arbitration award and this had " rattled the masters." The second reason, claimed Hicks, was that the employers were lining up with their capitalist colleagues to kill the new Labour Government. Although very much in a minority in the House the Labour Party, in January 1924, had taken office with

MacDonald as the Premier and the qualified support of the Liberal Party.

Poised on this political razor's edge the Labour Government nevertheless tried to push through measures which would benefit the working-class. One of these was a trail-blazing Housing Bill by John Wheatley. To this there had been embittered Tory opposition and George Hicks now suggested that the employers' declaration of a national lock-out " was admirably calculated to prejudice the Housing Bill, and our trouble has been used by the opponents of Wheatley's measure."

Because of the effect that the strike would have on housing production the Minister of Labour appointed a Court of Inquiry which made a preliminary examination into the causes of the struggle. When the Court had reported, negotiators for the two sides met again and finally thrashed out an agreement which was accepted by the joint executives of the unions affiliated to the Federation by 48 to 25 votes.

The agreement, in essence, was similar to the one from which the employers had withdrawn in June. It gave an increase of ½d. per hour on the wage rates, together with promises of investigation into lost time. It also specified that London and Liverpool should be given further consideration as " special areas." But, to the disgust of A.U.B.T.W. members, it re-emphasised that summer working hours were to be 46½ " other than in those localities that had agreed to vary the hours by mutual consent."

For this settlement the members had been out on strike nearly seven weeks. The cash " price " for the A.U.B.T.W. alone was £110,000 in strike pay. It seemed as if the bargain had certainly not been in favour of the unions and the fury of members was shown in the flood of resolutions, from branches in every division, insisting that the A.U.B.T.W. withdraw from the Federation and from the National Wages and Conditions Council. It was time, they urged, for all-out warfare—especially on the issue of guaranteed time—and affiliation to these two organisations would only restrict their freedom of action.

On Monday, the 13th October, 1924, the Executive Council of the Union met to hear the results of the ballots on the proposals for withdrawing from these two bodies. The scrutineers reported that the vote in favour of leaving the Wages and Conditions Council was 10,953 to 1,160. By only a slightly smaller majority the members had also endorsed withdrawal from the N.F.B.T.O.: 10,822 to 1,333 against.

Acting on these votes the Executive Council of the A.U.B.T.W. now formally tendered notice of secession to both organisations. And the union which had constantly preached closer unity between all of the organisations in the building industry now entered on a self-imposed four years' exile from its comrades within the Federation.

CHAPTER 22

THE TRUTH ABOUT CHURCHILL

WITHDRAWAL from the Federation was obviously tantamount to a rejection of the need for the other unions affiliated to it. Because of this the decision of the A.U.B.T.W. was met with unconcealed hostility from leaders of the other unions. It certainly was a difficult decision to understand when pictured against the background of the generally progressive steps being taken by the organisation. For almost immediately after 1921, without any question of passively going through a period of consolidation, the A.U.B.T.W. had commenced probing other societies about the prospects for a wider amalgamation. Even in the very year that it broke its bonds with the Federation the Union had held amalgamation talks with the Plasterers, the Scottish Masons, the Street Masons and Paviors, and the Woodworkers.

Nor had the progressive outlook been confined in this direction. Firmly believing that " emancipation can only come through education " the Union had become the very first in Britain to supply its members with an educational scheme through the National Council of Labour Colleges. For an annual *per capita* subscription, paid by the Head Office, members of the Union were able to have free correspondence courses on a number of subjects provided by the N.C.L.C.

The decision on the educational scheme had been taken at a gathering which was itself an indication of forward thinking—the first annual conference of the Union, which was held in 1922 at the Central Y.M.C.A. in Tottenham Court Road, London. By holding such conferences, to which came delegates from each district, the Executive thought it would be a constructive step towards binding the differing sections of the A.U.B.T.W. closely together.

Now with secession from the Federation the Union had taken a decision which was, at least to one member of it, a source of deep hurt. Dick Coppock had taken over the secretaryship of the N.F.B.T.O. at almost the worst time in its history: those first few years were the only ones in which there was the threat—and actuality—of national conflict. As an ex-organiser of the old London Bricklayers he had shown the ability for which he had been chosen to lead the Federation. Yet no one knew better than he that it would be a difficult task to soundly establish the organisation in face of the doubts and antagonisms being expressed by some of the unions in the industry. He had therefore looked in the direction of the A.U.B.T.W. —his own society—for moral and tangible support. And indeed the A.U.B.T.W. had been strongly in favour of the Federation in its first few years and George Hicks had been elected as president of the N.F.B.T.O.

Now Dick Coppock was left isolated and in the invidious position of trying to get other societies to accept policies which his own had completely rejected. Even worse for him was the necessity, in the interests of the Federation's future, that he must forthrightly condemn the A.U.B.T.W. for its action.

" There is nothing to be ashamed about in our Federation," he rebuked, " nay, it has become a great power in the trade union world and none of our affiliated members, no matter how advanced their views may be, can show a greater record of industrial activity than this young, vigorous organisation."

The hope of Coppock, and of those in the A.U.B.T.W. itself who had opposed withdrawal, was that the break would be short and without too much rancour. Instead it was to grow very much more serious with the angry exchanges between the A.U.B.T.W. and the other unions reaching a new depth of vindictiveness during the 1926 General Strike.

The builders' strike of 1924 was only one of a series of national industrial struggles by which the workers tried to fight the gradual depressing of their living standards during the early 'Twenties. The engineers and the miners—particularly the miners—had both suffered from the effects of lock-outs in their industries. Now the mine owners were returning to the attack in an effort to force the miner and his family to subsist on starvation wages. When negotiations between the coal owners and the men finally reached complete stalemate it was clear that the industry was heading towards another national stoppage. Aware of their own weakness contrasted with the strong economic position of the masters, the miners turned and appealed to the other unions for support. They emphasised that the attack on them, if successful, would trigger off a full-scale onslaught on conditions by all employers.

At 12 o'clock on the 1st May, 1926, the executives of the unions affiliated to the T.U.C. gathered in the Memorial Hall, Farringdon Street, London to hear a report from the General Council on developments in the coalfields. After the Council had indicated the critical situation which existed, and the appeal by the miners to their fellow trade unionists, the delegates present decided by 3,653,529 to 49,911 votes that on Monday, 3rd May, the miners would have every union in Britain standing by their side in resisting the employers. The General Strike was on.

Among the first to be ordered into the 'front line' with their comrades in the other heavy industries were building workers. Each union group was instructed to carry out the General Council's directive on the withdrawal of labour. It was in the interpretation of this directive that a row broke out between the A.U.B.T.W. and the other unions in the Federation. The General Council had advised that certain classes of work, particularly hospitals and council housing, could be continued.

But, claimed the A.U.B.T.W. Executive, even in these fields there was non-essential work that could be stopped. "As we felt that the fight had to be short and sharp we were concerned more with finding excuses for bringing men out in support of the miners than in finding reasons for keeping them in," they declared. " Under these circumstances our slogan ' if in doubt, all out ' was born."

But the other building unions were not so militant in supporting the strike, complained the A.U.B.T.W., and the row came to a head when the Federation was appointed by the General Council to supervise the strike organisation in the building industry. The A.U.B.T.W. condescended to attend the Federation committee but used it as a battleground rather than a field for co-operation. After the first meeting they wrote a letter to the T.U.C. accusing the other unions in the Federation of being " mainly concerned with finding excuses for keeping men at work."

The General Strike lasted only nine days. It was a unique demonstration of the power that could be exercised by the trade union movement acting on a principle of solidarity which, though not always in evidence, had long been cherished within the working class. But this alone could not guarantee success. There had been very little foresight; very little prior planning of the strike machine. On the other hand there had been a great deal of confusion, and few of the General Council leaders—if any at the outset—had fully appreciated the fundamental nature of the struggle in which they had engaged.

" The trade unions put themselves into a position where defeat was inevitable," wrote Francis Williams, " because they failed to appreciate that the weapon of a national strike could not by its very nature be used in a modern industrial state except as a revolutionary weapon, since it must inevitably call up against it all the forces of the state. They had, however, not thought of using it as a revolutionary weapon, and even if they had they would have had no support for such a course among either the great mass of trade unionists or Labour Party members."*

When the strike came to its abrupt end on the 12th May one of the few things it had achieved was a worsening of

**Fifty Years' March*, page 327.

the relationships between the A.U.B.T.W. and the other unions within the building industry. For George Hicks the aftermath was particularly unpleasant. From frustrated and furious members of his own Union he came under violent attack because, as a member of the T.U.C. General Council, they alleged he was " one of the guilty men who had betrayed the workers by calling off the strike."

Hicks now also realised, as a responsible trade union official, the General Strike had at least shown that the stand of the A.U.B.T.W. outside the Federation was completely untenable. But what he and his Executive still did not clearly appreciate was the necessity, in the interests of all the A.U.B.T.W. itself had fought for, that they must be proved on this occasion to be completely wrong in their attitude.

For if they had been right about withdrawing from the Federation, and able to secure better terms from the employers fighting on their own, their example would undoubtedly have been followed and the Federation would have collapsed. The basis of the national negotiating machinery would, in consequence, have been destroyed and the whole industry plunged back into the individualistic dog-fighting of the past.

It was inevitable that the other unions and the employers, recognising this, did all they could to ensure that the A.U.B.T.W. made no progress. And their resolve on this point became even stronger when, in September of 1926, the National Wages and Conditions Council was dissolved and the National Joint Council for the Building Industry took its place. The new joint body was much better in its control of the industry than any that had gone before. It was vitally essential that it should be protected in its formative period and allowed to develop. The stand of the A.U.B.T.W. was looked upon as a danger to the Council, and fought as such by both employers and the trade unionists attached to it.

Now aware of the inevitability of re-affiliating to the Federation, the A.U.B.T.W. made the first move at its

Annual Conference in 1927. After George Waddell, the President, had opened Conference by glumly admitting that the Union had got nowhere with its guaranteed time objective, or the National Charter it had proudly raised as a standard when leaving the Federation, the delegates went on to discuss the motion " that the time has arrived when the Union should re-affiliate with the N.F.B.T.O."

This proposal was supported by over 30 branches and district committees. There was only one motion on the agenda opposing re-affiliation and it came from Paisley Branch. The debate was long and bitter. There were the diehards who were still against federation, and being particularly violent in their denunciation because it was now shown that they needed it! There were also contributions in which delegates, almost in a spirit of self-flagellation, said that the only way to progress for the Union lay through re-affiliation. Of these speeches the one by Sid Stranks, No. 1 Divisional Organiser, was the most effective because it was the most brutally frank.

They had achieved nothing as an isolated unit, he said. The employers had challenged them to fight and they had refused the challenge because they knew, if they were beaten, the other unions would not be sympathetic but satisfied. Of course they had been attacked by other societies but, he said, " I am certain that our withdrawal was a purely sectional and selfish one. The other unions fully appreciated that point and there is the reason why they were bitter towards us."

When the vote was taken the motion for re-affiliation was carried by 43 to 7 and the Executive of the Union then proceeded to put the matter to the members for endorsement. In the national ballot there was a majority of two to one in favour and, at its meeting on the 22nd February, 1928, the Executive Council completed the process when it formally instructed George Hicks to make application for affiliation to the Federation.

It was as a much weaker organisation that the A.U.B.T.W. re-entered the fold. Its financial position, which the members had confidently felt would continually improve after amalgamation, had been severely affected by the strikes of 1924 and 1926. The depression years had also led to a drop in the membership of all British unions and the A.U.B.T.W. had not escaped the downward trend. From the 75,000 members it had started with in 1921 the A.U.B.T.W. had dropped to 60,000 seven years later.

Anxious as the officers were to improve on this position, however, there was one " prospective candidate for membership " who was decisively rejected by the entire Union in 1928. He was Winston S. Churchill, Chancellor of the Exchequer in the Tory Government of the day.

When feeling rather over-burdened by the cares of the Chancellory, Churchill used to slip down to his estate at Chartwell and relax by laying a few bricks. It was while he was at this favourite pastime, dressed in soft hat and with a cigar clenched between his teeth, that Jimmy Lane, the No. 2 Divisional Organiser of the A.U.B.T.W., made his round of the estate checking on the cards of the bricklayers. He spoke to Churchill and jocularly suggested that if he wanted to continue his career as a bricklayer he ought to have a union card.

Churchill responded by sending Lane a cheque for 5s. to cover his entrance fee—and subsequently leaked the story to the Press. By this time Lane had carried out his part of the episode by sending Churchill a union card with his name entered on it and what appeared to be George Hicks' signature in the appropriate place. A few days later the members of the A.U.B.T.W. opened their morning papers to find that they had acquired a distinguished new ' brother '. There was an immediate uproar of protest. Resolutions from districts and branches poured into head office vilifying Hicks and Lane for their part in the " humiliation of the Union."

From these protests it seemed clear that the Executive of the A.U.B.T.W. had two choices before it. The Union could consist of one member, Mr. Churchill, with 60,000 others leaving in a body. Or it could have 60,000 members minus one Chancellor of the Exchequer.

To the Executive Hicks denied having made Churchill a member, and Lane's attitude to the whole affair could best be judged from the fact that he had never sent Churchill's 5s. cheque to head office. Instead he had framed it and hung it up in his home.

When the Executive considered all these points at its meeting on the 20th October, they decided that there had been no serious attempt to complete an application for Churchill; that Jimmy Lane had not " wilfully violated the rules of the organisation in connection with this matter" and that " Mr. Winston Churchill is not eligible for membership of this Union."

And from all of this the press generally concluded that bricklayers, taken as a whole, had very little sense of humour. This judgement, however, was extremely superficial and was made without sufficient appreciation of immediate past history. For Churchill, as Tory Chancellor, had been directly responsible for the fiscal policies which had plunged the country into economic despair and had led directly towards the General Strike. And during that conflict Churchill had proved himself the arch strikebreaker. No other member of the Tory cabinet had been so violent in their denunciation of the men. Churchill had also vigorously prosecuted a policy of using all possible force, resulting in some broken heads and limbs for the workers, to crush the strike. Even worse, he had quite clearly shown that he relished the opportunity of waging war on the unions.

In the after-strike reprisals he had been a leading protagonist in pushing through Parliament the 1927 Trades Disputes and Trades Unions Act. This laid down the doctrine that a general strike was illegal and also any others aimed at coercing the Government, or which involved hardships for the community. On the right of trade unionists to picket a 'black' job the Act put the clock back nearly eighty years. To undermine the political effectiveness of the trade union movement, it also specified that money for political purposes could only be collected from members if they positively agreed to this by " contracting in " to political levies.

The years of 1926 and 1927, therefore, had brought defeat and punitive measures upon the trade union movement. Throughout this entire period Churchill had played a leading and revengeful role. The members of the A.U.B.T.W. therefore—or of any other union—would rather have welcomed the devil to membership than call Winston Churchill ' brother '.

Throughout 1928 and into 1929 the country's economic position worsened. The building industry, which had up till then been comparatively better off than some, faced mounting unemployment as the Tories cut back on housing expenditure. There were no exceptions now, no favoured industries, all sections of the working class found themselves faced with the stark consequences of recession. Isolated industrial action, they were beginning to see, could bring no real solution to their problems. For many of the members within the trade union movement their struggles became a grim educational course in which they learned one political lesson: only Labour offered them any hope for the future.

In 1929 they were able to put this lesson into effect when the Tories declared a general election. The trade union movement was out to obtain some revenge for the indignities it had so recently suffered. Restricted as they were by the 1927 Act they still fought a fierce campaign by the side of the Labour Party. When the results were declared Labour was once again the major party in Parliament. With 287 seats out of a total of 615, however, it still lacked an overall majority.

The major appeal of the Party during the election had been on three points over which the working class and the trade union movement had felt a deep grievance. The Party had pledged that if returned to power it would solve the growing unemployment, would repeal the Trade Disputes Act, and would abolish that degrading section of the Insurance Act which allowed petty-minded bureacrats to victimise unemployed persons on the pretext that they were " not genuinely seeking work."

It was obvious that to implement such a programme the Labour Party required at least a strong majority in

Parliament. Instead Ramsay MacDonald once more had to take office with a minority government which ultimately failed to realise most of its major objectives. And though the character of MacDonald and some of his colleagues was a contributory factor to Labour's weakness, the Government never looked capable of living up to its promises once the financial crisis became acute.

In the General Election of 1931 which was forced upon them, the Labour benches were decimated. From 287 the Parliamentary Party had shrunk to 46 M.P.s. One of those who did manage to hold his seat was George Hicks, who had entered the House as victor of a by-election at East Woolwich only a few months before the general election.

With 471 seats and the help of renegades MacDonald, Snowden and Thomas, the Tories were, unlike Labour, able to enforce legislation they thought necessary to control the economic situation. And control for them meant meeting depression with measures calculated to deepen it. This in turn implied an increase in the sufferings of the working class.

In the building industry the lack of capital investment brought operations almost to a halt. Men could go on the tramp for months without even the slightest prospect of a job. By January 1933 unemployment had reached a fantastic level. Out of an estimated total of 103,000 bricklayers and masons in the industry over 40,000, about 38 per cent, were without work.

The misery that lay behind these cold statistics was revealed in a huge demonstration of the unemployed on the 5th February of that slump year. 300,000 workers, from all sections of the trade union, co-operative and Labour movement, were gathered to march from the Embankment and other places to a huge rally in Hyde Park. It was the greatest show of strength by the working class for over a generation. Over the heads of the vast crowds were brilliant splashes of colour as trade union and Labour banners fluttered in the breeze. Among them was the banner of the old Operative Stonemasons' Society.

It held a special place in the hearts of those who regularly took part in the demonstrations organised by the movement. Nearly a century old the Masons' banner had been in the van of the battles over payment by the hour in Richard Harnott's day. In 1866 it had been a rallying standard for the crowds which tore down the railings at Hyde Park when Walpole's government had tried to prevent the right of free speech and free assembly. Throughout the national strikes, and the great political demonstrations, the appearance of the banner was the signal for cheering as if a beloved veteran had returned to do battle.

The 5th February was a wintry, blustery day. As the procession marched away from the Embankment the wind increased. Banners cracked and bellied in the sudden gusts: some reached breaking point and ripped in two. The Masons' banner was one of these. The standard bearers continued marching, however, until, by the time the procession had reached Hyde Park only a mass of flayed ribbons remained. A hundred years of history, and one of the last tangible links with the old Masons' Society, had gone.

CHAPTER 23

THE FIGHT AGAINST FASCISM

1933 was the worst year of the Depression. As unemployment increased, wages fell. On the 1st February they touched their lowest point with craftsmen in the Grade ' A ' areas sinking to 1s. 5½d. per hour. In the lowest graded district the rate was 1s. 1d. with labourers being paid, when they could get work, 9¾d. per hour.

Wages of A.U.B.T.W. full-time officials had also been cut—to show that officers were prepared to suffer with their members—and the Union's total membership had fallen to just over 50,000.

Speaking to the 1934 Conference of the Union the newly elected full-time president, Luke Fawcett, said that the unemployment position had begun to show a slight improvement but the terrible winters of 1931/32 and 1932/33 " have cost the Union at least £100,000. What it has cost our members, in privation and worry, it is impossible to tell."

The worst of that suffering, however, was now over. By January of 1935 unemployment had dropped to 25 per cent of the building labour force. Six months later, with the greater amount of work available in summer, the number of bricklayers without jobs had dropped as low as 3 per cent. And once more Union membership began to rise. It was a paradox typical of the movement as a whole: in bad times when workers might logically be expected to have greater need of organised protection the unions nevertheless lost members. With better conditions they came back. (It may be that in the desperate struggle to exist some were unable to continue paying contributions. Others perhaps felt they could not afford to carry the principles and discipline that trade union membership implied.)

The new upsurge of confidence in the future was revealed in the 1935 opening of the A.U.B.T.W.'s new office, "The Builders," at Clapham. For it was specially designed to allow for an expansion in membership and for the operation of a new system of accounts centralisation. Individual branch accounting, said the Executive, had not been completely effective and the organisation had lost a great deal of money through this. The loss in fact was put very high by George Hicks. In a speech to the Annual Conference about the new offices he said: "I think I can say, off hand, that this building has not cost the Union anything at all. The money saved by central administration and by judicious investment of funds has bought us our new offices and saved thousands of pounds in addition."

The expansionist outlook of the A.U.B.T.W. was being echoed in other unions. Work opportunities were definitely on the increase and men, some of whom had been idle for years, now found that their skills were in demand. The one grim shadow which clouded this more prosperous scene was the knowledge that, in part, the new economic stimulus was due to the grave international situation.

In Italy the bombastic, strutting Mussolini had established his fascist dictatorship. In the invasion of Abyssinia his fighting divisions had overcome the resistance of spear-armed tribesmen with bombing, gunfire and by drenching their women and children with mustard gas. The League of Nations had shown just how futile it was in face of this savage banditry and was thereby paving the way for its own extinction.

In Germany an even greater fascist menace was rising, led by the megolomaniac Adolf Hitler. And some of the early warnings of this danger to the peace of the world came through the international organisation of the building unions. Austrian and German trade unionists, co-operators and socialists were the first to suffer at the hands of their own people. In May 1936 members of the A.U.B.T.W. were told of an Austrian comrade, Rudolf Holowatji, who was sentenced to ten years' imprisonment for carrying on "clandestine" trade union activities after his union, the Austrian Woodworkers, had been suppressed by the fascists. "Confessions" against him had been obtained through the brutality that was to become the hallmark of the Gestapo.

Then there was Spain. Here the rebel Franco, with the help of Hitler and Mussolini, was waging a long and brutal civil war against the official Spanish Government because it represented a democracy which threatened the power of the capitalists and fascists in the country. Into this conflict members of the British trade union and Labour movement were sending money to help the Republican cause. And some of them made a one-way journey to Spain to give their lives fighting beside their Spanish comrades.

Increasingly the journals of the unions and the speeches of their leaders were turning on the Nazi menace spreading throughout Europe. The constant lesson being hammered home was that fascism, aided by benevolently disposed capitalists, among whom were some in Britain, was the direct enemy of the working-class and its aspirations. To meet the threat, it was constantly reiterated, "the movement must unite."

But while the trade union movement effusively supported these sentiments in theory, in practice they failed to reach anything like the unity of their opponents. The story in the building industry during this period was particularly depressing. Amalgamation discussions had taken place throughout the 'Thirties but had led only to disillusionment. After months of intensive effort, culminating in a two-day special amalgamation conference at Chester in October 1930, the unions affiliated to the Federation had agreed to hold a national ballot of their membership.

That year had been the start of the recession in trade. The few years previously had seen great national conflicts between masters and men. If ever the building unions had been graphically shown how much they needed each other it was then. Yet when the national ballot was taken on the Chester proposals at the end of 1931 the principle of amalgamation had been rejected by majorities in six unions. Five had recorded majorities in favour that were too small to be effective and only one had managed to obtain the required majority. It was a chastening experience which dampened the enthusiasm for total amalgamation for many years. Again the unions were thrown back on the much narrower possibilities of cognate trades merging together. But even this prospect looked far from encouraging when the A.U.B.T.W. got nowhere with offers to the Plasterers, and the Street Masons and Paviors.

In fact it had looked as if the unions were more likely to shatter apart when, in 1936, the A.S.W. suddenly gave notice that they were preparing to disaffiliate from the Federation. Speaking to the 1936 Delegate Conference of the A.U.B.T.W., the President, Luke Fawcett, said: "This news is staggering. I still find difficulty in believing it. How is it possible for the A.S.W. to justify its decision? . . . . . A great union like the A.S.W. with its splendid trade union history . . . to leave us at the present moment seems incredible." And although the A.S.W. ultimately withdrew the threat of secession the exercise at least proved that the A.U.B.T.W., which had burned its fingers with disaffiliation, had learned a thorough lesson.

One reason why there were diminishing prospects for amalgamation by 1936 was the much better general position of the unions. Societies were more amenable to mergers if their membership and funds were shaky and they were in need of a financial prop. If there was no direct and urgent need of assistance then the pull of vested interests became very much stronger.

The A.U.B.T.W. itself had begun to increase membership, and finances were better than they had ever been.

The organisation was also turning its attention to drawing the womenfolk of members into more active contact. At the 1936 Conference a Women's Section was set up with Mrs. Richard Coppock as the National President. The objective was that wives and daughters of members should meet in local guilds and carry on general social and supporting activities for the Union. As an ideal it was very desirable, even though it was launched a little dubiously by George Hicks in a pamphlet in which he claimed that " as regards many women of the working class, very little progress has been made on the Cave Period." He claimed that the guilds would " Abolish this Semi-Troglodyte Existence."

During this period the Union returned once more to cognate trades amalgamation as a possible source of increasing strength. In particular another attempt was made to agree terms with the Building and Monumental Workers' Association of Scotland (B.M.W.A.). Throughout 1936 and 1937 discussions were held leading towards the preparation of a ballot paper asking members for their approval for the merger. When the vote was taken, however, the Scottish Union's members had carried the principle by a bare majority in a total vote that was much too small to make the decision effective. David Black, general secretary of the B.M.W.A., promptly conveyed this decision to the A.U.B.T.W. and George Hicks and his Executive became suspicious that the leaders of the Scottish organisation were not particularly regretful about the result.

They therefore invited them to a joint meeting in London on the 27th October, 1938 at which they were bluntly castigated by George Hicks for having " no real desire or earnestness " on amalgamation. Since 1921, he said, his Union had tried to come to terms with them. Although the A.U.B.T.W. had the right to organise bricklayers throughout Scotland they had soft-pedalled any opposition to the B.M.W.A. in the hope that this would open the way to greater harmony and amalgamation. Now that it was clear they were giving all, and getting nothing, their officers were going to be instructed that as "the A.U.B.T.W. was the recognised trade union in Great Britain and Ireland for the organisation of bricklayers, it must insist upon its right to organise all persons so employed."

This also meant that, although the A.U.B.T.W. had been tolerant of mason members of the B.M.W.A. doing brickwork in the past, they would no longer be allowed to do this without a fight on the job. As a parting shot to the apparently unrepentant Scotsmen the Executive Council declared that, on the matter of amalgamation, "further approaches in this direction should emanate from the B.W.M.A." The possibility of further amalgamation developments, however, looked a little remote in view of the increasing preparations that were taking place for the Second World War.

It was becoming quite clear that Hitler was not to be satisfied with anything less than domination of Europe. No matter how Britain tried to follow the path of appeasement, in the long run the choice would be between submission or war. And when Hitler invaded Poland on 1st September, 1939, the Government had to recognise that even that choice no longer existed. Two days later Britain was at war with Germany.

It was a war in which the trade union movement was much more intensely involved compared with the 1914/18 conflict. Then, only occasional news items had appeared in journals and the war itself had seemed very much more remote. But the unions had already been campaigning for some years against Nazi Germany and, with the open declaration of war, their journals now became filled with articles urging their members to give all they had in the fight against Fascism. When Labour joined the Coalition Government set up under Churchill, George Hicks wrote:—

"The presence of Labour men in the Government, is evidence that the War will be kept to its liberating purpose . . . this is not the time to stand on ceremony or to tacitly follow the old traditions and formalisms . . . building workers, especially, need now to throw themselves, heart and soul, into the national effort."

Underlying this statement was a warning to members that some of their most cherished traditions would have to be judged as less important than the need to wage all-out war. Building workers soon found what this would mean with the introduction of the " Uniformity Agreement " in June 1940. This agreement was an attempt to solve the very real problems caused (and still being caused) by having two differing sets of national conditions covering building workers: the working rules of the National Joint Council for the Building Industry and the ones drawn up by the Civil Engineering Conciliation Board. Very often a struggle took place on the sites in order to determine what set of conditions should be applied. This was a luxury that could not be tolerated for priority building during the war. The Uniformity Agreement, therefore, provided for a general set of working conditions on all priority jobs specified as such by the Ministry of Labour and accepted by a joint board responsible for applying the agreement.

When it was reported that these conditions had been accepted by the Federation, and ratified by Fawcett and Hicks for the A.U.B.T.W., Camberwell (1) branch demanded that they be censured for their actions. And among eight other branch objections to the new agreement was one from Willesden urging that the Union, if necessary, withdraw all labour in order to have it rejected.

To all these protests the Executive were contemptuously indifferent. For, accepting that there might be disadvantages in the agreement, they nevertheless recognised that it gave official endorsement to two of the fundamental principles for which the Union had been fighting for years. The first and most vital was compensatory payment for 'broken time.' In fact this had been one of the sore points which had led to the Union leaving the Federation in 1924. It thought then that it could achieve this objective much quicker by fighting alone. In the years that followed, the A.U.B.T.W. had taken a leading part in framing policies on broken time payments and in holding campaign meetings to rally building workers behind the claim as a first priority.

Just before the war the combined efforts of the federated unions had led to an investigation by the Ministry of Labour into proposals for a " Wet Time Insurance Scheme " which had been formulated by the Federation. This scheme was based on men making joint contributions together with the employers. With the outbreak of hostilities the A.U.B.T.W. had despondently accepted that the scheme had little chance of being implemented. Now they had been presented with the Uniformity Agreement which provided compensatory payment for broken time up to 30 hours per week—and on a non-contributory basis. No wonder the Executive were prepared to approve the agreement and promise members that they were determined to try and get this section of it applied universally throughout the industry.

The other major reason why the A.U.B.T.W. turned a kindly eye on the new proposals for uniformity was that their very introduction underlined a principle which they had been proclaiming for some years—that the existence of two national agreements for the construction industry was bound to lead to problems of organisation and production. The stresses of war had now amply underlined that point.

Signing this agreement was one of the last official acts George Hicks was to perform for the Union. On the 15th November, 1940 he summoned a special meeting of the Executive and told them that he had recently had an interview with the Prime Minister. Churchill, he said, had invited him to become Parliamentary Secretary to the newly-established Ministry of Works and Buildings. Hicks, however, wanted the approval of the Council before accepting the post. Not unnaturally he also wanted to keep his job open in the Union until he saw how far he was committed to his Parliamentary career.

After a long discussion it was resolved that " This Council agrees to the General Secretary accepting the invitation of the Prime Minister to act as Parliamentary

Secretary of the Ministry and for this purpose grants him the necessary leave of absence, without payment of his trade union salary, on the understanding that he remains in close touch for consultative purposes."

Luke Fawcett was appointed to take over as acting general secretary until Hicks was able to resume full-time office. But this position was clearly impossible. Obviously Fawcett would not be amicably disposed to stand aside and let George Hicks resume as general secretary after he had carried the burden of office for any appreciable length of time. Nor were the members prepared to allow such a position to arise. When the Executive met some months later it had half-a-dozen letters before it demanding the resignation of George Hicks and an election to appoint his successor. All of them pointed out that Rule 18, Clause 9 of the Union had been broken. Under this rule the maximum period of leave of absence that could be allowed George Hicks—before proceeding to fill his position—was three months.

The Executive might have originally turned a blind eye to the rule but now it had been formally brought to their notice there was no alternative but to take action. George Hicks was asked to meet them and he stated that he quite realised the Council " had no option but to implement the rule in reference to the office of general secretary," and formally tendered his resignation. The Council expressed deep regret that the position had arisen and said it was their unanimous wish that his services be retained as " first Honorary President of the Union and in a consultative capacity, and also as honorary Political Secretary." For his work as a consultant he was to be paid £160 a year.

In the election for his successor, Luke Fawcett easily beat fourteen other candidates. With 13,336 votes his nearest opponent was Harry Adams with 3,284. But Harry Adams—a leader of the 1914 London lockout and now No. 1 Divisional Organiser of the Union—was in any case destined for national office. In the subsequent election to fill the office of president, vacated by Luke Fawcett, he beat J. Mounteny by 5,000 votes.

Fawcett and Adams were in fact the first two national officers of a Union which was effectively countrywide in its organisation of bricklayers. For, in 1942, a series of negotiations at last ended in merger between the Building and Monumental Workers of Scotland and the A.U.B.T.W.

After the heated meeting between the two executives, when original negotiations had broken down, the Scottish Executive had gone back and started an intensive propaganda campaign culminating in a decision by their members for amalgamation.

Throughout 1941 the final touches were put to the agreement under which the B.M.W.A. transferred its obligations to the A.U.B.T.W. Finally, on the 1st January, 1942, the B.M.W.A. entered the A.U.B.T.W., bringing with it a contribution of 5,000 members and a sum of nearly £18,000.

CHAPTER 24

A NEW EMINENCE

WITH the Second World War the trade union movement achieved a social status which, only a short time earlier, would have been almost inconceivable. In their early years the unions had been hounded as outright enemies of the State. At no time had they been conceded more than a grudging acceptance from a capitalist system which remained ready to justify legislative penalties against them. Now, with the loyalty they could command from their members, they were needed to wage total war. Trade unionists were members of the Government and the movement itself was helping to decide the course of national policies.

The building unions, particularly, found they had a new eminence. In the 1914/18 war the British Isles had been comparatively untouched, in a physical sense, by the clash in Europe. The aeroplane had been in an embryonic stage of development and the country had remained secure from threats of invasion. But during the Second World War, especially after Dunkirk, Great Britain almost ceased to be a country. It became an aircraft carrier launching offensives against the enemy: a huge pillbox standing protectively against the nightly air-raids—ready to resist invasion from across the English Channel. And the transformation was achieved with bricks, mortar, concrete and steel. Aerodromes were laid down and coastal defences and air-raid shelters built by men in the building industry. After the nightly destruction by Hitler's bombers they were feverishly working round the clock, patching, repairing, ready for further onslaught.

Never had the industry given greater service to the nation. From the men too there were sacrifices of time-honoured traditions to help the war effort. Working rules were often conveniently forgotten when emergencies arose; the ban on overtime had been relaxed and a system of payment by results—a practice vehemently resisted in normal times—had even been accepted for priority work.

But if the men made sacrifices it could justifiably be claimed they were being balanced by the progressive agreements demanded by their union leaders as the price of all-out effort. Judged by any other similar period the World War years saw a great advance in the fringe benefits secured. Wages were also steadily, if not spectacularly, rising. Undoubtedly one of the greatest gains was the agreement, signed on the 28th October, 1942, providing building workers with an annual paid holiday. For years this had seemed an insurmountable problem. No employer would give a man a paid holiday unless he had been with the firm for some considerable time. Yet the very nature of building operations implied a casual, nomadic form of employment for the men. Under these circumstances the great majority of building workers looked as if they would never have the benefit of paid holidays. The agreement of 1942, jointly reached between the building employers, the civil engineering employers and the unions, was a major advance for the entire industry because it was able to solve this problem. Each operative was to carry a card on which, for every week's employment, he would have a holiday credit stamp to the value of 1s. 6d. affixed by his employer. Even if he moved around from job to job during any year his various employers would give him the stamp credits due. These they purchased from the head office of the Holiday Scheme, and the sum of money that accrued from stamp sales was then used to pay operatives the total value on their cards when their holiday period became due.

The agreement of 1942 provided for the payment of holiday credits to start on the 1st February, 1943, and the first holiday period to take place between April 1st and 31st October, 1943.

The year 1943 also saw the inauguration of a National Apprenticeship Scheme on the 21st January. This scheme laid down the conditions of entry for young persons into the industry and dealt with the training they should receive. It was a step which the unions had been urging for some years and was now warmly welcomed by them. The warmth of the welcome, however, was considerably diminished because the National Apprenticeship Scheme was part of an all-inclusive offer that was being made to the unions. The unpalatable part of the deal was the Government's insistence that a system of adult training was required in order to meet post-war building needs.

By 1943 the prospects of victory and peace were strong enough for the country to be turning its attention to post-war requirements. For general rebuilding purposes, and the proposed new deal the people were to get on housing, the Government had estimated that 1,250,000 men were required in the building industry. But there had only been around one million operatives at the outbreak of hostilities. There had been almost no recruitment during the four years the war had already run, men had retired, died, or been called away to the Forces. It was calculated by Luke Fawcett that they could only count on a total labour force of 750,000 men after the War.

The National Apprenticeship Scheme, therefore, was seen as one method of stepping up traditional recruitment to the industry. This, however, would not produce the sharp build-up in the labour force that was required. The unions, insisted the Government, would have to accept the necessity for a training scheme aimed at pushing 200,000 men through a six months' training course to fit them for the building industry.

To this proposal for dilution they knew there would be the bitter hostility with which the men had fought such schemes in the past. "We can have serious unemployment for ten years or more," Luke Fawcett had said on one occasion, "and no one gives a damn for the men. But give us a few months in which labour seems unable to meet the demand and everybody wants to flood us with dilutees."

In addition to sweetening the bitter pill of dilution with an apprenticeship scheme, therefore, the Government assured the unions that it also favoured the adoption of a guaranteed week. This did not prevent a large number of branches in the A.U.B.T.W. attacking Luke Fawcett and Harry Adams for " accepting a special training scheme for adults " though, in fact, the building unions had still not agreed to the proposals.

The vital debate on dilution came at the 1944 Conference of the Union. There was a large number of motions on the agenda and the theme of many of them was that there should be no deal on adult training. The proper course of action to meet post-war needs, they urged, was to give priority demobilisation to skilled building workers in the Forces. The first motion to be debated was one from Leicester, and supported by five other branches, tacitly accepting the adult training scheme but demanding that unions be given greater control over it.

One of the emotional yet reasoned speeches that helped to sway conference was that by Harry Weaver, the No. 1 Divisional Secretary. Housing output had to be stepped up, he said, and therefore they could not avoid the necessity for the building labour force to be greatly increased. " If then we have to accept these workers into our industry," he cried, " then for goodness' sake let us welcome them with open arms and a generous spirit. Do not develop the position where we will have old sores going down through the years because we treated these men as pariahs . . . if they come to assist us to really build a better and brighter Britain, we should accept them with generosity and show them the spirit of trade union brotherhood."

When the vote was taken the Leicester motion was carried, and all the others accordingly fell. The A.U.B.T.W. was now committed to a qualified acceptance of dilution. This qualification was that the new apprenticeship scheme, with its local committee structure, be allowed to participate in the administration of adult special training. In this way the unions could ensure that no one unofficially " gained entry by the back door to the industry," and that adult training was not allowed to sap recruitment through the normal apprenticeship channels.

There was more than one form of dilution against which the A.U.B.T.W. felt it had to fight. A lowering of craft standards was one thing; a reduction of actual building standards was another—especially if it concerned housing. And there was no doubt in that year or two before the war ended, although there might be general political agreement on the need to provide a greater number of homes, there was a wide cleavage between the Labour Movement and the Tories over what constituted a reasonable house for the working class. In the fight for decent housing standards for the people the A.U.B.T.W. played a leading part.

Its opinion on the matter was made clear in a motion approved by the Executive in 1944. Moved by George Lowthian, the Executive member for the No. 9 Division, it pointedly condemned " the demands that are being made to lower housing standards, and to cheapen and debase, in size and construction, the dwellings in which the working people will have to live."

George Lowthian had been particularly incensed at a statement made by Lord Maugham that bathrooms were a luxury for working-class homes. This prompted the scorching reply from him that:

" The time has passed when the workers could tolerate being stabled as a class apart, in any wretched shelter, at the behest of Governments, or lordly aristocrats, or any other members of the ruling class . . . and we call on the members of our Union, and the building workers generally, to do all in their power not merely to defend the best in existing housing standards but to improve them in every way."

It was obviously a political speech and based on a recognition that, with the approaching end of war, the sinking of political identities was over. A post-war Britain had to be shaped and planned. The Government, of predominantly Tory persuasion, was producing a profusion of white papers calculated to impress the public about the honesty of Tory intentions. The trade unions however were sceptical about plans and promises likely to remain for ever at the white paper stage. Within the building industry they were, in any case, looking for much more than a larger crumb from the cake than they had been given in the past. They wanted, in fact, not a better joint status with the masters in influencing the industry but to take it over completely themselves. Public ownership of the building industry was now a well-established and priority political policy of the A.U.B.T.W.

With the end of hostilities the unions knew there existed the strong possibility of an end to the influential status they held. True there were roseate pictures of their prospective future being painted for them by the Government but they had seen similar promises fade to nothing in the past. Their efforts were therefore being directed to improving the status of their members while they could. At the beginning of 1945 they had another outstanding success with the achievement of an agreement for the introduction of a guaranteed week throughout the whole of the industry. " Here, probably, is our biggest gain. We have, for the first time in history the guaranteed week," said Luke Fawcett.

True there was something similar under the war-time agreement but this could not automatically be retained and consolidated into the National Working Rules for the industry. Now the guarantee of a thirty-two hour week was embodied in two of the most important working rules for the industry—2a and 2b—as from the first pay week after the 1st October, 1945.

There was not universal jubilation, however, over the new rules. Branches protested that the negotiators of the Federation should have refused to accept a guarantee of only thirty-two hours but should have insisted on a full week. Others complained, and with justification, that the rules were so hedged about with qualifications that the employers would find it easy to dodge their obligations. While conceding the validity of these objections the A.U.B.T.W. Executive nevertheless insisted that the major victory lay in obtaining the agreement. They could fight later to ensure its enforcement.

By May 1945 the Allies were victorious in Europe although, in the Far East, Japan was to carry on the war for another year. Labour decided it was now time that their emergency coalition with the Tories should end and, in July, a general election was held. It was fought in an atmosphere of amazing bitterness considering the co-operation and political truce there had been between the Parties for nearly six years. From Churchill there were attacks on the Labour Party which had hardly ever been equalled in venom or slanderous intent. Churchill claimed that his erstwhile Labour colleagues—who had held some of the toughest ministries and given him his most stable support—now possessed all the worst features of the Nazis they had just been fighting. Vote Labour he told the people and you will place yourself under the rule of the Gestapo.

But Churchill was only a pathetic, political Canute. His ranting made no impression on the huge wave of support that swept towards Labour. As the election results were broadcast over the radio, and one after another Tory seats fell to Labour victors, the jubilant workers in the trade union and Labour movement knew they had achieved an objective for which they and their forerunners had fought so long. Britain now had a workers' Government—and with the power required to carry out its policies.

To the building unions it looked, at last, as if they could make much faster progress in improving industrial conditions and in achieving their ultimate goal of public ownership. This confident mood might, in retrospect, seem naive in view of the tremendous job that had to be done to revive Britain's economic machine. But it was certainly maintained by the completely unique experience of the unions when they met the employers later in 1945 and demanded an increase of 4d. per hour on wage rates. It was, up to then, the largest single sum put forward by the operatives in a claim to the National Joint Council. And the employers created their own bit of history by agreeing that, as from January 1946, they would grant every single penny of it!.

1946 looked, in fact, as if it might well become a memorable year in the A.U.B.T.W.'s history when Luke Fawcett told the Executive Council that he had been asked by the Minister of Works to become chairman of a proposed National Building Corporation. The Council, at its meeting on the 23rd April approved his accepting the position and congratulated the Labour Government on the start it was making to the gradual public ownership of the entire building industry. Their congratulations, however, were more than a little premature.

When the Union held its Annual Conference at Cambridge, only three months later, Luke Fawcett made a halting—and obviously painful to him—speech in which he asked delegates not to press too strongly for information about the Building Corporation.

"I must deal with this question pretty carefully," he began, "and I would ask our friends at the Press table to be generous in their consideration of this matter. Not out of respect to my personal interests but because I must try to avoid giving general embarrassment.

"It is true that the Government is considering establishing a Building Corporation . . . certain overtures have been made to myself and a number of other persons but the Corporation is still in its embryo stages but has not yet been born. I hope nothing I might say might cause the Corporation to be stillborn or stifled at birth."

Although Luke Fawcett was attempting to be discreetly loyal to the Labour Government he was already apprehensively aware that it was almost certain they were going to abandon the scheme—even though the manager of the Corporation, the chairman and board of directors had been appointed. And though he continued to keep his lips sealed after it was quite clear that there was to be no Building Corporation, the information filtered through to the unions in the industry that the scheme had been given its death blow due to the hostility of Aneurin Bevan.

As Minister of Health and Housing, Bevan was determined to live up to the housing promises made by the Labour Party. In the economic realities of the immediate post-war years he felt that his first aim was to get the wholehearted co-operation of the builders in the industry. It was said, in fact, that the Building Corporation had been the sacrifice he felt compelled to make because the emnity from private contractors was such that they might, in revenge, have sabotaged the whole building programme.

At the 1947 Annual Conference of the Labour Party an open challenge to him on this point was made by Luke Fawcett. Fawcett said the President of the Employers' Federation had publically claimed that the employers had forced Labour to kill the Corporation. "That hurts," he told the Conference. Turning to Bevan on the platform he demanded to know if this were true. "If it is," he added, "it means that our Government that we have worked for, helped and struggled to bring into power, can respond to the blandishments of the enemy."

In his reply Bevan denied that he had been influenced by the employers but, in a scathing speech, left no doubt that he had little interest in forming a Building Corporation. "It is not new instruments for building that we need," he retorted, ". . . it would not help to solve the housing problem if, in addition to the 1,700 local authorities and thousands of building contractors, we had another Corporation."

It was a speech which embittered relationships between the building unions and the Minister. After all, following Bevan's line of logic there appeared to be no case for any extension of public ownership at all. And when a subsequent discussion took place on the matter at the Annual Conference of the A.U.B.T.W., the thoughts of a large number of members were expressed by T. Halliday representing the Cambridge district. "I wonder," he said, "if at Margate, Bevan would have used the same language on nationalisation to the miners as he used to building trade workers?" A motion "That this Conference condemns the action of the Minister of Health with respect to the State Building Corporation" was carried unanimously without a solitary voice being raised in Bevan's defence.

By then, however, he had completely estranged himself from the very men he depended upon for implementation of his housing policies. For, in at least one speech during 1947, he had ranged himself with the building masters who were trying to break down the resistance of operatives to incentive operations. This attack had commenced after the employers had rejected a wage claim by the unions, for 6d. an hour, in 1946. In February of the following year the claim was heard before an arbitration tribunal which again rejected it. The case of the employers was simply that they could not give any increase in wages unless it was directly linked to higher output. In other words they wanted to make permanent a system of payment by results and extend it to the entire industry.

The antagonism of the men to incentives was widespread. In part it was based on a feeling for craftsmanship. If the desire for money overcame all other considerations, the class of work would inevitably suffer. Many of those who were implacably against incentives also thought they would adversely affect human relationships on the job: older men would be driven out by those who would sweep aside all consideration in attempts to form high output bricklaying gangs.

All these feelings exploded to the surface when the employers declared, on the 2nd July, that they were preparing to unilaterally introduce incentive bonus working. The building unions immediately made it known to the employers and the Government that a national conflict might well be the outcome of such a rash action. On the 17th July a meeting was held between the employers and the unions under the auspices of the Ministry of Labour but, although they argued until late at night, both sides maintained their original positions. The employers said they could not consider the operatives' demand for an increase of 6d. and that any higher earnings must come through higher output. The unions insisted that they were entitled to an increase on the basic rate of wages.

It was at this crucial stage that Bevan, who must have been well aware of what was happening, made a speech the very next night at Morpeth which created uproar in the A.U.B.T.W. Plymouth and other branches insisted that the Executive Council demand the resignation of the Minister of Health for having " accused building trade operatives of not working satisfactorily, and contended that a mere rise in wages would not get the operatives to produce more, and that only incentives in the building trade were the solution to the problem."

It was an extremely dangerous comment for Bevan to have made on a situation that had already reached crisis point. The Minister of Labour, now convinced of the danger of national conflict, personally stepped into the breach with a suggestion for compromise. Both sides, he urged, should consider the introduction of a system of incentive payments which would give an additional 20 per cent on top of a basic wage rate which should be increased by 3d. per hour.

Reporting this to their members, the building unions said the employers had agreed to this proposal and it was now up to the unions to establish their attitude through a national ballot vote. And this vote was taken in an atmosphere of recrimination and mental anguish such as the industry has rarely seen.

To many men it seemed that a vote for incentives was equivalent to the signing away of their traditions of craftsmanship and consideration for their fellows on the site. Yet they were being subjected to both economic and political pressures, and a great amount of it from unexpected quarters. The bricklayers in particular were put under a Press microscope and abused to make a field day for readers. The number of bricks a man could lay in a day almost became public interest number one. People who had never soiled their shoes on a building site were setting themselves up as experts with one united, 'considered' opinion: bricklayers were less industrious than the legendary bricklayers of yesteryear. They were lazy rascals, exploiting the nation's need for houses.

It was a curious campaign of abuse. No one questioned the amount of doors a joiner could hang in a day; no scorn was directed against the plumber for not wiping sufficient joints in an eight-hour stint. The amount of cans of paint a painter might use was apparently his own business. But the bricklayer was treated almost like an actor on a stage, with constant critical notices appearing in the Press about the standard of his performance.

It was against this background that the national ballot was taken to its final conclusion. Out of the total membership of all building unions there was a high vote of approximately 50 per cent, and the proposition in favour of incentives plus an increase of 3d. per hour was carried by 165,606 to 77,868. And with the formal introduction of the agreement on the 16th November, 1947, the long traditional stand of the building unions against incentives came to an end.

CHAPTER 25

NO IVORY CASTLES

BUILDING workers had come home from the Forces, thousands of men had entered the industry through the adult training scheme, and the year 1947 brought the greatest craft membership the A.U.B.T.W. had ever had. There were 90,550 registered at head office and the worth of the Union had risen by over 6s. per member. "All previous records have been broken," enthused Luke Fawcett. "The valuation is the highest in our history. We now have a general fund amounting to £245,278 and additional funds totalling £28,165—altogether £273,443, over a quarter of a million pounds."

Nor did there seem any reason why the growth in numerical and financial strength should not continue. Employment prospects looked good and the adult training scheme had by no means reached its target figure of 200,000 trainees. Yet, within a matter of twelve months, Luke Fawcett had to report a serious and completely unforseen loss in membership of well over 4,000. Although he expressed the hope that this was only a temporary set-back, next year the Union lost another 3,424.

Luke Fawcett put the blame almost exclusively on an exodus of the new trainees from the industry: "A realisation that the builder's life was not easy, the passing on of the birds of passage, all affected the position and the sudden influx was offset very largely by a sudden exodus."

This, however, was certainly not the complete answer for throughout the whole of the trade union movement members began to drain away. There were some who saw a political significance in this paradox of trade union membership declining during an economic climate more favourable to its growth. They claimed that the growing Tory propaganda campaign to turn public opinion against the Labour Government—and which led to its defeat in 1951—was also having an adverse effect on the trade unions. There was probably an element of truth in this analysis and in Luke Fawcett's comment on the short-lived trainees. But, in fact, the unions were gradually to become aware that the fall in membership and loyalty was basically due to the completely new circumstances which now faced them, and which demanded a profound re-appraisal of their traditional role in industry.

In the A.U.B.T.W. the new problems would have to be met and tackled by new men for, within the space of two years, a completely new set of national officers had taken over responsibility for the Union. Luke Fawcett and Harry Adams were due to retire in 1951 and 1952 respectively. In addition to replacing the general secretary and national president, the Executive also decided to appoint for the first time an assistant general secretary.

In the national ballots that were held for these positions, George Lowthian was elected general secretary on the 23rd October, 1950, to take up his position when Fawcett retired in August of the following year. January of 1952 saw John Leonard taking over as assistant general secretary and, a few months later, Harry Weaver was elected national president.

There was a great similarity in the background of these new officials. Each was in his early forties when elected, and they were probably the youngest trio of national officers that had ever been responsible for a strong craft union with traditions going back well over a century. They had more than age in common for, not only had they all joined the Union when they were still very young men, each had been brought up in an intense building union environment.

Himself a bricklayer, George Lowthian had a father who had been a mason, and a grandfather who had also been of that craft. Both of these men had been active in the trade union movement and each had held the post of secretary of the Carlisle branch of the old Operative Stonemasons' Society. Following their example George Lowthian became secretary of the A.U.B.T.W. branch in Carlisle when he was 21 years of age. From his father Ernest Lowthian, who had been a prominent member of the old Social Democratic Federation, he had also inherited an awareness of the value of political action. Subsequently elected to the national executive of the Union, he resigned this position upon election to the full-time position as district organiser for the No. 9 Division.

The new president, Harry Weaver, was also a bricklayer as was his father and his grandfather before him. Both these men had been members of the old London Order of Bricklayers and his father, a long service member of the A.U.B.T.W., had been a militant in the 1914 London lockout. Joining the Union at the age of 18, Harry Weaver had been elected a full-time district organiser by the time he was 30. Five years later he assumed wider responsibilities when he was elected organiser for the No. 1 Division.

John Leonard, the assistant general secretary, was only a young apprentice bricklayer when his father had enrolled him in the Union. His father held the secretaryship of the Paisley branch under four different secretaries and two different unions—a record period of over 44 years. John Leonard had therefore been brought up in a trade union environment. His career in the A.U.B.T.W. was similar to the other new national officers; from being a full-time district officer to becoming elected as the organiser for the No. 10 Division.

The new men had certainly tradition and experience behind them but, unlike previous officials, they were facing problems which demanded more than the application of traditional solutions. Why was it that, even though the Union had achieved a new status and influence in society, apathy was rapidly denuding the branches of life? Why were operatives less demonstrably loyal to trade unionism on the sites; and why did they object to the payment of a reasonable trade union subscription when it was obviously the most rewarding investment a man could make? Above all, why was Union membership showing a continuing fall when employment and the economic situation remained good?

For a short time the gravity of the membership position was alleviated by amalgamation, in 1952, with the National Builders' Labourers' and Constructional Workers' Society. This amalgamation established a precedent within the building industry. It was the first time a craft union had broken the trade barrier to merge with a labourers' union. When Ted Lamerton, general secretary of the N.B.L. & C.W.S. brought over his 17,142 members with him on the 1st July, 1952, the membership total of the A.U.B.T.W. reached its zenith of 95,355.

But respite from the pressing problem of falling membership was only momentary. Again it began to plunge, and most seriously within the craft section, until an average of 5,000 members per year were being lost to the A.U.B.T.W. Accompanying this fall in membership there was also a heavy financial loss. An organisation which could once put an annual surplus of around £20,000 to reserves now found that, even with adding the interest on its sizeable investments to income, there was a net loss of thousands of pounds each year.

On the sites Union authority had been weakened and it was felt that this was largely due to incentive operations, which had opened the door to piece-work and labour-only sub-contracting. After a century of struggling for national wage negotiations the unions now saw men once more bargaining on their conditions at site level. The importance and status of the official joint consultative machinery obviously suffered by comparison.

In the branches there were fewer members available to carry out those local duties essential to the life of the Union and, while members expected a multiplicity of services, the contributions they paid were rapidly declining in real value. A wide survey of the problems showed that a situation of very real crisis faced the A.U.B.T.W.—in common with many other unions in the country. Ironically it was a crisis brought about in some measure by their own success in achieving reasonable living standards through political and industrial action.

Union branches, and the Labour Movement generally, had always been most active and vocal in times of depression or strife. In the Hungry Thirties there had been enthusiastic meetings and an upsurge of support for socialist objectives. But a great number of those men and women who flocked into the Movement saw socialism, naturally enough, in a very subjective light. To them it meant security, a job, food, and decent opportunities for their children.

By the 1950s the sharp hunger and unemployment of 20 years before was largely a memory that many people seemed determined not to recall. Trade Union, Labour and Co-operative organisations had been looked upon by these people as vehicles to be ridden towards their own limited objectives which had now been achieved. There remained no great compunction on them to give continued support to the Movement, and meeting rooms were now being left to the relatively few who realised that moral objectives would still remain after the material ones had been conquered.

After assessing the position the Executive Council of the A.U.B.T.W. decided on three immediate measures that should be taken. First, it was necessary to get to the interested members, especially the younger ones, and spend more time and money on them so that they were equipped for the task of carrying on the Union's work. Second, it was vital that even the disinterested member who probably never attended his branch, and also the non-unionist, should be kept in some form of contact with the organisation. Lastly there was the necessity to take immediate action to stop the loss in membership and money, or the Union would find itself almost unable to do anything but fight a rearguard battle.

In 1955, therefore, there began a series of progressive measures which were the most far-reaching that had been carried out by the Union for some years. Plans were laid for the launching of a membership campaign, in conjunction with instructions to officers to be on the lookout for younger members who would justify further encouragement. For these members the Executive decided that a full week's summer school should be held at which they would be taught subjects aimed at making them better equipped to play their part in the branches and in the wider Labour movement. The first of these schools was held at Beatrice Webb House near Dorking in the summer of 1955.

Towards the end of that year the Executive Council concentrated on the essential task of establishing the Union's finances on a sound basis. After a discussion at National Delegate Conference, in which the delegates were generally agreed that contributions must be increased, the Executive proceeded with a national ballot to obtain the necessary sanction from the membership. They were more than surprised when there was a majority vote against the proposal.

After all, the Conference delegates had been given a thorough understanding of the precarious financial position of the Union. Salaries, postal and printing charges, and the cost of materials were all rising. Members also demanded a much greater range of services than in the past. Yet Union contributions had hardly moved for years. Clearly it was impossible to be able to meet current expenditure, let alone make a surplus, under these conditions. But the vote against increased subscriptions appeared to indicate that the majority of members expected the impossible.

Surely, thought the national officers, they would not have rejected the proposal if they had known all about the Union's financial plight. It might well be that their failure to get increased contributions was precisely the kind of failure the whole trade union movement was meeting because it was not maintaining full and direct communication with membership. It was hardly fair to condemn members if they were not put in full possession of all the facts.

At a subsequent Executive Council meeting, therefore, a long discussion was held after which it was decided to hold another ballot asking for increased subscriptions. The proposal on this occasion was to be framed in radically different terms, for the Council realised that having to go to the members for every single increase was an unwieldy procedure. A national ballot was also a lengthy and costly business. This time, therefore, they asked the members to agree to a basic contribution which would move according to a sliding scale linked to the hourly wage rate. If wages increased, or were reduced, the Executive Council should be given the right to automatically adjust contributions.

It was a new and vital principle, and this time the Executive made sure that every member of the Union knew exactly where it stood financially. Graphic posters were produced for display in branch rooms, and leaflets setting out the detailed position were sent to all members together with an appeal signed by the four national officers: Harry Weaver, George Lowthian, John Leonard and Ted Lamerton. Members of the Executive Council and national, divisional and district officials toured the branches to meet members and answer their questions about the new contribution proposals.

It was a vigorous exercise in bringing the Union into closer contact with the members and, at its meeting on the 30th January, 1956, the Executive was shown the benefits of this policy. In the national ballot over 34 per cent of the membership had voted, one of the highest polls of recent years, and there was a large majority—24,025 to 8,051—in favour of the contribution proposals. It was the first time that a trade union's members had agreed to base its contributions on such a sliding scale.

The new rule, decided the Executive, was that contributions for craft members should rise or fall by 1d. per week for every rise or fall of 3d. per hour in the wage rate.

For labourers, contributions would move by 1d. according to a rise or fall of 4d. in their hourly wage.

The effect of the new rule was immediate. "I am pleased to report that, for the first time since 1952, there is a surplus of income over expenditure for the 12 months of 1956," George Lowthian was able to tell his members. The surplus was £16,494. "This is a definite improvement over 1955 when there was a deficit of £28,476."

George Lowthian had also good news about the membership campaign which had started towards the end of 1956. Divisional and district organisers had been directed to temporarily drop some of their other services to members and concentrate their time on recruitment. Though they had only swung into the campaign in the last quarter of the year the organisers had almost succeeded in wiping out the heavy losses of the previous months, and the year had ended with membership down just a few hundred.

While pleased with the improvements in money and members the Executive was well aware that other major industrial problems remained. There were the occasional demarcation disputes due to the uncontrolled introduction of new methods and new techniques. At the start of many of the larger jobs a struggle took place to decide which of the two agreements, Building or Civil Engineering, should apply to the work. Incentive operations seemed to be based on the law of the jungle rather than on any code of industrial ethics.

"When a man goes onto a job where the bonus mentality is supreme," said Harry Weaver in a presidential speech to Annual Conference, "he sometimes has to go through the degrading process of being sized up like a race-horse. Is he sound in wind and limb; will he have the stamina to last the pace of the bonus gang? If he hasn't these characteristics he can go to hell for all these people care. There are men in our industry who have, as trade unionists over a long number of years, given great service to their fellows and have assisted in improving their standards of life. Yet some of these men are amongst those who have been turned away from sites because they were not wanted by a bonus gang."

These problems were not exclusive to the A.U.B.T.W., however, and in 1959 a conference of all the building unions was held at Maritime House, Clapham, to try and thrash out a joint approach to them. For this conference the Executive Council of the Union had given very serious thought to the preparation of a document embodying the line of action they felt necessary. Introducing the document George Lowthian outlined its main points:

*New techniques which replace previously recognised craft operations should be integrated within agreed crafts.

*There should be established a national joint committee for the planned and agreed introduction of new techniques.

*The unions should consider the possibility of creating a central research unit capable of assessing new methods. This unit could also do valuable work in publicising the use of craft methods of construction.

*Apprenticeship to be reviewed with the objective of widening the basis of craft training so that, while fewer basic crafts remain in existence, the new operative is capable of adapting himself to a wide field of operations.

*There should be consideration of amalgamation or, at the very least, ways in which we can bring about greater co-operation between the unions.

*One constructional trades agreement to be brought into existence for the whole of the industry instead of two as at present.

During the two and a half days which conference delegates discussed all the proposals made by the various unions it was obvious that there was disagreement about whether any great need for urgency existed. Some contended that full employment acted as a cushion for change and demarcation disputes were therefore not widespread. The conference finally ended without any formal decisions being taken though the chairman, Jim Mills, said that on the question of two separate national agreements he hoped that " a small working party might be set up with the object of discussing these two agreements and what could be done at least towards bringing them closer together."

The rather tame ending to what had been an important event was probably some source of disappointment to Dick Coppock, who had convened the conference as secretary of the Federation. For him it had been an attempt to get joint policies established on outstanding problems before his impending retirement.

There was also another major objective that he wanted to achieve before handing over responsibility for the Federation to other hands. One of the early victories of the N.F.B.T.O. had been the obtaining of the 44-hour week. That had been nearly 40 years before, and Coppock keenly wanted to secure another reduction in hours as the climax to his own career as secretary of the Federation.

Throughout 1960 he, and a small committee representing the Federation, met the employers to argue for a reduction in hours with a wage increase to compensate for loss of earnings. The employers, however, were extremely reluctant to concede such a major claim. They protested that the unions, in their opinion, had made rapid advances in the past few years. Not only had the wage rate continued to rise but, by a continual policy of trying to eliminate the lower graded areas, the unions had been successful in wiping out all grades below Standard Rate. By October 1960 this was the only rate (together with the London and Liverpool super rates) that remained in existence, and the 46½ hour week had been finally abolished in the last of the areas and a universal 44 hours now applied.

In spite of these protests from the employers the union negotiators pressed on determinedly to their objective of a shorter working week. And in the January 1961 edition of the *Builders Standard* (the tabloid newspaper which had been started by the A.U.B.T.W. in 1960 as a new venture in publishing) a proud Dick Coppock announced that they had secured "The Best Package Deal Ever" from the employers. Wage rates were to go up by 6d. an hour and the working week was to be reduced to 42. The only drawback from the men's point of view, and it was big enough to take away a good deal of their initial pleasure about the new agreement, was that they had to wait ten months—until October 1961—until it was implemented.

To Dick Coppock, however, the reduction in hours was the great goal. "With this achievement I have completed my own life's work within the Federation," he wrote. "This is the last major negotiation I will undertake on behalf of the men in our industry." After 40 years as the chief official of the N.F.B.T.O., plus his position before then as district organiser with the London Bricklayers, Coppock had set up a long service record unequalled in Britain or in any other part of the world.

On the 23rd March, 1961, the unions within the Federation met to choose his successor. The man they elected was another bricklayer, Harry Weaver, president of the A.U.B.T.W. For the Union, which subsequently elected John Leonard in his place, the parting was a sad one because Harry Weaver had proved himself an exceedingly capable official who had won the loyalty of the members. General Secretary George Lowthian said, "The A.U.B.T.W. is far from happy at losing Harry Weaver and his guiding hand as national president. But in his new and onerous position he carries with him the best wishes and loyalty of every member of this Union."

The "onerous position" to which he had been elected was well understood by Harry Weaver. "I am conscious of the great responsibilities I am undertaking," he said. "Perhaps I am even more acutely aware of the almost impossible task of filling the role vacated by Sir Richard Coppock, a man who has become legendary in his own lifetime."

The first task to which Harry Weaver dedicated himself was to pick up the threads of the various important policy declarations made by the federated unions at various annual conferences, and weave a cohesive policy from them which would bind the unions closer together. The quickest avenue along which it seemed possible to proceed was the Federation's Amalgamation Committee. This Committee had been set up as a result of the motion passed at the 1959 annual conference calling for " one union for the building industry."

The Committee's task, however, was much more complicated than the mere drafting of a structure for the proposed one organisation. For, at the 1959 Conference, the largest union in the Federation, the Woodworkers, had gone against the motion and one or two others had expressed some doubt about whether it was possible to proceed in this direction. The difficulty facing the Amalgamation Committee, therefore, was to frame a set of proposals which would open the way to greater unity without antagonising those organisations which were reluctant to sacrifice too much of their autonomy.

Finally a document was drawn up which was presented to the leaders of all the building unions at the 1962 Federation Conference at Exmouth. It was a bold and realistic document—perhaps a little too realistic for some. For it bluntly stated that there was " no immediate possibility of establishing one union for the building industry." What the unions could do, however, was to attempt ' cognate ' amalgamations with the object of forming three main groupings: a building section, metal working section, and a woodworking section. Other measures proposed were centralisation of research and publicity services, the publication of a joint newspaper, and the gradual uniformity of membership contributions and benefits which would ultimately make the task of closer unity much easier.

In essence the Amalgamation Committee document propounded the principle that, by concentrating on the possible, the ' one union ' goal would gradually be accomplished. On the other hand, to have produced idealistic but impracticable proposals from which the unions would have shied away would have delayed any kind of progress whatsoever. In fact it was by no means certain that all of them would agree to the Committee's immediate suggestions because, while deliberately limited in their objectives, they still formed the most far-reaching steps that had ever been taken through the Federation.

This hesitation to commit themselves was made plain when, after Federation president Jim Mills had declared the document before delegates, there was a long silence in which no one made a move to open the debate. Finally George Lowthian, for the A.U.B.T.W., strode purposefully towards the rostrum. " My organisation stands as it has always done for closer unity," he began, " and we are open at any time to discussions with other bodies on this subject as outlined in this document.

" But we believe that we must get started on the job. It is no good coming here and paying lip-service and then going away to move even further than ever from each other. If we don't move with the times then some of us will not be in existence in the future. But we cannot move forward if we all insist on living in little ivory castles of our own.

" We cannot serve our members with prejudice and by constantly reliving past traditions. We can only serve them in terms of 1962 and the times that lie ahead."

The applause which greeted George Lowthian as he left the rostrum showed that he had made just the keynote speech necessary to set the pattern for the rest of the delegates. At the end of the debate, in which most speakers had declared themselves in favour of the document, Harry Weaver made an impassioned plea for the unions to give practical support and not merely lip-service to the ideals which had been put forward by the Amalgamation Committee.

When the vote was taken not one hand was raised against. It seemed as if the building unions had at last committed themselves to the first steps leading towards the goal of complete unity.

One union for the building industry. It was the vision which inspired the men who had created the short-lived Operative Builders' Union over 130 years before. It was an objective which had constantly been the banner of the three unions which had drawn together to form the A.U.B.T.W. in 1921. It was indeed the foundation stone upon which the new amalgamated union had been built.

Within the industry, and on the sites, it was recognised that the men of the A.U.B.T.W. were primarily dedicated to this ideal. Some, in fact, might believe that it had become almost a mania to the exclusion of other objectives. This view, however, ignores the significance behind the urge to create one vast, powerful building union.

The battle between capital and labour continues. It may take a rather more subtle form today because life, at least in Britain, has not the harsh and dramatic overtones of a century ago. But still the battle continues.

Due to the very nature of their industry building workers have been in at the start of the conflict, and will almost certainly be fighting to the end. The desire for one building union, therefore, is to create a united organisation in which petty rivalries, demarcation disputes and sectional vested interests are wiped out—and building workers of all trades stand shoulder to shoulder to ensure that the outcome of the struggle is a better life for themselves and their families.

APPENDIX A

FOUNDATION DATE OF THE OPERATIVE STONEMASONS

AT least two dates, other than 1831, have been given as the foundation date of the O.S.M. Sidney and Beatrice Webb in their *History of Trade Unionism* give it as approximately 1832.

Raymond Postgate in the *Builders' History* stated quite definitely: " The Stonemasons' exact date is 23rd March, 1833. (It is preserved in a notice in the *Working Man's Friend* of that date . . .)."

This notice, in full as printed, actually reads as follows:

" Public Meeting of Working Masons

Fellow Workmen. The Masons of Birmingham, Manchester, and every principal Town in the North of England, have formed themselves into a Union, for the purpose of watching over and promoting the interests of their trade, and have sent an invitation to the Masons of London to unite with them in this laudable object, and to join in one body all the Masons of England. Masons of London throw off your apathy and negligence, and be united with your brother workmen; it is practicable; it will be to your advantage; the subject is recommended to your serious consideration with purity of motive, and a firm conviction of its advantage. A Public Meeting of the trade will be held on Wednesday, 27th March at 7 o'clock at the Institute of the Working Classes, Theobald's Road, Red Lion Square, to discuss and devise means of carrying the same into effect. Your attention is earnestly requested."

Obviously this is not an announcement of the foundation of the O.S.M. but, quite conversely, proves that it was already in existence and so extensive as to embrace " every principal Town in the North of England." The notice, in fact, is an invitation to the London masons to link up with the Union.

Postgate's " exact date " of 23rd March, 1833, is not mentioned at all and is purely the date of the publication of that issue of the *Working Man's Friend.*

The importance of determining the foundation of the Stonemasons' Society is to put in correct perspective the part it played in the Operative Builders' Union, which was formed approximately in 1832. Obviously if the O.S.M. only came into existence in 1833 it would not have had the influence on the Operative Builders' Union which historical data definitely indicates.

The O.S.M., in fact, was formed in the autumn of 1831. This date is mentioned on a number of occasions in the records of the Union. Among the more important of these are as follows:

(*a*) At a large public meeting of masons in Wigan on the 29th July, 1848, one of the main speakers was a prominent member of the O.S.M., John H. Gibson. During part of his address he told the audience " Their Society had been instituted in 1831."

The Chairman of this meeting also claimed " he had been a member of their Society upwards of 16 years." This indicates that he must have joined around 1832. (See all this in O.S.M. Returns, 3rd August, 1848).

(*b*) The original minute book of the Warrington lodge is in the historical records of the A.U.B.T.W. On the fly-leaf is inscribed the information that it is " Lodge No. 3 In No. 2 District Opened September 15th, 1832." This confirms that the Union was already organised into a district structure and other lodges were in existence before Warrington joined in 1832.

(*c*) In the O.S.M. Returns for 16th July, 1863, a proposal was discussed that a presentation be given to Thomas

Fothergill, founder member of the Union. The Central Committee supported the proposal with the words: "Bro. Fothergill's idea in the year 1831, stands pre-eminent in trade societies, 32 years having elapsed since the formation of the Operative Stonemasons' Society."

(*d*) A collection was taken from the lodges for this presentation and given to Thomas Fothergill at a special event held by the Huddersfield lodge (which was the No. 1 lodge in the Union) on the 7th September, 1863. The lodge announced this event as the "Thirty-second Anniversary of the birth of our invaluable Society."

(*e*) In his reply to the presentation, old Thomas Fothergill confirmed that, "It is now thirty-two years since the commencement of this great work of enlightenment." (See O.S.M. Returns of 27th August, 1863).

APPENDIX B

REMAINING CIRCULAR OF THE O.B.U.

AT a Meeting of the Members of the Grand Central Committee, held in Manchester, on Thursday, the 28th day of November, 1833. *Proposed by Brother Rennie, Mason, Seconded by Brother Little, Plasterer, that the following MEMORIAL be forwarded to the different District Lodges for their consideration; and that they forward the same to the Lodges in their District.*

Brother LOWRY, *President.* JOHN EMBLETON, *Secretary.*

WE, the Members composing the Grand Central Committee of Manchester, deem it our bounden duty, in the present confused state of our government throughout the kingdom, to lay before you a plain statement of our difficulties in coming to any decisive measures, as to acting up to the purport of the Rules agreed upon at the last Delegate Meeting. After a laborious inquiry into the state of our affairs in different parts of England, we are obliged to confess, that no regular systematic plans are adopted amongst the Trades in general, to uphold those laws which are established for our guidance.

In order to remedy these difficulties, and to adopt some conclusive measure for our future prosperity, we respectfully lay a Programme of our intentions before you, which we deem highly indispensable, and by which alone we can carry into effect the principle of sound general government.

We are of opinion, the Law requiring all monies to be sent to the District on strike is wholly inefficient; as it is impossible to make a correct division of the money by sending it according to the present rules; as money is sent to several districts who are on strike at the same period, when some Towns send more money than others, and by these means is unequally divided. To avert this serious evil, we recommend the whole of the Money to come through one source, viz. The Grand Central Committee wherever the seat of government exists. And that all Money appropriated for the use of the Turnouts, be paid into the Central Committee of the different Towns where the General Government exists; and them to forward such money to the Grand Central Committee for equal division throughout England, where the Turnouts are situated. And that a regular return of Turnouts be sent to the said Committee weekly, and that a regular return of payable Members be given to the Grand Lodge Central Committee on the First Tuesday of every month, so that an equal levy be given with accuracy: owing to the gross neglect of the different Districts not sending the amount of Levy passed at the last Delegate Meeting: in them neglecting to give the return of Payable Members: in Lodges taking upon themselves to affix their levies which has caused anarchy and confusion in those Lodges who do pay the regular stipend. By these neglects, the pay of the Turnouts is upon an average from 4s. to 8s. per week. And strange to say, this mismanagement has been thrown upon the seat of government, who have been contending with almost insurmountable difficulties, which we cannot remove but by the zealous co-operation of the different Districts, or the Central Committee must cease to exist in Manchester, as the oracle of government. We feel confident that Manchester has done its duty to the present Turnout. If other Towns had paid as well as the bodies we represent, families would not have suffered the privations they have from such miserable pittance received. We unanimously give our decided disapprobation of the conduct of many of the District Lodges for their lukewarm exertions in not supporting our society in the present dilemma and in not endeavouring to ensure the firm stability of general government.

You will take these measures into your consideration, and by adopting and strictly adhering to the same, you will eventually restore that confidence to the Society in general, which is nearly eradicated for want of zealous co-operation.

Signed by—

Masons: GEORGE BEVAN, *Secretary*, and two others.

Plasterers: EDWARD WOLSTENHOLME, *Secretary* and two others.

Slaters: WILLIAM MEDCALF, *Secretary*, and two others.

Painters: WILLIAM WHITE, *Secretary*, and two others.

JOHN EMBLETON,
Secretary of the Grand Central Committee.

Engravers' Arms, Brazennose Street.

BIBLIOGRAPHY

1. Some of the books which were found particularly helpful in writing this history and from which occasional quotes are taken, are as follows:—

BUILDING IN ENGLAND ...	L. F. Salzman, F.S.A.
HISTORY OF TRADE UNIONISM	Sidney and Beatrice Webb
THE MEDIAEVAL MASON ...	D. Knoop and G. P. Jones
SHORT HISTORY OF THE BRITISH WORKING CLASS	G. D. H. Cole
THE BUILDERS' HISTORY ...	R. W. Postgate
SIX CENTURIES OF WORK AND WAGES	J. E. Thorold Rogers
FREEMASON'S GUIDE AND COMPENDIUM	B. E. Jones
ECONOMIC INTERPRETATION OF HISTORY	J. E. Thorold Rogers
HISTORY OF THE BRITISH TRADES UNION CONGRESS	W. J. Davis
A SHORT HISTORY OF THE BUILDING CRAFTS ...	Martin S. Briggs
HISTORY OF THE NATIONAL FEDERATION OF BUILDING TRADES OPERATIVES (UNPUBLISHED)	Harry Heumann
FIFTY YEARS' MARCH ...	Francis Williams
OUR SOCIETY'S HISTORY (WOODWORKERS' HISTORY)	S. Higenbottam

2. There are a number of journals in the British Museum which deal with the period 1832/34 when the Operative Builders Union was in existence. Though the main news they carry is more of a general social and political nature, occasional references to the Operative Builders Union are made in their pages. These journals are:—

The Pioneer, or Trades Union Magazine. A weekly journal published at Birmingham. Editor: James Morrison.

The Poor Man's Advocate and People's Library. Published from Manchester.

The Destructive and Poor Man's Conservative. Editor: Bronterre O'Brien.

The Crisis. Robert Owen and J. E. Smith.

The Man. Editor: R. E. Lee.

The Poor Man's Guardian. Editor: H. Hetherington

The True Sun. Editor: H. Cartwright.

3. The most valuable source of information was, of course, the records contained in the archives of the Amalgamated Union of Building Trade Workers. While none of the material is complete from the date of the foundation of the various organisations which comprise the A.U.B.T.W., the records of the Operative Stonemasons' Society are perhaps the finest individual trade union documents which remain in existence.

Operative Stonemasons' Society

Founded in 1831 the Operative Stonemasons' Society, or the O.S.M. as it is often referred to in this book, left continuous records going back to 1834. The major source of information is the set of Fortnightly Returns from this time through to 1910, when a change was made to a more formal type of journal. This was continued until the amalgamation in 1921.

In addition to this set of journals are a number of annual accounts, rule books and miscellaneous items which provide a great deal of information about the O.S.M. and the unions with which it came into contact from time to time.

Operative Bricklayers' Society, London Order

Though the London Order of the O.B.S. was formed in 1848 there are no records in existence before the 1862 monthly circulars, annual and quarterly reports. In addition to this information there are also various rules, etc. of value in following the development of the Union.

Operative Bricklayers' Society, Manchester Order

Until 1848, when there was the split which led to the formation of the London Order, the Union was known as the Friendly Society of Operative Bricklayers. Although its foundation date is 1829, no records exist before the rules and financial reports of 1844. No reports or journals of the organisation are in existence before the 1868 set.

Like many other unions the Manchester Bricklayers changed their title occasionally, becoming frequently known as the Manchester Unity or the Manchester United Operative Bricklayers, etc.

4. Though a number of other unions, including the Scottish Building and Monumental Workers' Association, are dealt with in this book no records of these organisations are at Head Office of the Union. The Scottish Building and Monumental Workers' Association has records dispersed in various parts of Scotland while the National Builders' Labourers and Constructional Workers' Society, which joined up with the A.U.B.T.W. in 1952, lost all its old records due to a bombing attack in the second World War.

INDEX